THE STUDENT'S DICTIONARY

OF

MUSICAL TERMS

—

ARTHUR J. GREENISH

The Student's Dictionary of Musical Terms

PART I

ENGLISH AND FOREIGN TERMS AND EXPRESSIONS,
WITH THEIR SIGNIFICATION.

PART II

A SELECTION OF ENGLISH TERMS AND WORDS,
WITH THEIR EQUIVALENTS IN ITALIAN,
GERMAN, AND FRENCH.

BY

Arthur J. Greenish

JOSEPH WILLIAMS
STAINER & BELL, LONDON

ISBN 0 85249 228 6

PREFACE

It is hoped that this Dictionary of Musical Terms may prove useful to students and others as a book of reference in connection with their musical studies. In addition to the majority of terms usually met with, it includes tables of notes and keys in various languages, the helpful French time-names (which now form such a prominent feature in aural training), and a comprehensive list of abbreviations.

A special and novel feature of the book is the provision of a list of English words, with their equivalents in Italian, German and French; a feature which — so far as the compiler is aware — is not contained in any similar publication.

ARTHUR J. GREENISH

TABLE OF CONTENTS.

PART I.

PART II.

NAMES OF NOTES IN VARIOUS LANGUAGES.

English.	Italian.	French.	German.
C	Do	Ut	C
C sharp	Do diesis	Ut dièse	Cis
C flat	Do bemolle	Ut bémol	Ces
D	Re	Ré	D
D sharp	Re diesis	Ré dièse	Dis
D flat	Re bemolle	Ré bémol	Des
E	Mi	Mi	E
E sharp	Mi diesis	Mi dièse	Eis
E flat	Mi bemolle	Mi bémol	Es
F	Fa	Fa	F
F sharp	Fa diesis	Fa dièse	Fis
F flat	Fa bemolle	Fa bémol	Fes
G	Sol	Sol	G
G sharp	Sol diesis	Sol dièse	Gis
G flat	Sol bemolle	Sol bémol	Ges
A	La	La	A
A sharp	La diesis	La dièse	Ais
A flat	La bemolle	La bémol	As
B	Si	Si	H
B sharp	Si diesis	Si dièse	His
B flat	Si bemolle	Si bémol	B

THE FRENCH TIME-NAMES OF AIMÉ PARIS.*

(N.B.—aa = ah ; é = eh ; i = short i (as in "pity").)

Simple Time.
(Binary division of the beat.)

𝅝 = Four-pulse sound, called Ta aa aa aa.

𝅗𝅥. = Three-pulse sound, called Taa aa aa.

𝅗𝅥 = Two-pulse sound, called Taa aa.

♩ = One-pulse sound, called Taa.

♫ = Half-pulse sounds, called Ta-té.

♬♬ = Quarter-pulse sounds, called Tafa-téfé.

Compound Time.
(Ternary division of the beat.)

♫♩ = Third-pulse sounds, called Ta-té-ti.

♬♬♫ = Sixth-pulse sounds, called Tafa-téfé-tifi.

Examples of combinations of the Binary division of the beat (Simple Time):—

= One 1½-pulse and one ½-pulse sounds, called Taa-até.

= One ½-pulse and two ¼-pulse sounds, called Ta-téfé.

= Two ¼-pulse and one ½-pulse sounds, called Tafa-té.

= One ¾-pulse and one ¼-pulse sounds, called Ta-éfé.

= One ¼-pulse and one ¾-pulse sounds, called Tafa-é.

* From *Aural Culture*, by STEWART MACPHERSON and ERNEST READ.

NAMES OF KEYS IN VARIOUS LANGUAGES.

English.	Italian.	French.	German.	Key Signature
C major ...	Do maggiore ...	Ut majeur ...	C dur	⎱ No sig-
A minor ...	La minore	La mineur ...	A moll	⎰ nature
G major ...	Sol maggiore ...	Sol majeur ...	G dur	⎱ 1 sharp
E minor ...	Mi minore	Mi mineur ...	E moll	⎰
D major ...	Re maggiore ...	Ré majeur ...	D dur	⎱ 2 sharps
B minor ...	Si minore	Si mineur ...	H moll	⎰
A major ...	La maggiore ...	La majeur ...	A dur	⎱ 3 sharps
F sharp minor	Fa diesis minore ...	Fa dièse mineur	Fis moll	⎰
E major ...	Mi maggiore...	Mi majeur ...	E dur	⎱ 4 sharps
C sharp minor	Do diesis minore ...	Ut dièse mineur	Cis moll	⎰
B major ...	Si maggiore ...	Si majeur ...	H dur	⎱ 5 sharps
G sharp minor	Sol diesis minore ...	Sol dièse mineur	Gis moll	⎰
F sharp major	Fa diesis maggiore...	Fa dièse majeur	Fis dur	⎱ 6 sharps
D sharp minor	Re diesis minore ...	Ré dièse mineur	Dis moll	⎰
C sharp major	Do diesis maggiore...	Ut dièse majeur	Cis dur	⎱ 7 sharps
A sharp minor	La diesis minore ...	La dièse mineur	Ais moll	⎰
F major ...	Fa maggiore.. ...	Fa majeur ...	F dur	⎱ 1 flat
D minor ...	Re minore	Ré mineur ...	D moll	⎰
B flat major...	Si bemolle maggiore	Si bémol majeur	B dur	⎱ 2 flats
G minor ...	Sol minore	Sol mineur ...	G moll	⎰
E flat major...	Mi bemolle maggiore	Mi bémol majeur	Es dur	⎱ 3 flats
C minor ...	Do minore	Ut mineur ...	C moll	⎰
A flat major...	La bemolle maggiore	La bémol majeur	As dur	⎱ 4 flats
F minor ...	Fa minore	Fa mineur ...	F moll	⎰
D flat major...	Re bemolle maggiore	Ré bémol majeur	Des dur	⎱ 5 flats
B flat minor...	Si bemolle minore ...	Si bemol mineur	B moll	⎰
G flat major...	Sol bemolle maggiore	Sol bémol majeur	Ges dur	⎱ 6 flats
E flat minor...	Mi bemolle minore...	Mi bémol mineur	Es moll	⎰
C flat major...	Do bemolle maggiore	Ut bémol majeur	Ces dur	⎱ 7 flats
A flat minor...	La bemolle minore...	La bémol mineur	As moll	⎰

ABBREVIATIONS.

A ...	...	... Alto	Cor.	...	...	{ Cornet / Corno
A² ...	...	... A due				
Accel.	...	... Accelerando	C. p.	...	... Colla parte	
Accomp.	...	... Accompaniment	Cres.	...	... } Crescendo	
Adg° or Ad°	...	... Adagio	Cresc.	...	...	
Ad lib.	...	... } Ad libitum	C. S.	...	... Colla sinistra	
Ad libit.	...	...	C. voc.	...	... Colla voce	
Affett°	...	... Affettuoso				
Affrett°	...	... Affrettando				
Ag°	...	... } Agitato	D ...	...	... *See* D (page 23)	
Agit°	...	...	D. C.	...	... Da capo	
All°	...	... Allegro	Dal S.	...	... Dal segno	
Allgett°	...	... Allegretto	Dec.	...	... Decani	
All' ott.	...	... All' ottava	Decres	...	... } Decrescendo	
Al seg.	...	... Al segno	Decresc.	...	...	
And.	...	... Andantino	Diap.	...	... Diapason	
And.	...	... Andante	Dim.	...	... { Diminished / Diminuendo
Anim.	...	... Animato				
Arc. ...	...	... { Coll' arco / Arcato	Div.	...	... Divisi	
			Dol.	...	... Dolce	
Arp.	...	... Arpeggio	Dolciss.	...	... Dolcissimo	
A t. ...	...	... } A tempo	Dopp. ped.	...	... Doppio pedale	
A temp.	...	...	D. S.	...	... Dal segno	
B ...	...	... *See* B (page 8)	Esp.	...	... } Espressivo	
B. C.	...	... } Basso continuo	Espress.	...	...	
Bass Con. ...	...	...				
Br. ...	...	... Bratsche	F ...	...	... { Fine / Forte
Brill.	...	... Brillante				
			Fag.	...	... Fagotto	
C ...	...	... *See* C (page 13)	ff. or fff.	...	... Fortissimo	
C. a.	...	... Coll' arco	Fl.	...	... Flute	
Cad.	...	... { Cadence / Cadenza	F. O.	...	... } Full organ	
			F. Org.	...	...	
Cal. ...	...	... Calando	For.	...	... Forte	
Calm.	...	... Calmato	fp. ...	...	... Forte piano	
Can.	...	... Cantoris	Forz.	...	... { Forzando / Forzato
Cantab.	...	... Cantabile	fz. ...	...	...	
C. B.	...	... { Contra basso / Col basso				
			G ...	...	... Gauche	
Cb. ...	...	... Contre-basse	G. O.	...	... } Great organ	
C. D.	...	... Colla destra	G. Org.	...	...	
'Celli	...	... Violoncelli	Graz.	...	... Grazioso	
'Cello	...	... Violoncello	Gt. ...	...	... Great organ	
C. F.	...	... { Canto fermo / Canto firmus				
			Hauptw. ...	...	... Hauptwerk	
Ch. ...	...	... Choir organ	Haut.	...	... } Hautboy	
Cl., Clar. ...	...	... Clarinet	Htb.	...	...	
Col. c.	...	... Col canto	Hr. ...	...	... } Hörner	
Coll' ott.	...	... } Coll' ottava	Hrn.	...	...	
Coll' 8va	...	...				

Incalz.	... ...	Incalzando
Introd.	... ...	Introduction
Inv....	... ...	Inversion
L ...	... ...	Left
Leg.	... ...	Legato
Legg.	... ...	Leggiero
L. H.	... ...	{ Left hand
	... ...	{ Linke Hand
Lo. ...	... ...	Loco
Lusing.	... ...	Lusingando
M ...	... ...	*See* M (page 53)
Maesto.	... ...	Maestoso
Magg.	... ...	Maggiore
Man.	... ...	Manual
Manc.	... ...	Mancando
Marc.	... ...	Marcato
M. D.	... ...	{ Mano destra
	... ...	{ Maine droite
Men.	... ...	Meno
Mez.	... ...	Mezzo
mf ...	... ...	Mezzo forte
M. G.	... ...	Main gauche
M. M.	... ...	Maelzel's metronome
Mod.	... ...	} Moderato
Modto	... ...	}
Mor.	... ...	Morendo
Mov.	... ...	Movimento
mp ...	... ...	Mezzo piano
M. S.	... ...	{ Manuscript
	... ...	{ Mano sinistra
M. V.	... ...	Mezza voce
Ob. ...	... ...	Oboe
Obbl.	... ...	Obbligato
Oberw.	... ...	Oberwerk
Op. ...	... ...	Opus
Org.	... ...	Organ
Ott. ...	... ...	}
O ...	... ...	} Ottava
8va ...	... ...	}
P ...	... ...	*See* P (page 63)
Ped.	... ...	Pedal
Perd.	... ...	}
Perden.	... ...	} Perdendosi
Perdendo. ...	... ...	}
P.F. or Pfte.	...	Pianoforte
p.f. ...	... ...	Più forte
Piang.	... ...	Piangendo
Pianiss.	... ...	Pianissimo
Pizz.	... ...	Pizzicato
pp or ppp ...	... ...	Pianissimo
Ima ...	... ...	Prima
Imo ...	... ...	Primo

Raddol.	... ...	Raddolcendo
Rall.	... ...	Rallentando
Recit.	... ...	Recitativo
rf, rfz, rinf.	...	Rinforzando
R. H.	...	{ Right hand
		{ Rechte Hand
Rit....	... ...	} Ritardando
Ritard.	... ...	}
Riten.	... ...	Ritenuto
S ...	... ...	*See* S (page 77)
Scherz.	... ...	Scherzando
Seg.	... ...	Segue
Sem. or Semp.	...	Sempre
sf. sfz.	... ...	Sforzando
Sim.	... ...	Simile
Sin....	... ...	Sinistra
Sinf.	... ...	Sinfonia
Smorz.	... ...	Smorzando
Sost. or Sosten.	...	Sostenuto
Spirit.	... ...	Spiritoso
S. sord.	... ...	Senza sordini
Stacc.	... ...	Staccato
St. Diap. ...	...	Stopped diapason
Stent.	... ...	Stentando
String.	... ...	Stringendo
Sw....	... ...	Swell organ
Sym.	... ...	Symphony
T ...	... ...	Tempo, Tenor, Tutti
T. C.	... ...	Tre corde
Tempo I ...	...	Tempo primo
Ten.	... ...	Tenuto
Timp.	... ...	} Timpani
Tymp.	... ...	}
Tpt.	... ...	Trumpet
Tr. ...	... ...	{ Trill
		{ Trumpet
Trem.	... ...	{ Tremolando
		{ Tremulant
Tromb.	... ...	{ Trombe
		{ Trombone
T. S.	... ...	Tasto solo
U. C.	... ...	Una corda
Unis.	... ...	Unison
V ...	... ...	Voce *or* Volti
Va ...	... ...	Viola
Var.	... ...	Variation
Vc., Vcl., Vcllo. ...		Violoncello
Viol., Vl., Vno. ...		Violino
V. S.	... ...	Volti subito
VI ...	... ...	Violini primi
V2 ...	... ...	Violini secondi
Vv., Vni. ...	...	Violini

PART I.

ENGLISH AND FOREIGN TERMS AND EXPRESSIONS WITH THEIR SIGNIFICATION.

In the case of Italian words which have two genders, such as :—Diretto (mas.), Diretta (fem.), the feminine form is indicated by -a after the masculine form, thus :—Diretto, -a ; Mezzo, -a.

With a few exceptions, adverbial forms are not included. In Italian they are formed by the addition of the suffix " -mente " to the adjective, the final vowel " o " being, at the same time, changed to " a," for example :— Delicato (adj.), Delicatamente (adv.). In French the corresponding suffix is usually " -ment."

A.

A (*It.*)—In, at, to, by, for, etc. *A tempo*, in time. *A piacere*, at pleasure.

A (*Fr.*)—In, at, to, by, for, etc. *À deux mains*, for two hands. *À première vue*, at first sight.

Ab (*Ger.*)—Off (in organ music).

A ballata (*It.*)—In the ballad style.

Abandon, avec (*Fr.*)
Abbandonatamente (*It.*)
Abbandono, con (*It.*)
With unrestrained emotion ; with a burst of passion.

Abbellire (*It.*)—To add embellishments to a melody.

Abbreviatura (*It.*)
Abréviation (*Fr.*)
An abbreviation.

Abellimento (*It.*) — Embellishment,
Abellitura ornament.

Abendlied (*Ger.*)—An evening song.

A bene placito (*It.*)—At pleasure.

Aber (*Ger.*)—But.

Abgeleiteter Akkord (*Ger.*) — An inverted chord.

Abgemessen (*Ger.*)—In strict time.

Abgerissen (*Ger.*)—Abruptly.

Abgestossen (*Ger.*)—Detached, staccato.

Abkürzung (*Ger.*)—Abbreviation.

Abnehmender Ton (*Ger.*)—A decrease of the tone.

Abnehmendes Tempo (*Ger.*) — A decrease of the speed.

Absatz (*Ger.*)—A cadence.

A cappella (*It.*)—(1) In the style of church music. (2) Unaccompanied vocal works. (3) Sometimes considered as synonymous with *Alla Breve* time.

A capriccio (*It.*)—At will : according to individual fancy.

Accarezzevole
Accarezzevolmente
(*It.*)Caressingly, coaxingly.

Accelerando (*It.*)—Getting gradually faster.

Accelerato (*It.*)—Livelier, at a quicker speed.

Accent.—Stress or emphasis. Also the stress laid upon a certain note or upon certain notes of a bar, at more or less regular intervals of time.

Accent (*Fr.*)—Accent.

Accento dobole (*It.*)—The up-beat in a bar.

Acciaccatura (*It.*)—A short grace note, played as quickly as possible.

Accidentals.—Sharps, flats, or naturals which inflect—or contradict the inflection of—the notes of the scale indicated by the key-signature.

Accident (*Fr.*)—An accidental.

Accompagnamento (*It.*)
Accompagnement (*Fr.*)
Accompaniment.

Accord (*Fr.*)—A chord. The mode of tuning an instrument.

1

Accordando (*It.*)—Being in tune, agreeing.

Accordare (*It.*)—To tune.

Accord brisé (*Fr.*)—A broken chord.

Accorder (*Fr.*)—To tune an instrument.

Accordion.—A free reed instrument of the concertina type, invented by Damian, of Vienna, in 1829.

Accordo (*It.*)—A chord.

Accresciuto (*It.*)—Augmented, as applied to intervals.

Achtel (*Ger.*)—Eighth; octave. *Achtel* (*note*), quaver. *Achtelpause*, quaver rest.

Acoustics.—The science which treats of the phenomena and laws of sound.

Act.—The principal division of an opera or play. The sub-division of an act is termed a scene.

Acte (*Fr.*)—An act in an opera or play.

Action. — The mechanism of the pianoforte, organ, etc.

Acute.—Sharp, shrill. High in pitch, as opposed to grave.

Adagietto (*It.*)—A speed somewhat faster than adagio. The term applied to a short adagio movement.

Adagio (*It.*)—Slow. The term applied to a movement in slow tempo. This term, as indicating the speed of a movement, is frequently qualified; for example:—*Molto adagio*, very slow; *adagio sostenuto*, slow and sustained; *adagio, ma non troppo*, not too slow.

Adagissimo (*It.*)—Extremely slow.

Additato (*It.*)—Fingered.

Additional accompaniments. — Instrumental parts added to a composition by some person other than the original author ; sometimes necessary in the case of older writers, who left portions of their works with only a " figured bass " indication of their harmonies.

Addolorato (*It.*)—Sorrowfully, with an expression of grief.

À demi-jeu (*Fr.*)—With half the power of the instrument.

À demi-voix (*Fr.*)—With half the power of the voice (mezza voce).

À deux (*Fr.*) — For two voices or instruments. (A due.)

À deux mains (*Fr.*)—For two hands.

À deux temps (*Fr.*)—Duple time.

Adjunct notes.—Notes not essential to the harmony, occurring on unaccented parts of the bar.

Ad libitum (*Lat.*)—At pleasure. In passages so marked, the tempo and expression are left to the judgment of the performer. The term also indicates that any vocal or instrumental parts may, or may not, be rendered.

A due (*It.*)—For, or divided between, two voices or instruments. This direction is indicated thus, *a²*, and when employed for two instruments—such as violins playing in unison—it signifies that they are to divide ; but if employed for instruments playing two separate parts—such as the clarinets—it signifies that they are to play in unison.

A due corde (*It.*)—On two strings.

A due tempi (*It.*)—Two beats in a bar.

A dur (*Ger.*)—The key of A major.

Affabile
Affabilità, con }(*It.*)—In a pleasing, kindly manner.
Affabilmente

Affanoso (*It.*)—Anxious, restless.

Affectueusement (*Fr.*)—Lovingly.

Affetto, con } (*It.*) With passion, emotion; very expressively.
Affettuoso

Affezione, con (*It.*)—In a style expressing tender emotion.

Affrettando } (*It.*)—Hurrying, pressing on the speed.
Affrettoso

After-beat.—The ending of a trill, consisting of the lower auxiliary and the principal note.

Agilità, con (*It.*)
Agilité, avec (*Fr.*) } A passage so marked is to be executed lightly, and with agility.
Agilmente (*It.*)

Agitamento (*It.*)—Agitation, restlessness.

Agitato (*It.*)—An agitated, restless style of performance.

Agité (*Fr.*)—Restless, agitated.

Agnus Dei (*Lat.*)—"Lamb of God." One of the principal numbers of the Mass.

Agrémens (*Fr.*)—Ornaments, graces.

Ähnlich (*Ger.*).—Similar.

Aigu (*Fr.*)—Sharp, acute, high.

Air.—A tune or melody.

Air (*Fr.*)—Air, tune, melody.

Ais (*Ger.*)—The note A sharp.

Aisis (*Ger.*)—The note A double sharp.

Akkord (*Ger.*).—A chord.

Akt (*Ger.*)—An act.

À la (*Fr.*) } To the, in the,
Al, All', Alla (*It.*) } at the; in the style of, like.

À la même (*Fr.*)—In the original time.

À la mesure (*Fr.*)—In time. The equivalent of *a tempo* or *a battuta.*

Alberti Bass.—A bass consisting of broken chords.

Albumblätter (*Ger.*) — Albumleaves, short pieces.

Alcuna (*It.*)—Some, certain. *Con alcuna licenza,* with a certain freedom as to time.

Aliquot tones.—Overtones, harmonics.

À livre ouvert (*Fr.*)—At first sight.

Alla (*It.*)—In the style of.

Alla breve (*It.*)—Formerly, a time having 4 minims to a measure. At the present day the term is usually applied to the time having 4 crotchets in the measure, but in which the pulse or beat is a minim.

Alla caccia (*It.*)—In the hunting style.

Alla camera (*It.*)—In the style of chamber music.

Alla cappella (*It.*)—The same as *A cappella.*

Alla marcia (*It.*)—In the style of a march.

Alla polacca (*It.*)—In the style of a polonaise.

Allargando (*It.*)—Enlarged; broadening out.

Alla stretta (*It.*)—Getting faster and faster. In the style of a stretto.

Alla zingara (*It.*)—In the style of gipsy music.

All' 8va alta (*It.*)—In the octave higher.

All' 8va bassa (*It.*)—In the octave lower.

Allegretto (*It.*)—Lively, and moderately fast; rather slower than *allegro.*

Allegrezza (*It.*)—Lively, with vivacity.

Allegrissimo (*It.*)—Extremely fast.

Allegro (*It.*)—Quick, lively. This term is very commonly used in conjunction with other terms, which qualify or intensify its meaning, such as:—*Allegro ma non troppo,* not too quickly; *allegro moderato,* moderately quick; *allegro assai,* or *allegro di molto,* extremely fast, etc., etc. This term is also used as a substantive, to designate a movement or piece in quick tempo.

Allegro di bravura (*It.*)—A movement containing difficulties intended to display the executive skill of the performer.

Allemanda (*It.*) } One of the move-
Allemande (*Fr.*) } ments of a suite.
It is written in 4–4 time, is moderately quick, and generally commences upon the last semi-quaver of the bar.

All'espagnuola (*It.*)—In the Spanish style.

All'improvisata (*It.*)—Without preparation, extemporaneously.

All'inglese (*It.*)—In the English style.

All'italiana (*It.*)—In the Italian style.

Allmählich (*Ger.*)—Gradually, by degrees. (Also spelt *allmählig, allmälig.*) *Allmählich schwächer,* softer by degrees.

Al loco (*It.*)—In, or to, the place. A term used to contradict a previous direction to play an octave higher or lower.

All'ottava (*It.*)—"At the octave." A direction to play an octave higher. Generally indicated by the abbreviation 8va.

All'unisono (*It.*)—In unison.

Al rigore di tempo (*It.*)—In strict time.

Al riverso } (*It.*)—By contrary mo-
Al rovescio } tion ; that is, answering an ascending interval by one descending the same distance, or *vice versa.*

Al segno (*It.*)—To, or at, the sign. (Dal Segno.)

Alt (*Ger.*)—The alto voice or part.

Alt (*It.*)—Notes "in alt" are those contained in the octave which commences with the G first above the treble staff. The notes in the next higher octave are said to be "in altissimo."

Alta (*It.*)—High. *Ottava alta,* an octave higher.

Alterato (*It.*) } Altered in pitch, raised
Altéré (*Fr.*) } or lowered a semitone.

Alternando (*It.*) } (1) Alternating.
Alternativo (*It.*) } (2) A part of a composition played alternately with another.

Altgeige (*Ger.*)—The tenor violin, the viola.

Alt-horn.—The alto saxhorn.

Altissimo (*It.*) — Highest, extremely high. (Alt.)

Alto (*It.*)—The deeper of the two principal classes of women's and boys' voices. In England the female voice of this pitch is more generally known as *contralto.*

Alto, -a (*It.*)—High ; as *ottava alta,* an octave higher.

Alto (*Fr.*)—The tenor violin. (Viola.)

Alto clef.—The C clef on the third line of the staff, making the note on that line Middle C. It is used for the alto part when writing in vocal score, and for the viola, etc.

Alto-trombone (*Fr.* and *It.*) } Alto-
Altposaune (*Ger.*) } trom-
bone.

Altschlüssel (*Ger.*)—Alto clef.

Altviole (*Ger.*)—Viola.

Am (*Ger.*)—By, to, at, on the.

Amabile (*It.*)—Sweet, tender, gentle.

Amabilità, con (*It.*)—With sweetness ; tenderly.

Amarevole (*It.*) } Bitterly, sadly,
Amarezza (*It.*) } mournfully.

Amateur (*Fr.*)—One who admires and takes an interest in music, and who, while possessing knowledge of one or more of its branches, does not pursue the art as a profession.

Ambrosian Chant.—The most ancient form of Church-song, introduced by St. Ambrose, Bishop of Milan.

Âme (*Fr.*)—The sound-post of the violin, or other stringed instrument of the same class.

American organ.—A keyboard instrument, the tone of which is produced by the vibration of reeds. It differs from the harmonium, in that the air is sucked, instead of being blown, through the apertures over which the reeds are placed.

A mezza voce (*It.*)—With half the power of the voice. Also occasionally used to indicate the subdued tone of an instrument.

A moll (*Ger.*)—The key of A minor.

Amore, con }
Amorevole } (*It.*) Lovingly, fondly,
Amoroso } tenderly.

Amphibrach (*Gk.*)—A metrical foot, consisting of a long syllable between two short ones, ◡ — ◡

Amphimacer.—A metrical foot, consisting of a short syllable between two long ones, — ◡ —

Anacrusis.—One or two unaccented syllables beginning a verse of poetry ; in music, the unaccented note or notes which precede the first accented note of a phrase.

Anapest.—A metrical foot, consisting of two short syllables followed by a long one, ◡ ◡ —

Anche (*Fr.*)—The reed in the mouthpiece of a hautboy, bassoon, etc.; the reeds in an organ, harmonium, etc., are termed *anches.*

Anche (*It.*)—Also, still, likewise.

Ancia (*It.*)—The same as the French *anche*, a reed.

Ancor ⎫ (*It.*)—Again, also, yet, still.
Ancora ⎭ *Ancor più mosso*, still faster.

Andacht, mit ⎫ (*Ger.*)-With devotion;
Andächtig ⎭ devoutly.

Andante (*It.*) — This term, which means literally "walking," indicates a somewhat slow tempo.
This term is frequently qualified: as for example, *andante con moto*, slowly, but with some movement; *andante affettuoso*, slowly and with tender feeling, etc.

Andantino (*It.*)—Diminutive of *andante*, meaning a little slower than *andante* ; the term is however frequently interpreted as meaning a little faster than *andante*.

Andare diritto (*It.*)—Go straight on.

Andauerend (*Ger.*)—Continually.

Anemometer.—An instrument to shew the weight or pressure of wind in an organ.

Anfang (*Ger.*) — Beginning. *Vom Anfang*—the same indication as *Da capo*.

Anfangsritornell (*Ger.*) — Introductory symphony.

Anglican Chant.—The form of musical composition to which the Canticles and Psalms are sung in the Anglican Church. There are two forms in general use, named " Single " and " Double " chants. The former is seven bars in length, divided into two phrases, the first of which is three bars, and the second four bars, long. The form of a double chant is that which would equal two single ones.
Another form, less frequently used, is the " Quadruple " chant, the dimension of which is that of two double chants.

Angore (*It.*)—Anguish, grief, distress.

Angoscia ⎫ (*It.*)—Expressive of suf-
Angoscioso ⎭ fering and anguish.

Ängstlich (*Ger.*)—Anxiously, fearfully.

Anhang (*Ger.*)—A coda.

Anima, con (*It.*)—With soul; with deep expression. This term is frequently confused with " *animato* " (*q.v.*)

Animando (*It.*) ⎫
Animato (*It.*) ⎬ With animation; with increased life.
Animé (*Fr.*) ⎭

Animosamente ⎫ (*It.*)—Lively, with
Animoso ⎭ energy.

Anklang (*Gre.*)—Tune, harmony, accord.

Anklingen (*Ger.*)—To accord, to be in tune.

Anlaufen (*Ger.*)—To increase or swell out the sound.

Anmut(h)svoll (*Ger.*) — Gracefully, suavely, sweetly.

Ansatz (*Ger.*)—(1) Attack. (2) The mode of tone-production in the case of a wind instrument.

Anschlag (*Ger.*)—(1) Touch. (2) The mode of tone-production on a keyed instrument.

Anschwellen (*Ger.*)—To increase the tone. (Crescendo.)

Answer.—In a fugue, the presentation of the theme in a second voice and in a different key, forming a response to the initial entry in the first voice.

Antecedent.—The theme or motive proposed for imitation in a canon.

Antérieur (*Fr.*) – Previous.

Anthem.—A sacred vocal composition, set to words selected from the Scriptures. There are different styles of anthems, such as : Full anthem, for chorus only ; Verse anthem, in which some portion is sung by one voice for each part; and Solo anthem, in which some portion is set for a single voice.

Antibacchius.—A metrical foot, consisting of two long syllables followed by a short one, — — ◡

Anticipation.—The introduction of a note before the harmony which would naturally accompany it.

Antico (*It.*)--Antique, ancient. *All' antico*, in the ancient style.

Antiphon.—Originally, a responsive system of singing by two choirs, or a divided choir, as practised in the early Catholic service.

Also, a short sentence from the Bible sung before or after the Psalms for the day, or the Canticles.

Antiphony.—In ancient Greek music antiphony meant "sounds in octaves."

In the modern sense, the term indicates the responsive singing of two choirs, or of the two sides of a divided choir.

Antispastus.—A metrical foot, consisting of two long syllables between two short ones, ◡ — — ◡

Antistrophe. (See Strophe.)

Antithesis.—(1) A contrasted thought; (2) a countersubject in a fugue.

Antwort (*Ger.*)—Answer; the response to the subject in a fugue.

Anwachsend (*Ger.*)—Swelling; increasing in tone. (Crescendo.)

Aperto, -a (*It.*)—Open. The use of the damper-pedal in pianoforte music. *Allegro aperto*, an allegro with broad, clear phrasing.

A piacere   } (*It.*)—At the pleasure
A piacimento } of the performer. The equivalent of *ad libitum*.

Aplomb (*Fr.*)—Self-possession, coolness, steadiness.

A poco a poco (*It.*)—By degrees; little by little. The term is used in connection with a gradual increase or decrease of tone, or of speed.

Appassionamento (*It.*)—With passion, ardour.

Appassionatamente (*It.*)—Passionately, ardently.

Appassionato, -a (*It.*)—With strong emotion, passionately.

Appena (*It.*)—Hardly, very little. *Appena animato*, a trifle more animated.

Appenato (*It.*)—In a manner expressive of grief.

Application (*Fr.*) } Method of finger-
Applicatur (*Ger.*) } ing, or of using
Applicatura (*It.*) } the fingers, upon an instrument.

Appoggiando } (*It.*)—Drawing out,
Appoggiato } leaning upon. The term indicates the gliding from a note to the next one, as in *portamento*. Also, in the case of repeated notes or chords, the effect is that of *mezzo staccato*.

Appoggiatura (*It.*)—A leaning. The name applied to a grace-note which carries the accent, and takes a certain portion of the value of the principal note which follows it.

À première vue (*Fr.*) }
A prima vista (*It.*) } At first sight.

A punta d'arco (*It.*)—With the point of the bow.

A punto (*It.*)—Exact, precise. In accurate time.

À quatre mains (*Fr.*) } For four hands
A quattro mani (*It.*) } on one instrument—that is, a duet for two performers on the pianoforte or organ.

À quatre voix (*Fr.*) } For four voices
A quattro voci (*It.*) } in harmony.

A quattro parti (*It.*)—In four parts.

Arbitrio (*It.*)—Will, pleasure. *A suo arbitrio*, at pleasure. The term conveys the same indication as *a piacere* and *ad libitum*.

Arcato (*It.*)—With the bow, as opposed to *pizzicato*.

Archet (*Fr.*)—The bow with which stringed instruments are played.

Arco (*It.*)—A bow. *Arco in giù*, down bow; *Arco in su*, up bow.

Ardente (*It.* and *Fr.*)—Ardently fervently.

Arditezza, con. (*It.*)—With boldness, spiritedly.

Ardito (*It.*)—Bold, spirited.

Aretinian syllables.—The names, ut, re, mi, fa, sol, la, given to the notes of the hexachord by Guido d'Arezzo.

Aria (*It.*)—(1) An air; a song; a melody. (2) A movement for a single voice or instrument, with an instrumental accompaniment.

Aria buffa (*It.*)—An aria of a humorous or burlesque character.

Aria concertante (*It.*)—An air with obbligato instrumental accompaniment.

Aria di bravura (*It.*)—An aria florid in style, and containing brilliant and ornamented passages calculated to display the dexterity of the performer.

Aria parlante (*It.*)—A declamatory aria.

Arietta (*It.*) ⎱ The diminutive of aria ;
Ariette (*Fr.*) ⎰ a short air or song.

A rigore di tempo (*It.*)—In strict time.

Arioso (*It.*)—In the style of an air ; melodious. In instrumental music the term indicates a rendering in *cantabile* style.

Armonia (*It*).—Harmony.

Armonica (*It.*) — (1) Harmonic. (2) Harmonica (*q.v.*).

Armonioso (*It.*)—Harmonious.

Armure de la clef (*Fr.*)—A signature.

Arpa (*It.*)—A harp. *Arpa doppia*, a double harp.

Arpeggiando ⎫ (*It.*)—The notes of a
Arpeggiare ⎬ chord played in suc-
Arpeggiato ⎭ cession. (Arpeggio.)

Arpeggio.—The notes of a chord played in succession.

Arpicordo (*It.*)—A harpsichord.

Arrangement. — An adaptation of one or more parts, or the whole, of a composition, for voices or instruments other than those for which it was originally designed.

Arranger (*Fr.*) ⎱ To arrange.
Arrangiren (*Ger.*) ⎰

Arsis (*Gk.*)—The weak beat.

Articolare (*It.*) ⎫ To articulate, to
Articuler (*Fr.*) ⎬ pronounce dis-
Articuliren (*Ger.*) ⎭ tinctly.

As (*Ger.*)—The note A flat.

As dur (*Ger.*)—A flat major.

As moll (*Ger.*)—A flat minor.

Aspirando ⎫ (*It.*) — To breathe
Aspirare ⎬ audibly ; bad manage-
Aspirato ⎭ ment of the breath in singing.

Assai (*It.*)—Very. *Allegro assai*, very fast.

Assonance (*Fr.*) ⎱ Agreement of
Assonanz (*Ger.*) ⎰ sound ; consonance.

Assourdi (*Fr.*)—Muffled.

A suo arbitrio ⎫ *It.*—At the will
A suo bene placito ⎬ or pleasure of
A suo comodo ⎭ the performer.

A tempo (*It.*)—In time. An indication that the original speed is to be resumed, should any temporary alteration have been made.

A tempo primo (*It.*)—Return to the original tempo.

A tre mani (*It.*) ⎱ For three hands.
À trois mains (*Fr.*) ⎰

A tre parti (*It.*) ⎱ In three parts.
À trois parties (*Fr.*) ⎰

A tre voci (*It.*) ⎱ For three voices.
À trois voix (*Fr.*) ⎰

Attacca (*It.*)—Begin what follows without any pause or break. *Attacca subito*, attack instantly.

Attack.—The precise, vigorous, entry of voices or instruments at a leading point.

Attaquer (*Fr.*)—To attack ; to begin.

Attendant keys.—Related keys. These are the relative major or minor of the original key, also the dominant and sub-dominant, with *their* relative major or minor keys.

Atto (*It.*)—An act of an opera or play.

Audace, con (*It.*)—With boldness ; audaciously.

Auf (*Ger.*)—Upon.

Aufgeregt (*Ger.*)—Excitedly ; in an agitated style.

Aufgeweckt (*Ger.*)—Brisk, lively, animated.

Aufhalt (*Ger.*)—Suspension.

Aufhalten (*Ger.*)—To retard, to keep back.

Auflösung (*Ger.*)—The resolution of a discord.

Auflösungszeichen (*Ger.*)—A natural (♮).

Aufschlag (*Ger.*)—An up-beat, an unaccented beat.

Aufschwung (*Ger.*)—Lofty, soaring. *Mit Aufschwung*, in a lofty, impassioned style.

Aufstrich (*Ger.*) — The up-bow in violin playing.

Auftakt (*Ger.*)—The unaccented part of a bar ; the commencement of a phrase on the unaccented part of a bar.

Auftritt (*Ger.*)—A scene.

Augmentation.—Increasing the time value of the notes of a theme, or point of imitation.

Augmenté (*Fr.*)—Augmented.

Augmented interval.— An interval which is a chromatic semitone greater than a major or perfect interval.

Aumentato, -a (*It.*)—Augmented.

Au mouvement (*Fr.*)—In time.

A una corda (*It.*)—On one string. In pianoforte music, a direction to use the soft pedal.

Ausdruck (*Ger.*)—Expression. *Ausdrucksvoll*, expressively.

Ausführung (*Ger.*)—Performance, execution.

Ausgedehnt (*Ger.*)—Extended.

Aushaltung (*Ger.*)—The sustaining of a note. *Aushalten*, to hold.

Ausserordentlich hoch (*Ger.*) — Extremely high.

Ausweichung (*Ger.*) — Modulation, change of key.

Authentic cadence.—(See Cadence.)

Authentic mode.—A term used in the Ecclesiastical modes, each mode having two forms named respectively Authentic and Plagal.

The octave is divided into two parts, one containing five notes—from the final (key-note) to the dominant above, the other containing four notes—from the dominant to the final above.

When the notes extend from the final to its octave, the division will be at the dominant, and the lower part will consist of five notes and the upper part of four. This constitutes the *Authentic* mode. If the same series of notes be arranged so as to extend from the dominant to its octave, the division at the final will reverse the position of the two parts. This constitutes the *Plagal* mode.

Authentic part of a scale.—That portion situate between the tonic and the dominant above.

Auxiliary notes.—Notes foreign to the harmony, lying either immediately above or below an essential note. They differ from passing notes in that they do not move by degrees from one harmony note to *another*, but return to that from which they started.

Avec (*Fr.*)—With. *Avec âme*, with soul ; *avec le* (or *la*), with the ; *avec la voix*, the same as *colla voce*, or *col canto*.

Avec ardeur (*Fr.*)—Longingly.

Avec délicatesse (*Fr.*)—With delicacy.

Avec douleur(*Fr.*)—With grief ; sadly.

Avec la main droite (*Fr.*)—With the right hand.

Avec la main gauche (*Fr.*)—With the left hand.

Avec sentiment (*Fr.*)—With sentiment.

Ave Maria (*Lat.*)—Hail, Mary ! A hymn of the Roman Catholic Church.

A vista (*It.*)—At sight.

Avoided cadence.—(See Cadence.)

B.

B.—The name of the seventh degree of the scale of C major. In German, B stands for the note B flat, B natural being called H. B is also the abbreviation for *Bass* or *Basso*.

Bacchius.—A metrical foot, consisting of one short and two long syllables, ⏑ — —

Backfall.—(1) An obsolete musical ornament. (2) A horizontal lever in an organ.

Bagatelle (*Fr.*)—A short piece, a trifle.

Bagpipe.—An ancient wind instrument, still in use in many countries. It consists of a leathern bag which acts as the wind reservoir, two or three pipes which are called drones, and a short pipe pierced with finger-holes, upon which the tune is played.

Baguettes (*Fr.*)—Drumsticks.

Balance swell-pedal.—A foot-lever in an organ, which enables the tone of certain manuals to be increased or diminished, and which will remain in any fixed position.

Ballad.—Originally, a song intended for a dance-accompaniment. The popular meaning in English is " a simple song," usually with an accompaniment for the pianoforte. It also includes compositions for a single instrument, and for chorus with or without accompaniment.

Ballade (*Fr.*) ⎫
Ballade (*Ger.*) ⎬ A ballad.
Ballata (*It.*) ⎭

Ballet.— (1) A spectacular dance introduced into an opera or stage-piece. (2) The representation of an action by pantomime and dancing, with suitable musical accompaniment.

Ballet (*Fr.*) ⎫
Ballett (*Ger.*) ⎬ A ballet.
Balletto (*It.*) ⎭

Ballo (*It.*)—A dance; a ballet. *Balli ungaresi*, Hungarian dances. *Da ballo*, in dance-style, light and spirited.

Band.—(1) A body of instrumental performers. (2) A section of the orchestra playing instruments of the same class (*e.g.*, string-band, brass-band).

Banda (*It.*) ⎫ A band.
Bande (*Fr.*)⎭

Banjo.—A long-necked string instrument, the body of which consists of a hoop with skin stretched over it. It has from five to nine strings, tuned to notes of different pitch.

Bar.—(1) The name given to each of the perpendicular lines drawn across the staff, which lines divide the music into portions of equal

duration. (2) The name given to the music comprised between two such lines; which, though generally used, is really hardly as correct as " measure."

Barcarole (*E.* and *Ger.*) ⎫ An Italian
Barcarola (*It.*) ⎬ (Venetian) boatman's
Barcarolle (*Fr.*) ⎭ song. Also a vocal or instrumental piece in imitation of, or similar in character to, such a song.

Bard.—A poet and minstrel among the various Celtic nations.

Bare fifth.—An interval of a fifth unaccompanied by the third.

Bariton (*Fr.* and *Ger.*)—Baritone, or barytone (*q.v.*).

Baritone or ⎫ (1) The male voice with
Barytone ⎭ a range between bass and tenor. Also a singer having such voice. (2) An obsolete bowed-instrument like the viola da gamba. (3) The euphonium.

Baritono (*It.*)—Baritone.

Baritone clef.—The F clef on the third line, now obsolete.

Barocco (*It.*) ⎫
Barock (*Ger.*) ⎬ Whimsical, strange, odd.
Baroque (*Fr.*) ⎭

Barré (*Fr*).—The temporary alteration of the pitch in guitar or lute playing, by pressing the forefinger of the left hand across the strings.

Barre de mesure (*Fr.*)—Bar-line.

Barre de répétition (*Fr.*)—A double bar with dots, indicating a repeat.

Barsch (*Ger.*)—Brusquely.

Bas-dessus (*Fr.*)—Mezzo-soprano.

Bass.—(1) The lowest note of chord. (2) The lowest member of any family of instrument. (3) The lowest male voice.

Bassa (*It.*)—Low. *Ottava bassa*, or *all'ottava bassa*, indicates that the notes thus marked are to be played an octave lower than they are written.

Bass clef.—The F clef on the fourth line of the staff.

Basse (*Fr.*)—Bass.

Basse chantante (*Fr.*)—A baritone voice. (*See* also Basso Cantante.)

Basse chiffrée }
Basse continue } (*Fr.*)-Figured bass.

Basse contrainte (*Fr.*)—Ground bass.

Basse contre (*Fr.*)—(1) A deep bass voice. (2) The double-bass.

Basse de viole (*Fr.*)—Bass viol.

Basse fondamentale (*Fr.*)–(1) Fundamental bass. (2) Root.

Basse recitante (*Fr.*)—A solo bass.

Basse-taille (*Fr.*) — The baritone voice.

Basset-horn.—A transposing instrument of the clarinet family, with a soft, rich quality of tone. The pitch of the notes it produces is a perfect fifth lower than those written. It is now practically obsolete.

Basse-trombone (*Fr.*)—Bass trombone.

Bassgeige (*Ger.*)—Violoncello. *Grosse Bassgeige*, double bass.

Basso (*It.*)—(1) A bass voice or singer. (2) The double bass. (3) The bass part.

Basso buffo (*It.*)—A comic singer with a bass voice.

Basso cantante (*It.*)—The lighter, more flexible "singing bass," differing from the heavy "deep bass" (Basso profondo).

Basso continuo (*It.*)—A figured bass part for the organ or pianoforte.

Basso figurato (*It.*)—(1) Basso continuo. (2) A bass part with running passages.

Basso fondamentale (*It.*)—The fundamental bass, or root.

Basson (*Fr.*)—The bassoon.

Basso numerato (*It.*)—A figured bass.

Basso ostinato (*It.*)—Ground bass.

Basso profondo (*It.*)—A deep bass.

Basso ripieno (*It.*)—The bass played by all the performers, as distinguished from that played by only one, or a few.

Bassoon.—A wood wind instrument with a double reed mouthpiece. It has a compass of rather more than three octaves, upwards from

and forms the bass of the group of wood-wind instruments in the orchestra.

Basso-Trombone (*It.*)—Bass trombone.

Bass-Posaune (*Ger.*) — Bass trombone.

Bass Schlüssel (*Ger.*)—Bass clef.

Bass Stimme (*Ger.*)—Bass voice.

Bass tuba.—(Tuba.)

Bass viol.—(Viol.)

Bâton (*Fr.*)—The stick used by a conductor for beating time.

Bâton de reprise (*Fr.*)—The sign of repeat.

Battement de mesure (*Fr.*)—A beat.

Battuta (*It.*)—(1) A bar, a measure. (2) A beat. *A battuta*, in time.

B-doppel B.—The German name for B double flat.

B dur (*Ger.*)—The key of B flat major.

Beat.—(1) The movement of the hand or bâton in beating time. (2) The musical pulse. (3) The term occasionally applied to a transient trill, or mordent. (4) The "throbbing" sensation produced by sounding together two notes not quite identical in pitch.

Beaucoup (*Fr.*)—Much.

Bebung (*Ger.*)—The pulsating, trembling effect given to a sustained note. On stringed instruments the effect is produced by the oscillation of the finger when pressing the string down. More particularly, the word refers to the effect capable of production on the old clavichord, where the continuous repetition of a note was effected by a movement of the tip of the finger on the key without quitting it. The modern equivalent would be *Tremolo* or *vibrato*.

Bécarre (*Fr.*)—The natural (♮).

Bec (*Fr.*) }
Becco (*It.*) } A mouthpiece.

Becken (*Ger.*)—Cymbals.

Bedeckt (*Ger.*)—Stopped.

Begleitung (*Ger.*)—Accompaniment.

Beisser (*Ger.*)—A mordent.

Beitöne (*Ger.*)—Harmonics.

Bel canto.—The cantabile style of singing usually associated with the Italian school. It may be described as being opposed to the modern, declamatory style.

Belebend (*Ger.*)—Enlivening.

Belebt (*Ger.*)—Animated, lively.

Bell.—(1) The termination of the tube in the majority of wind instruments. (2) An instrument of percussion.

Bell diapason. — An organ-stop, usually of 8 ft. pitch, with open, bell-mouthed pipes.

Bell gamba. — An organ-stop, the pipes of which are conical and surmounted by a bell.

Bell metronome.—A metronome with a small bell which automatically indicates the first beat of the bar.

Belly.—(1) The upper side of the sound-box of the violin, etc. (2) The soundboard of the pianoforte.

Bémol (*Fr.*) ⎫
Bemolle (*It.*) ⎭ Flat.

Ben ⎫ (*It.*)—Well. *Ben marcato*,
Bene ⎭ well marked.

Bene placito (*It.*)—At pleasure.

Bequadro (*It.*) ⎫
Béquarre (*Fr.*) ⎭ The natural.

Berceuse (*Fr.*)—A cradle song, lullaby.

Bes (*Ger.*)—B double flat.

Beschleunigtes tempo (*Ger.*)— A gradual increase of the speed.

Bestimmt (*Ger.*)—With decision, energy.

Betont (*Ger.*)—Emphasised, marked.

Betonung (*Ger.*)—Accent, emphasis.

Bewegt (*Ger.*)—Moved, agitated, impassioned.

Bewegter (*Ger.*)—Faster ; *più mosso*.

Bewegung (*Ger.*)—Motion, movement, agitation, emotion.

Bezifferter Bass(*Ger.*)—Figured bass.

Bianca (*It.*)—A minim.

Bichord.—Having two strings tuned in unison, to each note.

Bien (*Fr.*)—Well. *Bien rhythmé*, well accented.

Binary.—Two-fold. *Binary measure*, a measure, or bar of music, having an accent on alternate notes. *Binary form*, a form of movement divided into two parts (*e.g.*, most of the movements in the suites of Bach and Handel).

Bind.—A curved line joining together two notes identical in pitch, the second being sustained but not re-sounded. (Tie.)

Binde ⎫
Bindebogen ⎭ (*Ger.*)—A bind, or tie.

Bindung (*Ger.*)—Syncopation, suspension.

Bis (*Lat.*)—Twice. (1) A direction that a passage is to be played or sung twice. (2) Again, *encore*.

Bis (*Ger.*)—Until.

Biscroma (*It.*) ⎫
Biscrome (*Fr.*) ⎭ A demisemiquaver.

Bis diapason.—The interval of a double octave, or fifteenth.

Bisser (*Fr.*)—To " encore."

Bizarr (*Ger.*) ⎫ In a whimsical,
Bizzarramente (*It.*) ⎬ fantastic, extravagant
Bizzarria, con (*It.*) ⎭ style.

Bizzarro, -a (*It.*)—Odd, whimsical.

Blanche (*Fr.*)—A minim.

Blanche pointée (*Fr.*) — A dotted minim.

Blasinstrument (*Ger.*)—Wind instrument.

Blatt (*Ger.*)—A reed.

Blechinstrument (*Ger.*)—Brass instrument.

B moll (*Ger.*)—The key of B flat minor.

Bocal (*Fr.*)—The mouthpiece of the horn, trumpet, etc.

Bocca (*It.*)—Mouth.

Body.—(1) The resonance-box of a string instrument. (2) The portion of a wind instrument remaining after the mouthpiece, crooks, and bell have been removed. (3) The tube of an organ-pipe above the mouth.

Bogen (*Ger.*)—(1) A bow, such as is used for playing the violin, etc. (2) A slur or tie.

Bogenstrich (*Ger.*)—A stroke of the bow.

Bolero (*Sp.*)—A Spanish national dance in triple time and lively *tempo*, usually accompanied with castanets.

Bombard.—(1) A large kind of oboe, or shawm, now obsolete. (2) A 16 ft. reed-stop in the organ.

Bombarde (*Fr.*) ⎱ A bombard.
Bombardo (*It.*) ⎰

Bombardon.—A powerful brass wind instrument which executes the bass part in military bands.

Bon temps de la mesure (*Fr.*)—The accented part of a bar.

Bouche (*Fr.*)—Mouth. *À bouche fermée*, with closed lips.

Bourdon (*Fr.*) — (1) A drone bass. (2) An organ-stop, consisting of stopped pipes, generally of 16 ft. tone.

Bourrée (*Fr.*) — A lively dance of French origin. It forms one of the movements in the earlier suites, and is in 𝄵 time. Though similar in character to the *Gavotte*, it has this important point of difference, viz., that the *Gavotte* commences upon the third crotchet of the bar, while the *Bourrée* begins upon the fourth.

Bow.—An instrument used for playing the violin and other string-instruments.

B quadro (*It.*)—The sign ♮.

Brace.—(1) A bracket joining two or more staves together. (2) One of the leather slides upon the cords of a drum.

Branle, or **Bransle** (*Fr.*)—A brawl (*q.v.*) ; an old French dance.

Bratsche (*Ger.*)—The viola, or tenor violin.

Bravour (*Ger.*) ⎱
Bravoure (*Fr.*) ⎰ (Bravura.)

Bravura (*It.*)—Boldness, dash, spirit, brilliancy.

Brawl.—An old country dance, in which the performers joined hands in a circle.

Break.—(1) In the voice, the point which marks the change from one register to another. (2) In the clarinet the break occurs between

(3) A break, in an

organ-stop, occurs when a change is made from the natural ascent of a scale to the octave below.

Breit (*Ger.*)—In a broad, stately manner.

Breve.—The note equal in length to two semibreves.

Breve (*It.*)—Short.

Bridge.—The piece of wood which rests upon the resonance-box of string instruments such as the violin, etc., and over which the strings are stretched.

Brillant (*Fr.*) ⎱ Brilliant, showy,
Brillante (*It.*) ⎰ sparkling.

Brio, con ⎱ (*It.*)—With spirit, vigour
Brioso ⎰ and vivacity.

Brisé (*Fr.*)—Broken, arpeggiated In violin-playing, short, detached strokes of the bow.

Broken cadence.—A term sometimes used to signify an *Interrupted* cadence.

Broken chord.—Any position, or successive positions of a chord, in which the notes are played one after the other in any order.

Bruscamente (*It.*) — Brusquely, roughly, strongly accented.

Brusco (*It.*)—Rough, harsh.

Brusquement (*Fr.*)—Brusquely.

Brust (*Ger.*)—Chest.

Buccolico, -a (*It.*) ⎱ Rustic. *À la buco-*
Bucolique (*Fr.*) ⎰ *lique*, in a rustic manner.

Buffo, -a (*It.*) — Comic, burlesque. *Aria buffa*, a comic air. *Opera buffa*, a comic opera.

Bugle.—A brass wind instrument, chiefly used for the purpose of giving military signals.

Buona nota (*It.*)—An accented note.

Burden.—(1) The chorus or refrain of a song. (2) The drone of a bagpipe. (3) A dance accompaniment sung without instruments.

Burlando (*It.*)—In a jesting, comic manner.

Burlesco, -a (*It.*) ⎰ Burlesque, merry,
Burlesk (*Ger.*) ⎱ comic. *Burlesca*, a movement of a jocular character.

Burlesque. — A dramatic extravaganza.

Burletta (*It.*)—A comic operetta.

C.

C.—The name of the first degree, or key-note, of the normal diatonic scale. A capital C indicates the note written in the second space of the bass staff, and is termed Tenor C. A small c indicates the note an octave above Tenor C, and the note at this pitch is called *Middle* c.

Cabaletta (*It.*)—A simple melody.

Caccia (*It.*)—Chase, hunting. *Alla caccia*, in the hunting style.

Cachuca (*Sp.*)—A Spanish dance, after the style of the bolero.

Cacofonia (*It.*) ⎫
Cacophonie (*Fr.*) ⎬ Confused, ill-sounding music.
Cacophony ⎭

Cadence.—A close, or ending. A progression of two chords indicating a point of rest, complete or incomplete.
Cadences are of four kinds :—
(1) Perfect, the dominant chord followed by that of the tonic. Also spoken of as (*a*) an Authentic cadence, (*b*) a Full close.
(2) Plagal, the subdominant followed by the tonic. This is sometimes called the " Amen " cadence.
(3) Imperfect or Half close, a temporary point of arrest (usually upon the chord of the dominant).
(4) Interrupted, the chord of the dominant followed by some chord other than the tonic. This cadence is sometimes spoken of as a " False," " Deceptive," " Broken " or " Evaded " cadence.
Some authorities apply the term " Mixed cadence " when a Perfect cadence is preceded by the chord of the sub-dominant.
The term " Cadence " is applied to a shake or brilliant passage which leads up to the close of a movement, or part of a movement.

Cadence (*Fr.*)—(1) A shake. (2) The close of a musical phrase.

Cadence imparfaite (*Fr.*)—An imperfect cadence, a half close.

Cadence interrompue (*Fr.*)—An interrupted cadence.

Cadence parfaite (*Fr.*) ⎰ A perfect
Cadenza perfetta (*It.*) ⎱ cadence.

Cadence pleine (*Fr.*)—A plagal cadence.

Cadenz (*Ger.*)—A cadence.

Cadenza (*It.*)—(1) A cadence. (2) A brilliant passage introduced towards the close of a movement. Such cadenzas are met with in vocal and instrumental compositions, and in the concerto the cadenza is of a very elaborate nature, practically a fantasia upon the principal themes of the movement.

Cadenza d'inganno ⎰ (*It.*)—An interrupted cadence.
Cadenza finta ⎱

Cadenza imperfetta (*It.*)—An imperfect cadence.

Cæsura. — A momentary point of rest, a cutting off : a break between phrases or musical figures.

Caisse (*Fr.*)—A drum. *Grosse caisse*, bass drum.

Calando (*It.*)—Decreasing in tone, frequently associated with a slackening in speed.

Calcando (*It.*).—Pressing on the time.

Calmando ⎰ (*It.*) — Calmly, tranquilly.
Calmato ⎱

Calme (*Fr.*)—Calm, tranquil.

Camera (*It.*)—Chamber. *Musica da camera*, chamber music.

Campana (*It.*)—A bell.

Campanella (*It.*)—A small bell.

Cancrizans (*Lat.*)—Retrogressive; moving backwards.

Canna (*It.*)—A reed ; a pipe. *Canne d'organo,* organ pipes.

Cannello (*It.*) — A reed-stop on an organ.

Canon.—A form of composition in which the theme announced in one part is, after a short rest, reproduced in another part.

A canon is said to be 2 in 1, when two parts perform one subject ; 3 in 1, when three parts perform one subject ; 4 in 2, when four parts perform two subjects.

The part which announces the theme is termed the Antecedent, and the part reproducing it, the Consequent.

A canon by diminution is one in which the notes of the Consequent are shorter than those of the Antecedent ; by augmentation, when the notes of the Consequent are longer than those of the Antecedent.

A canon by retrogression is one in which the Consequent performs the notes of the Antecedent backwards.

Canon Cancrizans (*Lat.*) — A canon by retrogression.

Canone (*It.*)—A canon.

Canone chiuso (*It.*)—A concealed canon ; one having only one part written out, the other parts having to be discovered, or being indicated by signs or words.

Canone enigmatico (*It.*)—Enigmatic canon. (Canone chiuso.)

Canone infinito or **canone perpetuo** (*It.*)—An infinite canon, one without a conclusion.

Canone sciolto (*It.*)—A free canon, in which the imitation is not exact.

Canonic imitation.—Strict imitation of one part by another.

Cantabile (*It.*)—In a singing style. A term frequently used in pianoforte music to indicate that the tone must be made to " sing."

Cantando (*It.*)—(Cantabile).

Cantare (*It.*)—To sing.

Cantata (*It.*)—Originally this term meant something sung, as distinguished from something played. At the present time it is the title given to a vocal composition consisting of solos and choruses, the subject of which may be sacred or secular.

Cantatore (*It.*)—A male singer.

Cantatrice (*It.*)—A female singer.

Canticle (*It.*)—A song or hymn of the Church.

Cantico (*It.*)—Canticle.

Cantilena (*It.*)
Cantilene (*Ger.*) } A short, song - like composition.
Cantilène (*Fr.*)

Cantique (*Fr.*)—A canticle.

Canto (*It.*)—A song, a melody. The highest part in concerted music. *Col canto,* "with the melody," a direction for the accompanist to follow the singer.

Canto a capella (*It.*)—Vocal church music.

Canto armonico (*It.*)—A part song.

Canto fermo (*It.*)—(Cantus firmus.)

Canto figurato (*It.*)—(Cantus figuratus.)

Canto plano (*It.*)—Plain-chant.

Canto primo (*It.*)—First soprano.

Cantor (*Lat.*)—A singer, a precentor.

Cantore (*It.*)—A singer, a chorister.

Cantoris (*Lat.*)—The side in a choir upon which the precentor sits, usually the north side.

Canto secondo (*It.*) — Second soprano.

Cantus (*Lat.*)—A song, a melody.

Cantus figuralis (*Lat.*) — (Cantus mensurabilis.)

Cantus figuratus (*Lat.*)—" Figured song." A *cantus firmus,* accompanied by figured, or florid counterpoint. Also used in the same sense as *cantus mensurabilis.*

Cantus firmus (*Lat.*)—(1) A fixed or given melody, originally sung by the tenor voice ; afterwards given to the treble-part, hence the term *canto* (*q.v.*) (2) Plain-song, plainchant. (3) A fragment of plainsong or other melody chosen for contrapuntal elaboration.

Cantus mensurabilis (*Lat.*)—Measured song, as distinguished from *cantus planus*, or plain-chant:—*i.e.*, consisting of notes of different time-values.

Canzona ⎱ (*It.*)—(1) A song, a melody.
Canzone ⎰ (2) An instrumental composition of former times, contrapuntal in character.

Canzonetta (*It.*)—The diminutive of *canzone.*

Capellmeister (*Ger.*)—The musical director in a church. The conductor of a band or an opera.

Capo (*It.*)—(1) The head; the beginning. *Da capo*, from the beginning. (2) A leader.

Capotasto (*It.*)—The nut on the fingerboard of stringed instruments.

Cappella (*It.*)—(1) A church. (2) A choir; an orchestra; or both together. The word is frequently spelt *capella*. (A cappella.)

Capriccietto (*It.*)—A short *capriccio.*

Capriccio (*It.*)—A whim, a caprice, An instrumental composition not written in any particular form. *A capriccio*, at pleasure.

Capriccioso (*It.*)—In a capricious, fanciful style.

Caprice (*Fr.*)—(Capriccio.)

Capricieux (*Fr.*)—Fancifully; with humour.

Caractères de musique (*Fr.*)—The signs used in the notation of music.

Caressant (*Fr.*) ⎫
Carezzando (*It.*) ⎬ Caressingly, soothingly.
Carezzevole (*It.*) ⎭

Carillon (*Fr.*)—(1) A set of bells, played either by hand or by some form of mechanism. (2) A tune played on bells; also, a composition intended to produce such an effect.

Carol.—(1) To sing joyously. (2) A song of mirth, or praise, usually associated with Christmas-tide.

Cassa, or **cassa-grande** (*It.*)—The big drum.

Castagnette (*It.*) ⎫
Castagnettes (*Fr.*) ⎬ Castanets.
Castañuelas (*Sp.*) ⎭

Castanets.—Two small pieces of hard wood or ivory, concave in shape, attached to the hand by a chord and struck together. They form a prominent feature in the accompaniment of Spanish dances and songs.

Catch.—A round or canon for three or four voices, each singer having to "catch" or take up his part at the right moment.

Catgut. — General name for gut strings.

Cathedral music.—The music composed in a style suitable for use in a cathedral service. Usually applied to the settings of the canticles, and to anthems.

Cavatina (*It.*)—A short and simple form of *aria*, without a second part, or "da capo."

C barré (*Fr.*)—The time signature which indicates *alla breve* time.

C clef.—The clef which indicates that the line of the staff upon which it is written is "middle C." For the *Soprano* staff the C clef stands upon the first line, for the *Mezzo-soprano* upon the second line, for the *Alto* upon the third line, and for the *Tenor* upon the fourth line.

C dur (*Ger.*)—The key of C major.

Celere (*It.*)—Quick, nimble.

Celerità, con (*It.*)—With swiftness, nimbly.

Céleste (*Fr.*)—A direction for the use of the soft pedal.

Celli (*It.*)—Abbreviation of *violoncelli*, plural of violoncello.

Cello (*It.*)—Abbreviation of *violoncello.*

Cembalo (*It.*)—A harpsichord. The same as *clavicembalo.*

Ces (*Ger.*)—The note C flat.

Ces dur (*Ger.*)—The key of C flat major.

Chacona (*Sp.*) ⎫ A slow dance in 3-4
Chaconne (*Fr.*) ⎬ time, constructed over a ground-
Ciaconna (*It.*) ⎭ bass.

Chalumeau (*Fr.*)—(1) An ancient reed instrument. (2) The lower register of the clarinet. The word " chalumeau " in clarinet music indicates that the notes have to be played an octave lower.

Chamber music.—Compositions suitable for performance in a room, as distinguished from *Concert music*— *i.e.*, music performed by a large number of executants.

Changer de jeu (*Fr.*)—To change the stops of an organ or harmonium.

Changes.—The varying order of a peal of bells.

Changing notes.—The term " changing notes " is applied in harmony, or perhaps more frequently in counterpoint, to two passing notes, the first of which is approached by step from a harmony note, and then leaps an interval of a third to another—over the same, or another, harmony note — immediately returning to the harmony note lying between the two passing notes.

Chanson (*Fr.*)—A song.

Chansonette (*Fr.*)—A little song.

Chant.--The form of composition to which the canticles and psalms are sung in the Church. There are two kinds in general use—the Anglican and Gregorian. Anglican chants are usually of two kinds, single and double. A single chant contains two phrases, the first three bars in length, and the second four bars.

A double chant is equal to two, a triple chant to three, and a quadruple chant to four, single ones.

A Gregorian chant contains five parts — the intonation, reciting-note, mediation, second reciting-note, and the ending.

Chant (*Fr.*)—Song; singing; melody.

Chanter (*Fr.*)—To sing.

Chanterelle (*Fr.*)—The highest string on a violin, etc.

Chanteur (*Fr.*)—A male singer.

Chanteuse (*Fr.*)—A female singer.

Characters.—The signs employed in musical notation.

Charakterstücke (*Ger.*)—Characteristic pieces ; those descriptive of some mood, scene, or impression.

Charme, avec (*Fr.*)—With charm ; gracefully.

Chasse (*Fr.*)—Chase, hunting. *À la chasse*, in the hunting style.

Chef d'attaque (*Fr.*)—The leader of a chorus, or of an orchestra.

Chef d'œuvre (*Fr.*)—The chief work of any composer.

Chef d'orchestre (*Fr.*) — The conductor of an orchestra.

Chest of viols.—A set of viols, consisting of two trebles, two tenors, and two basses.

Chest-register.—The term applied by some authorities to the lower register of the male or female voice. The tone thus produced is also termed chest tone, or chest voice.

Chevalet (*Fr.*)—The bridge of a stringed instrument.

Cheville (*Fr.*)—A peg for the violin, guitar, etc.

Chiarezza, con (*It.*)—With brightness, clearness.

Chiaro, -a (*It.*)—Clear, pure. *Chiara quarta*, a perfect fourth.

Chiave (*It.*)—A clef or key. *Chiave di tenore*, the tenor clef.

Chiesa (*Fr.*)—Church. *Sonata da chiesa*, a sacred sonata.

Chiffré (*Fr.*)—Figured. *Basse chiffré*, figured bass.

Chime.—To play on bells by means of hammers, or by swinging their clappers, the bells themselves not being moved. It is opposed to *ringing*, in which the bells are made to swing.

Chitarra (*It.*)—A guitar.

Chiuso, -a (*It.*)—Closed. *A bocca chiusa*, with closed mouth, humming.

Chœur (*Fr.*)—Choir, chorus.

Choir.—(1) A body of singers. (2) That part of the church set apart for the singers. (3) A sub-division of a chorus.

Choir organ.—That part of an organ containing stops of a rather subdued tone, as distinguished from that of the more powerful " great organ."

Chor (*Ger.*) — (1) A choir. (2) A chorus.

Choragus (*Lat.*)—(1) The leader of the chorus in the Greek drama. (2) The title of a musical official at Oxford University.

Choral.—(1) Belonging to the choir. (2) *Choral service*, a service with music.

Choral, or **Chorale** (*Ger.*)—A hymn tune of the early German Protestant Church, or one similar in style.

Chord.—(1) A combination of two or more sounds. (2) A string.

Choriambus.—A metrical foot, consisting of two short syllables between two long ones, — ⌣ ⌣ —

Chorist (*Ger.*) ⎫
Choriste (*Fr.*) ⎬ A member of a choir or chorus.
Chorister ⎭

Chorstimmen (*Ger.*)—Chorus parts.

Chorus.—(1) A body of singers. (2) The whole or portion of a composition in which each part is assigned to several voices. (3) The refrain of a song.

Christe eleison (*Gk.*)—A portion of the Kyrie in the Mass.

Chroma (*Gk.*)—In Greek music the chromatic alteration of the tetrachord ; also a chromatic semitone.

Chromatic.—Notes contrary to a given key signature ; opposed to diatonic.

A chromatic *scale* is one proceeding by semitones. A chromatic *interval* is one not found in a diatonic *scale*. A chromatic *chord* is one having one or more of its notes inflected by an accidental, but which chord does not cause a modulation.

Chromatique (*Fr.*) ⎫
Chromatisch (*Ger.*) ⎬ Chromatic.

Church modes.—The scales which were in use up to the period when the present major and minor scales became generally accepted. They are formed of the " natural " notes only, and may commence upon any one of these, the lowest note being repeated an octave higher to complete the octave.

These modes, which differ only in the position of the semitones, are divided into Authentic and Plagal. The seven Authentic modes are :—Dorian, commencing on D ; Phrygian, on E ; Lydian, on F ; Mixolydian, on G ; Æolian, on A ; Hyperæolian, on B ; and Ionian, on C. In the Authentic modes the lowest note is the Final (the equivalent of the modern term Tonic) ; and each Authentic mode has its corresponding Plagal mode, which commences on the note a fourth below, and is signified by the prefix " Hypo " ; for example—the Plagal mode of the Dorian is the Hypo-Dorian. The difference between an Authentic and a Plagal mode depends upon the position of the Final, which will be seen if the notes a b c d e f g a be taken as a scale. If A be the Final, the notes form the Æolian mode ; but if D be the Final, the notes form the Hypo-Dorian.

Ciaccona (*It.*)—Chaconne.

Cimbales (*Fr.*) ⎫
Cinellen (*Ger.*) ⎬ Cymbals.
Cinelli (*It.*) ⎭

Cimbalo (*It.*)—(1) A cymbal. (2) A harpsichord. (3) A tambourine. (4) A dulcimer.

Cipher.—The constant sounding of an organ pipe, caused by defective mechanism.

Circular canon.—A canon ending in the key a semitone above that in which it began, which process, if repeated twelve times, would cause it to pass through the " circle " of twelve keys.

Cis (*Ger.*)—C sharp.

Cis dur (*Ger.*)—The key of C sharp major.

Cisis (*Ger.*)—C double sharp.

Cis moll (*Ger.*)—The key of C sharp minor.

Cithara (*Gk.* and *Lat.*)—A species of lyre used by the Greeks and Romans.

Cither.—A species of lute or guitar, strung with wire instead of gut, and played with a quill or plectrum.

Cittern.—An old English name for the cither.

Clairon (*Fr.*)—(Clarino.)

Clang.—A fundamental note with its harmonics.

Clarabella.—An organ - stop constructed of wood, of soft tone, and usually of 8 ft. pitch, invented by Bishop.

Claribel flute.—A 4 ft. clarabella.

Clarichord.—(Clavichord.)

Clarinet.—A transposing wood-wind instrument, cylindrical in shape, played with a single reed, said to have been invented about the year 1690. It has a compass of about 3½ octaves upwards from tenor E. It is in three keys—C (non-transposing) ; B flat, transposing a tone lower; and A, transposing a minor third lower. In military bands a smaller one in E flat is used, transposing a minor third higher.

Clarinette (*Fr.*)
Clarinetto (*It.*) }(Clarinet.)
Clarionet

Clarino (*It.*)—(1) A shrill-toned trumpet. (2) A bugle. (3) A reed-stop in the organ, usually of 4 ft. pitch.

Clarion.—(1) A trumpet. (2) A reed-stop in the organ, usually of 4 ft. pitch.

Clausula (*Lat.*)—A close or cadence : *e.g.*, *clausula finalis*, a final cadence ; *clausula ficta*, an interrupted cadence.

Clavecin (*Fr.*)—A harpsichord.

Claviatur (*Ger.*)—The keyboard of a pianoforte, organ, etc.

Clavicembalo(*It.*)—The harpsichord.

Clavichord.—One of the precursors of the pianoforte ; a keyboard stringed instrument, the strings being struck by upright metal wedges called tangents, fixed at end of the keys.

Clavier (*Ger.*) ⎰ (1) The pianoforte.
Clavier (*Fr.*) ⎱ (2) A row of keys on an organ.

Clavierauszug (*Ger.*)—A pianoforte score, as distinguished from *Partitur*, a full score.

Clavierstück (*Ger.*)—A piece for the pianoforte.

Clavis (*Lat.*)—A key ; a clef.

Clef.—The sign placed at the commencement of a staff, which determines the name and absolute pitch of the line upon which it is placed, and from which all the other notes are calculated. Clefs are of three kinds—G, F and C or.

Clef de Ténor (*Fr.*)—The tenor clef.

Cloche (*Fr.*)—A bell.

Clochette (*Fr.*)—A small bell.

Close.—A cadence.

Close harmony.—When the three upper notes of a chord are so arranged that no note of the same chord can be inserted between any note and the one next above it, or below.

C moll (*Ger.*)—C minor.

Coda.—(*Lit.*, " a tail.") The passage which is added at the end of a movement, in order to emphasize the conclusion.

Codetta.—(1) The term frequently applied to a short coda. (2) In a fugue the term is applied to the passage which links together two entries of the theme, either in the exposition, or at a later stage.

Col, coll', colla, collo (*It.*)—With the.

Col canto (*It.*)—With the vocal part, or with the melody.

Coll' arco (*It.*)—With the bow.

Colla destra (*It.*)—With the right hand.

Colla parte (*It.*)—With the solo part.

Colla punta dell' arco (*It.*)—With the point of the bow.

Colla sinistra (*It.*)—With the left hand.

Colla voce (*It.*)—With the voice.

Col legno (*It.*)—With the wood—*i.e.*, to strike the strings of the violin with the back of the bow.

Collet de violon (*Fr.*)—The neck of the violin.

Color (*Lat.*)—Timbre ; quality.

Coloratura (*It.*)—Ornamental passages, runs, trills, &c., in vocal music. Also applied to instrumental music.

Combination pedals.—Part of the mechanism of the organ, being foot levers which enable the player to alter the draw-stops.

Combination, or **combinational, tones.** (Resultant tones.)

Come (*It.*)—As, like.

Come da lontano (*It.*)—As from a distance.

Come prima (*It.*)—As before ; as at first.

Comes (*Lat.*)—The answer to the subject (*Dux*) in a fugue.

Come sopra (*It.*)—As above.

Come sta (*It.*)—As it stands ; as it is written.

Comma.—The difference which exists between a major tone, the two notes of which vibrate in the ratio 9 : 8, and a minor tone with a ratio of 10 : 9.

Commodo (*It.*)—Easily, at a convenient speed.

Common chord.—A chord composed of a bass-note, with its major or minor third, and perfect fifth.

Common metre.—A verse of four lines, containing the following number of syllables—first line, 8 ; second line, 6 ; third, 8 ; and fourth, 6.

Common time.—A species of time in which the measure, or bar, contains two, or four, divisions, whatever the value of each division. The term is generally associated with 4-4 time.

Comodo (*It.*)—(Commodo.)

Compass.—The range of sounds which a voice or instrument is capable of producing.

Complement.—The interval which must be added to any other interval, in order that the whole shall be equal to an octave.

Composition pedal. — Combination pedal.

Composizione (*It.*)—A composition.

Compound interval. — An interval which exceeds the compass of an octave, *i.e.*, one which contains more than eight notes in alphabetical order.

The number or name of a compound interval is found by adding seven to that of a simple interval ; thus, a third becomes a tenth ; a fifth a twelfth, etc. Conversely, the simple form of an interval is obtained by deducting the number seven from the number of a compound interval.

Compound time.—When each pulse is divisible into three equal parts, *e.g.*,

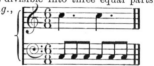

Compound time may be duple, triple, or quadruple, as the case may be.

Compressed score.—(Short score.)

Con (*It.*)—With ; in a style expressive of. "Con" is a word constantly used as a prefix to another, such as *con espressione*, with expression ; *con moto*, with movement, etc.

Concave pedals.—A pedal-board so constructed that the pedals are not on the same level, being so arranged that from the centre to the right and left they gradually rise.

Concert (*Ger.* and *Fr.*)—(1) A concert. (2) A concerto.

Concertante (*It.*) — (1) A concert piece. (2) A composition in which one or more instruments play prominent parts. (3) A composition for two or more solo instruments.

Concerted Music.—Vocal or instrumental music for two or more performers, as distinguished from a solo performance.

Concertina.—A musical instrument which is of the accordion type, but a great improvement thereon. It is hexagonal in form, and has a compass of about three and a-half octaves.

Concertino (*It.*)—(1) A small concerto. (2) The principal instrument in a concerto, as *violino concertino*.

Concertmeister (*Ger.*)—The leader of the band, the conductor.

Concerto (*It.*)—(1) A concert. (2) A composition consisting of three, very occasionally of four, movements for some solo instrument, with orchestral accompaniment.

Concerto da camera (*It.*)—A chamber concerto.

Concerto grosso (*It.*)—A grand concerto. It was distinguished from the *concerto da camera* by the greater number of instruments employed.

Concert overture.—An independent composition written in sonata form.

Concertspieler (*Ger.*)—A solo performer; the player of a concerto.

Concertstück (*Ger.*)—A concert piece; a concerto.

Concord.—An interval or chord which does not require resolution.

Concordant. — Harmonious, consonant.

Conduct.—To direct the performance of a composition; to beat time.

Conductor.—The director of an orchestra or chorus.

Con fretta (*It.*)—In haste.

Congiunto (*It.*)—Conjunct movement.

Conical.—Cone-shaped. A conical tube is one tapering gradually.

Conjunct degree.—The note next above or below a given note.

Conjunct motion. — Movement by conjunct degrees (*i.e.*, by step).

Consecutives.—The term applied to the movement of two or more parts in parallel motion. In strict harmony consecutive unisons, fifths, and octaves, are forbidden.

Consequent.—(1) The answer to a fugue subject. (2) The part which takes up the imitation in a canon. (3) The term is also applied to a responsive phrase in a musical sentence.

Conservatoire (*Fr.*)
Conservatorio (*It.*)
Conservatorium (*Lat.*)
} A public institution for the study of music.

Consonance.—Concord. Two or more notes sounded together, which do not require resolution.

Consonant.—Concordant; harmonious.

Consonanz (*Ger.*)
Consonanza (*It.*)
} Consonance.

Con sordini (*It.*)—With mutes.

Con stromenti (*It.*)—With the instruments.

Contano (*It.*)—(*Lit.*, "They count.") In a score this expression indicates that certain parts have to be silent.

Continuato (*It.*)—Sustained, held down.

Continued bass
Continuo (*It.*)
} (Basso continuo.)

Contra (*It.* and *Lat.*) — Against. When prefixed to the names of instruments, it means an "octave below." (*See* following terms.)

Contrabass
Contrabasso (*It.*)
} A double-bass.

Contra fagotto (*It.*) — (1) A double bassoon. (2) A 16 ft. reed-stop on the organ.

Contralto (*It.*)—The lowest of the female voices. The tone is very full, and the compass about two octaves upwards from F below the treble staff.

Contralto - Trombone (*It.*) — Alto trombone.

Con tranquillità (*It.*) — With tranquillity : calmly.

Contra octave.—The notes an octave below the Great octave (*q.v.*). They are frequently indicated by repeated capitals, CC, DD, EE, etc.

Contra-posaune.—An organ-stop of 16 ft. and 32 ft. pitch.

Contrappunto (*It.*)—Counterpoint.

Contrappunto doppio (*It.*)—Double counterpoint.

Contrappunto sopra il soggetto (*It.*) —Counterpoint above the subject.

Contrappunto sotto il soggetto (*It.*) —Counterpoint below the subject.

Contrapunkt (*Ger.*)—Counterpoint.

Contrapuntal.—Belonging to, or in the nature of, counterpoint.

Contr' arco (*It.*)—Incorrect bowing on the violin, etc.

Contrary motion.—When parts move in the opposite direction; one ascending, the other descending.

Contra-soggetto (*It.*)—Counter-subject.

Contra tempo (*It.*)—Against the time ; syncopation.

Contraviolone (*It.*)—The double-bass.

Contre-basse (*Fr.*)—The double-bass.

Contrepoint (*Fr.*)—Counterpoint.

Contre-sujet (*Fr.*)—Countersubject.

Contre-temps (*Fr.*) — Against the time ; syncopation.

Conversio (*Lat.*)—Inversion.

Con violenza (*It.*)—With vehemence.

Coperto (*It.*) — Covered, muffled. *Timpani coperti*, muffled kettle-drums.

Copyright.—The exclusive right of printing, publishing, and selling, allowed by law to an author or publisher.

Cor (*Fr.*)—A horn.

Corale (*It.*)—A hymn tune ; a plain chant.

Cor anglais (*Fr.*)—" English horn." This instrument is a large sized oboe, a fifth lower in pitch, with a compass of similar extent. It is a transposing instrument, the notes sounding a perfect fifth lower than written.

Corda (*It.*) — A string.   (Plural, *corde*, strings.)

Corde (*Fr.*)—A string.

Corde à jour⎫
Corde à vide⎭(*Fr.*) An open string.

Corde fausse (*Fr.*)—A false string.

Cornet.—(1) An obsolete instrument of the serpent class.   (2) A reed-stop on the pedals in some German organs.   (3) *Mounted cornet*, a solo-stop on old organs.   (4) A *cornet-à-pistons* (*q.v.*).

Cornet-à-pistons (*Fr.*) — A modern brass instrument of the trumpet family. It is fitted with three valves which enable the complete chromatic scale to be produced. The natural scale is usually B flat, but by means of crooks it can be tuned to the keys of A, A flat, and G.

Cornetta (*It.*)—(1) A small horn. (2) A cornet.

Cornetto (*It.*)—(1) A cornet.   (2) An obsolete wind instrument.   (Cornet.)

Corno (*It.*)—A horn.

Corno di bassetto (*It.*)—A basset-horn.

Corno di caccia (*It.*)—A hunting horn.

Corno Inglese (*It.*)—The English horn.   (Cor anglais.)

Cornopean.—(1) The name sometimes given to the *Cornet-à-pistons*. (2) An organ-stop, usually found upon the swell-manual.

Coro (*It.*)—A choir, a chorus.

Coro della chiesa (*It.*)—A church choir.

Corona (*It.*)—A pause.

Corpo (*It.*)—The body of an instrument.

Corrente (*It.*)—(Courante.)

Corta, cortamente (*It.*)—Short.

Cotillion⎫A lively, spirited
Cotillon (*Fr.*)⎭dance, without any set step.

Cottage piano.—A small style of upright piano.

Coulé (*Fr.*)—(1) A slur.   (2) An ornament in harpsichord music.

Counter-exposition.—In many fugues, on the completion of the exposition, a re-entry of the subject and answer in the original keys, but in different order, takes place in some or all of the voices, and this is termed the " counter-exposition."

Counterpoint.—Before the introduction of notes, music was expressed by dots called "*points*"; and in the writing of one "*point*" against another originated the term "*counterpoint.*"

Nowadays, the term implies the art of adding one or more parts to a given melody, or, "harmonising a theme by adding parts which are in themselves melodious."

For a list of the various species into which counterpoint is divided, a text-book on the subject should be consulted.

Double counterpoint consists of two parts so constructed that they are invertible; *i.e.*, when each part will serve equally well as the higher or lower of the two; *triple counterpoint* when three, and *quadruple* when four, parts are similarly invertible.

Counter-subject.—(1) The theme which serves as a counterpoint against the principal subject in a double fugue; also spoken of as a second subject, and the whole, as "a fugue upon two subjects." (2) The theme which accompanies the *answer* in a fugue, provided that it is heard against the theme at each appearance.

Counter-tenor.–The name sometimes applied to the male alto voice.

Country-dance.—A rustic dance, in which the performers are arranged face to face, gentlemen on one side and ladies on the other. It may be danced to music in duple or triple time.

Coup d'archet (*Fr.*)—Stroke of the bow.

Couper le sujet (*Fr.*)—To abbreviate a musical theme.

Coupler.—The mechanism in an organ which connects two manuals together, or the pedals to the manuals.

Couplet.—(1) Two lines of verse which rhyme. (2) Two equal notes with the number 2 placed over or under them to indicate that they are to be played in the time of three of the same value.

Courante (*Fr.*)—An old French dance in 3-2 time, moderate in speed, and characterised by the prevalence of dotted notes. There is also an Italian form of this dance, in 3-4 or 3-8 time, consisting almost entirely of "running" passages.

Cracoviak (*Pol.*) **Cracovienne** (*Fr.*) } A Polish dance in duple time, with frequent syncopations.

Credo (*Lat.*)—One of the numbers in a Mass.

Cremona.—(1) A violin made in Cremona, Italy. (2) A reed-stop on the organ, the name being a corruption of Krummhorn.

Crescendo (*It.*)–Gradually increasing the tone.

Croche (*Fr.*) **Croma** (*It.*) } A quaver.

Cromatico (*It.*)—Chromatic.

Crooks.—Short tubes, which are inserted into horns, trumpets, etc., for the purpose of altering the pitch of these instruments.

Crotchet.—A note one-fourth of the value of a semibreve. A *quarter note.*

Crowd **Crwth** (*Welsh*) } An ancient instrument of the violin type, having six strings, four of which were played with a bow, the other two being plucked with the thumb, and serving as an accompaniment.

Crushed-note.—An *acciaccatura.*

Csárdás.—A national Hungarian dance.

C Schlüssel (*Ger.*)—The C clef.

Cue.—After a voice or an instrument has had a rest of considerable length, and just before its re-entry, the notes of some other part which lead up to this point are given (usually in small type) to serve as a guide to the performer. Such notes form a "cue."

Cuivré (*Fr.*).—Damped.

Cupped mouthpiece.—The shallow, cup-shaped mouthpiece for brass wind instruments.

Cyclic form.—A cycle or set of movements which, though separate in themselves, form collectively one whole composition. The sonata, symphony, and concerto are in cyclic form.

Cymbales (*Fr.*)—Cymbals.

Cymbals.—Musical instruments of percussion, made of metal. They are concave in shape, have broad, flat rims, and are attached to the hands by means of straps. Generally speaking, they are played by being struck together, and are used to mark strong accents.

D.

D.—The second degree of the normal scale of C. D also stands for :—Da (D.C., abb. of **Da capo**); Dal (D.S., abb. of **Dal segno**), **Destra**, and **Droite.**

Da (*It.*)—From, by, of, for, etc.

Da ballo (*It.*)—In dance style.

Da capo (*It.*) or abbreviated, **D.C.** From the beginning. A direction to repeat from the beginning, it being generally understood that such repetition is to conclude at the word *Fine*, or at a double-bar marked with a pause.

Da capo al fine (*It.*)—From the beginning to the word *Fine*, or to a double-bar with a pause.

Da capo al segno (*It.*)— From the beginning to the sign 𝄋. This expression is sometimes interpreted " Repeat from the sign."

Da capo dal segno (*It.*)—Repeat from the sign.

Da capo senza replica (*It.*)—From the beginning, but without observing any intermediate repeats.

D'accord (*Fr.*)—In tune.

Dach (*Ger.*)—Sound-board. Resonance-body of an instrument.

Dactyl.—A metrical foot, containing three syllables, the first long, the two others short, — ⌣ ⌣

Dagli, dai, dal, dalla, dalle, dallo (*It.*)—Of the, by the, for the, from the, etc.

Dal segno (*It.*)—From the sign.

Damper. — (1) That part of the mechanism of the pianoforte which checks the vibration of the strings immediately the key is released. (2) The mute of a brass wind-instrument.

Damper pedal. — The right - hand pedal of the pianoforte, which acts upon, and raises, the complete set of dampers.

Dämpfer (*Ger.*)—A damper ; a mute.

Dämpfung (*Ger.*) — (1) Damping, muffling. (2) The dampers of the pianoforte.

Dash.—(1) In figured bass a line drawn through a figure indicates that the note represented by such figure is to be raised a semitone. (2) A dash placed over or under a note implies the shortest form of *staccato*.

Dasselbe Tempo (*Ger.*)—The same time. (L'istesso tempo.)

Débile (*Fr.*) ⎫
Debile (*It.*) ⎬ Languid, feeble, weak.

Début (*Fr.*)—A first appearance.

Débutant (*Fr. mas.*) ⎫ A performer
Débutante (*Fr. fem.*) ⎬ appearing for the first time.

Decachord (*Ger.*) ⎫ An instrument of
Decacorde (*Fr.*) ⎬ the guitar family with ten strings.

Decani (*Lat.*)—The side of the choir upon which the Dean sits ; usually the south side.

Deceptive cadence.—An interrupted cadence.

Décidé (*Fr.*)—Firmly ; with decision.

Decima (*Lat.* and *It.*)—A tenth, the interval of a tenth. The word *decima* adds a tenth to the name of any other interval; for example :— *tertia*, a third, *decima tertia*, a thirteenth, etc.

Decimole.—A decuplet.

Deciso (*It.*)—Decided ; with firmness.

Declamando (*It.*) ⎫
Declamato (*It.*) ⎬ In a declamatory style.
Déclamatoire (*Fr.*) ⎭

Declamation.—Rendering words with proper pronunciation, accentuation, and expression, whether in speaking or singing.

Décoration (*Fr.*)—The signature of a piece of music.

Decrescendo (*It.*) — Gradually decreasing the tone. Generally indicated by the abbreviations *dec.*, *decres.*, or by the sign >

Decuplet.—A group of ten notes played in the time of eight of the same value.

Deferred resolution.—The delayed progression of a discord to its resolution.

Degré (*Fr.*)—Degree.

Degré conjoint (*Fr.*)—Conjunct movement.

Degree in music.—The title conferred by a University upon a candidate who has passed the necessary examinations.

Degree of a scale.—(1) One of the consecutive tones in a diatonic scale. (2) A step.

Dehnung (*Ger.*)—Expansion, extension.

Dehnungstrich (*Ger.*)—A long stroke with the bow.

Deklamatorisch (*Ger.*) — Declamatory.

Deliberato (*It.*) ⎱ In a deliberate
Délibérément (*Fr.*) ⎰ manner.

Délicatesse (*Fr.*) ⎱ Delicacy of per-
Delicatezza (*It.*) ⎰ formance.

Delicato (*It.*)—In a delicate, refined manner.

Délié (*Fr.*)—Delicate, light, easy.

Delirante ⎱ (*It.*)—In an excited,
Delirio, con ⎰ frenzied manner.

Dell, dell', della, delle, dello (*It.*)—Of the.

Démancher (*Fr.*)—(1) To cross hands in playing on a keyboard. (2) To shift, in playing the violin, etc.

Demande (*Fr.*)—The subject in a fugue.

Demi (*Fr.*)—Half.

Demi-cadence (*Fr.*)—A half, or imperfect, cadence.

Demi-jeu (*Fr.*)—Half power. Though usually met with in organ and harmonium music, its general meaning is equivalent to *mezza voce* and *mezzo forte*.

Demi-mesure (*Fr.*)—Half a bar.

Demi-pause (*Fr.*)—A minim rest.

Demi-quart de soupir (*Fr.*)—A demi-semiquaver rest.

Demisemiquaver.—The note having the value of a quarter of a quaver, and the thirty-second part of a semibreve. A *thirty-second note*.

Demi-soupir (*Fr.*)—A quaver rest.

Demi-ton (*Fr.*)—A semitone.

Derivative.—(1) The generator, from the harmonics of which a chord is derived. (2) An inversion of a chord.

Des (*Ger.*)—D ♭ ; *Deses*, D ♭♭.

Descant.—(Discant.)

Des dur (*Ger.*)—The key of D flat major.

Desiderio, con (*It.*)—With desire, longingly, yearningly.

Dessin (*Fr.*)—Design, or plan, of a composition.

Dessus (*Fr.*)—The treble or highest part.

Destra (*It.*)—Right; *mano destra*, the right hand.

Détaché (*Fr.*)—Detached, staccato.

Détonner (*Fr.*)—To sing out of tune.

Deutlich (*Ger.*)—Clear, distinct.

Deutsche Flöte (*Ger.*)—The German flute.

Deux (*Fr.*)—Two. *À deux mains*, for two hands.

Deuxième fois (*Fr.*)—Second time.

Deuxième position (*Fr.*)—(1) The second position on the violin. (2) The second fret on the guitar.

Deux quatre (*Fr.*)—*Mesure à deux quatre* is 2-4 time.

Development.—The working out of a theme by means of harmonic and other devices.

Devoto } (*It.*)—With devotion.
Devozione, con }

Dextra (*Lat.*)—Right. *Manus dextra,* the right hand.

D-flute.—The orchestral or German flute.

Di (*It.*)—By, of, from, with, etc. *Di grado,* by step ; *i.e.,* conjunct movement. *Aria di bravura,* an air with florid passages.

Diapason (*Gk.*)—(1) An octave. (2) Standard or definite pitch ; *normal diapason* is an accepted standard of pitch. (3) The " diapasons " are the most important foundation stops on an organ.

Diapente (*Gk.*)—The interval of a fifth.

Diaphony.—(1) In ancient Greek music the term meant dissonance, as opposed to *symphony,* which meant consonance. (2) One of the earliest attempts at harmonic combination of sounds. It preceded *discant.*

Diatonic.—The term has several applications : (1) In the ancient Greek system, it was one of the three *genera* employed, the two others being chromatic and enharmonic. (2) In modern music it means " according to the key or scale," *i.e.,* having no chromatic alterations. (3) A *diatonic scale* is one composed of tones and semitones. (4) *Diatonic semitone,* one formed by two notes in alphabetical order. (5) *Diatonic interval,* one formed by two notes of a diatonic scale, unaltered by an accidental. (6) *Diatonic chord,* one formed from the diatonic notes of a key or scale, unaltered by accidentals. (7) *Diatonic modulation,* when a change is made to a key closely related to the original key.

Dichord.—(1) An ancient instrument having two strings. (2) Any instrument having two strings to each note. (Bichord.)

Di colto (*It.*)—Suddenly, at once.

Diesare (*It.*) } To sharpen.
Diéser (*Fr.*) }

Dièse (*Fr.*) } A sharp (♯).
Diesis (*It.*) }

Diesis (*Gk.*)—The difference between a diatonic and chromatic semitone; the ratio which represents the difference is 128 : 125.

Dièze (*Fr.*)—A sharp.

Difference tones.—(Resultant tones)

Difficile (*Fr.* and *It.*)—Difficult.

Digital.—A key on the keyboard of the piano, organ, etc.

Digitorium.—A small, dumb instrument with five keys, used for strengthening the fingers.

Digne (*Fr.*)—In a dignified manner.

Di grado (*It.*)—By step.

Dilettante (*It.*)—An amateur.

Diminished.—Made less.

Diminished interval.—An interval which is a chromatic semitone less than major or perfect.

Diminished subject.—A subject presented in notes of less value than the original, generally one-half.

Diminished triad.—A triad consisting of a bass note, with its minor third, and diminished fifth.

Diminué (*Fr.*) } Diminished.
Diminuito (*It.*) }

Diminuendo (*It.*)—Decreasing the tone.

Diminutio (*Lat.*)—(Diminution.)

Diminution.—The presentation of a phrase or figure in notes of less value than the original.

Diminuzione (*It.*)—(Diminution.)

Di molto (*It.*)—Very ; *allegro di molto,* very fast.

Direct.—A sign (ᵥᵥ) placed at the end of a staff to indicate the note with which the same part commences in the next line, or on the next page.

Directeur (*Fr.*)—A director ; a conductor.

Direct motion.—The progression of two or more parts in similar motion.

Diretto, -a (*It.*)—Direct, straight. *Alla diretta,* in direct or similar motion.

Direttore (*It.*)—(Directeur.)

Dirge.—A composition of a mournful character, associated with funeral rites.

Diriger (*Fr.*) To conduct, or di-
Dirigiren (*Ger.*) rect, a performance.

Dis (*Ger.*)—D♯; *Disis*, D✕.

Discant.—(1) The early attempts at counterpoint, use being made of contrary motion in the parts, as opposed to *Organum*, in which parallel motion prevailed. (2) The highest voice or part, *i.e.*, soprano or treble.

Discantus (*Lat.*)—(Discant.)

Discord. — An interval, or chord, which does not produce a sense of finality, and which requires resolution.

Discordant.—Not agreeing; requiring resolution.

Disdiapason (*Gk.*)—An interval of two octaves; a fifteenth.

Disinvolto (*It.*)—Free, easy, graceful.

Disis (*Ger.*)—D double sharp.

Disjunct motion.—The movement of a part by skip, as opposed to *conjunct motion*; *i.e.*, movement by step.

Disperato (*It.*) Despairing,
Disperazione, con with desperation.

Dispersed harmony.—The converse of close harmony; *i.e.*, having the notes so arranged that any two adjacent parts must be separated by an interval of a fifth or more.

Dissonance.—A combination of two or more sounds requiring resolution.

Dissonanza (*It.*)—(Dissonance.)

Dissonant.—Discordant. (See Discord.)

Distanza (*It.*)—Distance, an interval.

Distinctement (*Fr.*) Clear, distinct.
Distinto (*It.*)

Distonare, or Stonare (*It.*)—To sing or play out of tune.

Diteggiatura (*It.*)—Fingering.

Dithyrambus (*Gk.*)—A hymn in honour of Bacchus. A composition of a wild, impetuous character.

Dito (*It.*)—A finger.

Divertimento (*It.*) (1) An instru-
Divertissement (*Fr.*) mental composition of a light character,

usually containing several movements. (2) An entr'acte in an opera. (3) A short ballet.

Divisi (*It.*)—Divided. In an orchestral score, if two string parts are written upon a staff usually occupied by one part, the term "divisi" indicates that the two parts are not to be played as double-stops, but divided between two instruments.

Division.—(1) A variation upon a simple theme. (2) A melodic series of notes constituting a rapid ornamental passage.

Divotamente (*It.*) Devoutly. *Con divozione*, with devotion.

Dixième (*Fr.*)—Tenth. The interval of a tenth.

D moll (*Ger.*)—D minor.

Do.—The Italian name for the note C. On the fixed-Do method, Do is used for C, whether it be the key-note, or any other degree of the scale; while on the movable Do (Doh) method, Do is always the key-note, whatever the actual pitch.

Doch (*Ger.*)—Yet, still.

Dodecuplet.—A group of twelve equal notes played in the time of eight of the same value.

Doh.—The Tonic Sol-fa name for the key-note of any scale.

Doigt (*Fr.*)—Finger.

Doigté (*Fr.*) — Fingered. *Doigter*, (verb) to finger; (noun) fingering.

Dolce (*It.*)—Sweet, soft.

Dolcezza, con (*It.*)—With sweetness, delicacy.

Dolciano
Dolcin (*It.*)—(Dulciana.)
Dolcino

Dolcissimo (*It.*)—With the utmost delicacy and sweetness.

Dolente (*It.*)—Plaintive, doleful, sad.

Dolore, con.—With sadness.

Doloroso (*It.*)—Sad, sorrowful, pathetic.

Dolzflöte (*Ger.*)—(1) An obsolete kind of flute. (2) A soft-toned 8 ft. flute-stop on the organ.

Dominant.—(1) The fifth degree of the scale. (2) In plain-chant the dominant is, in some of the modes, the fifth of the scale ; in others it is the third, the fourth, etc.

Dominante (*Fr. Ger.* and *It.*)—Dominant

Doppel (*Ger.*)—Double.

Doppel-B (*Ger.*)—A double flat.

Doppelchor-(*Ger.*)—Double chorus.

Doppelcis (*Ger.*)—C double sharp.

Doppelflöte (*Ger.*)—An organ-stop constructed of wooden pipes, each having a double mouth.

Doppelfuge (*Ger.*)—A double fugue.

Doppelgriffe (*Ger.*)—Double stopping on the violin, etc. ; double thirds and sixths played on the pianoforte.

Doppelkreuz (*Ger.*) — A double sharp.

Doppeloctave (*Ger.*)—A double octave.

Doppelschlag (*Ger.*)—A turn.

Doppel so schnell.—Twice as fast.

Doppeltaktstrich (*Ger.*)—A double bar.

Doppelte Geschwindigkeit (*Ger.*)—Double the speed.

Doppeltriller (*Ger.*)—Double shake.

Doppio (*It.*)—Double.

Doppio movimento (*It.*)—Indicates that the speed is to be twice as quick as that of the preceding matter.

Doppio pedale (*It.*)—This indicates, in organ music, that the pedal part is to be played in octaves.

Dorian.—The first of the Authentic Gregorian modes, having D as the final.

Dot.—(1) A dot placed after a note, rest, or another dot, prolongs the duration by half the value of what precedes it ; thus ♩. is equal to ♩♪; ♩.. is equal to ♩♪♬ (2) A dot placed over or under a note, indicates that the note is to be played *staccato*. (3) Two, sometimes four, dots placed before a double-bar, indicate a repeat, which will be from the preceding double-bar if dots are placed after it, or, if there be no such double-bar, from the beginning of the movement. (4) A dot over a note also implies that, under certain conditions, such note is to be accented.

Double.—(1) A 16 ft. stop on the organ. (2) To write the same note in a chord, either in the unison, or an octave or more apart.

Double (*Fr*).—(1) A turn. (2) An old term for a variation. (3) Double.

Double bar.—Two thick lines drawn across the stave, shewing—(*a*) the end of a piece or movement, or a portion of either ; (*b*) the end of a portion to be repeated ; (*c*) the commencement of a change of key or of time ; (*d*) the end of a line of words, as in a hymn-tune.

Double bass.—The largest and deepest toned instrument of the violin family. It has either three strings, tuned to

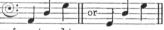

or four, tuned to

Double bassoon.—A reed instrument an octave lower in pitch than the bassoon.

Double bémol (*Fr*).—Double flat.

Double bourdon.—An organ stop of 32 ft. tone.

Double chorus.—A chorus, usually in eight parts, for two choirs, named respectively first and second choir.

Double concerto.—A composition for two solo instruments accompanied by the orchestra.

Double counterpoint.—(See Counterpoint.)

Double croche (*Fr*).—A semiquaver.

Double demisemiquaver. — Another name for a semidemisemiquaver ; a note which is half a demisemiquaver, and the 64th part of a semibreve. A sixty-fourth note.

Double diapason.—An organ-stop of 16 ft. pitch.

Double dièse (Fr.)—A double sharp.

Double flat. — The sign ♭♭, which lowers a natural note two semi-tones, and a note which is already flat, one semitone.

Double fugue.—A fugue on two subjects. Sometimes spoken of as a fugue with one counter-subject.

Double harp.—A harp with two sets of strings.

Double mouvement (Fr.)—Twice as fast.

Double octave.—The interval of a fifteenth.

Double pedal-point.—The sustaining of two notes—usually the tonic and dominant—in the lowest parts, the parts above them forming various harmonies.

Double quartet.—A composition for two sets of four solo voices or instruments.

Double reed.—(1) The vibrating reed of the instruments of the oboe family. (2) A reed-stop on the organ, of 16 ft. tone.

Double sharp.—The sign x, which raises a natural note two semitones, and a note which is already sharp, one semitone.

Double stopping.—To stop two strings simultaneously, producing two-part harmony on the violin, viola, etc.

Double temps (Fr.)—Duple time.

Double-tongueing. — The action of the tongue used in playing the flute and certain brass instruments, for producing the rapid repetition of any note.

Double trumpet.—An organ reed-stop of 16 ft. tone.

Doublette (Fr.)—(1) An organ-stop of 2 ft. pitch. (2) An organ-stop having two ranks of pipes.

Doucement⎫(Fr.) — Soft, sweet,
Doux   ⎬ gentle. Très doux,
          ⎭ very soft.

Douloureux (Fr.)—Sad, doleful.

Douzième (Fr.)—A twelfth.

Down-beat.—The first or accented beat in a bar.

Down-bow.—Drawing the bow across the strings from the heel (or holding part) of the bow to the point, in playing the violin, viola, etc. Indicated thus ⊓

Doxology (Gk.)—A hymn of praise and honour to God. There are two versions : the "Gloria in excelsis Deo," sung at the celebration of the Holy Eucharist, which is the Greater Doxology (doxologia major); and the Gloria Patri, sung at the end of the Psalms and Canticles in the Anglican service, which is the Lesser Doxology (doxologia minor).

Dramatic music. — (1) Programme music. (2) Music which illustrates, or serves as an accompaniment to, a drama on the stage.

Dramma lirico   ⎫(It.) — Musical
Dramma musicale ⎭ drama; opera.

Drammatico (It.)—Dramatic.

Drängend (Ger.)—Hastening, press-ing on the time.

Draw-stop.—Any stop on an organ which is drawn by the hand.

Drei (Ger.)—Three.

Dreichörig (Ger.)—A pianoforte hav-ing three strings to each note ; a trichord.

Dreiklang (Ger.)—A triad, consisting of a bass note, its third, and fifth.

Dreit(h)eilig (Ger.)—Ternary.

Dritta (It.)—(Diritta.)

Driving notes.—Syncopation ; notes anticipating the succeeding accent.

Droite (Fr.)—Right ; main droite, right hand.

Drone.—The notes on the bagpipe which form the continuous accom-paniment to the melody. This effect is often a characteristic of the old dance called the Musette.

Drum.—An instrument of percussion, consisting of a hollow body, cylin-drical in shape, over one or both ends of which a membrane is tightly stretched. Drums are of several kinds, the important ones being the kettle-drum, side-drum, and the bass (or big) drum.

D-string.—The third string on the violin ; and the second on the viola, 'cello and double-bass.

Du début (*Fr.*)—From the beginning.

Due (*It.*)—Two. *A due,* (*a*) for two voices or parts ; (*b*) both together, signifying that if a part for any orchestral stringed instrument has been divided, the unison is to be resumed. Also, if two parts are written upon one staff, in the case of the wind instruments, etc., in an orchestral score, the term *a due* indicates that the two instruments are to play in unison. *Due pedali,* use both of the pianoforte pedals together.

Due corde (*It.*)—Two strings ; a direction that the same note is to be played upon two strings simultaneously. In pianoforte music the term *due corde* has sometimes to be interpreted as indicating the release of the soft pedal.

Duet.—(1) A composition for two voices or instruments. (2) A composition for two performers on one instrument, such as the pianoforte.

Duett (*Ger.*)⎫
Duetto (*It.*) ⎬A duet.

Due volte (*It.*)—Twice.

Dulciana.—(1) An organ-stop of soft tone. (2) A small reed-stop of delicate tone.

Dulcimer.—An ancient stringed instrument, having the strings stretched over a soundboard or resonance-box. It was played upon by the strings being struck with two hammers.

Duo (*It.* and *Fr.*)—A duet.

Duodecima (*It.*)—The interval of a twelfth.

Duolo (*It.*)—Grief. *Con duolo,* with grief, dolefully.

Duple time.—Time in which each alternate pulse is accented.

Dur (*Ger.*)—Major ; as C *dur,* C major.

Dur (*Fr.*)—Hard, coarse.

Durchaus (*Ger.*)—Throughout.

Durchführung (*Ger.*)—The working-out or development of a theme.

Durchgangston (*Ger.*)—A passing note.

Durchgehend (*Ger.*)—Passing, transient.

Durezza, con (*It.*)—With harshness.

Dux (*Lat.*)—The proposition, or subject, of a fugue, the answer being called *Comes.*

Dynamic marks. — Indications of variation of tone.

E.

E.—(1) The third degree of the scale of C major. (2) The key-note of the major scale, having four sharps in the key-signature.

E (*It.*)—And. When occurring before a word commencing with the vowel " *e,*" it should be written " *ed* " ; before other vowels *e* or *ed* may be used ; before a consonant, always *e.*

Eccedente (*It.*)—Exceeding. Applied to intervals, it means augmented.

Eccitato (*It.*)—Excited.

Ecclesiastical modes.—(Church modes.)

Échelle (*Fr.*)—A scale.

Echo.—(1) An acoustic phenomenon produced by the vibrations of a sound being reflected, thus causing the sound to be heard again, more or less faintly. (2) In music, the soft repetition of a note, or series of notes.

Écho (*Fr.*) ⎫The soft repetition of a
Echo (*Ger.*)⎭ previous passage.

Echo-organ.—A set of pipes enclosed in a box within the organ, or placed at some distant point in the building, the sound produced giving the effect of an echo. In large instruments they are governed by a separate manual ; on others, they are connected to one of the other rows of keys.

Eco (*It.*)—Echo.

Ecole (*Fr.*)—A school or style of music.

Écossaise (*Fr.*)—An ancient dance of Scotch origin.

Ed (*It.*)—And. (E.)

Edel (*Ger.*)—Noble.

E dur (*Ger.*)—The key of E major.

Eguale (*It.*)—Equal, even, smooth. *Voci equali*, equal voices.

Eifrig (*Ger.*) — Ardently, passionately.

Eighth.—An octave.

Eilen ⎱ (*Ger.*)—(Stringendo.)
Eilend ⎰

Eilig (*Ger.*)—Hurriedly ; rapid, swift.

Ein (*Ger.*)—One.

Einfach (*Ger.*)—Simple. *Einfache Intervalle*, simple intervals.

Eingang (*Ger.*)—Introduction.

Eingestrichen (*Ger.*) — Having one stroke, or accent. *Eingestrichene Oktave*, the one-lined, or once-accented octave, a¹, d¹, etc.

Einige (*Ger.*)—Certain, some.

Einklang (*Ger.*)—Unison.

Einleitung ⎱ (*Ger.*) — An introduction, an over-
Einleitungssatz ⎰ ture.

Einmal (*Ger.*)—Once.

Einstimmen (*Ger.*)—To tune.

Ein wenig (*Ger.*)—A little ; rather. *Ein wenig lebendig*, rather lively.

Eis (*Ger.*)—E sharp.

Eisis (*Ger.*)—E double-sharp.

Élan, avec (*Fr.*)—With dash.

Élargissez (*Fr.*)—Broaden out the time.

Élégant (*Fr.*) ⎫
Elegante (*It.*) ⎬ In an elegant, refined style.
Eleganza, con (*It.*) ⎭

Elegia (*It.*) ⎫
Elegie (*Ger.*) ⎬ (Elegy.)
Élégie (*Fr.*) ⎭

Elegiac.—Expressing sorrow.

Elegy.—A poem or musical composition of a mournful character, a species of dirge.

Elevato (*It.*)—Lofty, sublime.

Elevazione, con (*It.*)—In a lofty, sublime style.

Élevé (*Fr.*)—Lofty.

Eleventh.—An interval of an octave and a fourth ; a compound fourth.

Embellimenti (*It.*)—Embellishments; ornaments.

Embellishment.—An ornament.

Embouchure (*Fr.*)—The mouthpiece of a wind instrument.

E moll (*Ger.*)—E minor.

Emozione, con (*It.*)—With emotion.

Empfindung (*Ger.*) — Emotion, feeling.

Empfindungsvoll (*Ger.*)—With emotion, full of feeling.

Emphase, avec (*Fr.*) ⎱ With
Emphase, mit (*Ger.*) ⎰ emphasis.

Emphasis. Stress.

Emporté (*Fr.*)—Passionate, hurried.

Empressé (*Fr.*)—Eager, hurried.

En animant (*Fr.*)—With increased animation ; faster. *En animant peu à peu*, faster by degrees.

Enarmonico (*It.*)—Enharmonic.

En badinant (*Fr.*)—(Scherzando.)

Encore (*Fr.*)—Yet, still. A term used in English-speaking countries for the recall of a performer.

Encore plus vite.—Still faster.

Ende (*Ger.*)—The end.

En dehors (*Fr.*)—Prominently.

En élargissant (*Fr.*) — Broadening out the time.

Energia, con (*It.*) ⎫
Energico (*It.*) ⎬ With energy and decision.
Energisch (*Ger.*) ⎭

Enfasi, con ⎱ (*It.*)—With emphasis.
Enfatico ⎰

Enfler (*Fr.*)—To swell, to increase in tone.

Englisches Horn (*Ger.*) ⎱ (Cor
English horn ⎰ anglais.)

Enharmonic.—(1) One of the three genera in Greek music, the other two being diatonic and chromatic. (2) Enharmonic notes : notes written upon different degrees of the staff, but not differing in pitch, *e.g.*, F♯ and G♭. (3) Enharmonic chords : chords differing in notation but not in sound, according to the tempered scale. (4) Enharmonic modulation: modulation effected by means of enharmonic chords.

Enharmonique (*Fr.*) } Enharmonic.
Enharmonisch (*Ger.*) }

En mesure (*Fr.*)—In time.

En pressant (*Fr.*)—Accelerating the speed.

En retenant (*Fr.*)—Decreasing the speed.

Ensemble.—Together; the whole. It is applied (1) to the general effect of a performance; (2) to the unanimity existing between the performers in rendering a composition.

En se perdant (*Fr.*)—Dying away.

En serrant (*Fr.*)—Increasing the speed.

Entr'acte (*Fr.*)—(1) The interval between the acts of a dramatic performance. (2) The music played during such interval.

Entrante (*It.*) }
Entrata (*It.*) } An entry; an introduction; a prelude.
Entrée (*Fr.*) }

Entschlossen(*Ger.*)–Firm, deliberate.

Entwurf (*Ger.*) — Design; plan; sketch.

Eolian harp. — An instrument the strings of which, enclosed in a box, are set in motion by the wind.

Eolian mode.—The fifth of the Gregorian modes, having A as its keynote.

Epilogue.—A concluding piece; the final section or part of a work.

Épinette (*Fr.*)—A spinet.

Episode.—(1) In a Sonata, an episode is a theme or subject matter, of secondary importance to, and occurring between, two presentations of the principal theme. The Episode is a prominent feature in Rondo form; and further, a movement built upon the design of principal theme, Episode, and principal theme repeated, is regarded as being in *Episodical* form. (2) On the other hand, an episode in a Fugue is of a different nature, and serves to give relief to the several

appearances of the theme, and is the medium for modulation from one key, or group of keys, to another.

Equabile (*It.*)—Equable; even; uniform.

Equal temperament.—The system of tuning which, by means of a slight modification of the true ratio of certain intervals, divides the octave into twelve equal semitones.

Equivocal chords.—Chords which are common to two or more keys.

Ergriffen (*Ger.*)—Affected, stirred.

Ergriffenheit (*Ger.*)—Emotion, agitation.

Erhaben (*Ger.*)—Lofty, sublime.

Erhabenheit (*Ger.*)—Loftiness, subblimity.

Erhöhung (*Ger.*)—Elevation, raising. *Erhöhungszeichen*, a sign chromatically raising a note.

Erniedrigung (*Ger.*)—Lowering. *Erniedrigungszeichen*, a sign chromatically lowering a note.

Ernst (*Ger.*)—Earnest, serious.

Eroico, -a (*It.*)—Heroic.

Erschüttert (*Ger.*)—Agitated.

Erst (*Ger.*)—First. *Erster Satz*, first movement; first theme. *Erstes Mal*, first time.

Erste Bewegung (*Ger.*)—Return to original speed.

Ersterben (*Ger.*)—To die away.

Erweitert (*Ger.*) — Extended, augmented.

Es (*Ger.*)—The note E flat.

Esacordo (*It.*)—The interval of a sixth.

Es dur (*Ger.*)—E flat major.

Esercizio (*It.*)—Exercise.

Eses (*Ger.*)—The note E double flat.

Espace (*Fr.*)—Space; a space on the staff.

Espagnol (*Fr.*) } In the Spanish
Espagnolo (*It.*) } style.

Espandendosi (*It.*)—Getting broader and fuller; with increasing intensity.

Espirando (*It.*)—Dying away; expiring.

Espressione, con ⎰ (*It.*)–With expres-
Espressivo ⎱ sion ; expres-
                 sively.

Essential notes.—Notes which form a constituent part of a chord, not passing notes or suspensions.

Estinguendo (*It.*)—Dying away.

Estinto (*It.*)—Barely audible ; the extreme degree of pianissimo.

Estremamente (*It.*)—Extremely.

Etendue (*Fr.*)—Compass.

Étincelant (*Fr.*)—Sparkling.

Étouffé (*Fr.*)—Stifled ; damped.

Étouffoir (*Fr.*)—Damper.

Étude (*Fr.*)—A study. Music under this head may be written with a view to the improvement of technical dexterity, or the study of expression, phrasing, etc. There is, in addition, the *Étude de concert*, which is designed for public performance.

Etwas (*Ger.*)—Rather, somewhat. *Etwas langsam*, rather slow.

Eufonia (*It.*) ⎰
Euphonie (*Fr.*) ⎱ (Euphony.)

Euphonium.—The bass saxhorn ; a brass instrument used in a military band.

Euphony.—A concordant combination of sounds.

Evaded cadence.—An interrupted cadence.

Éveillé (*Fr.*)—Sprightly, lively.

Exactement (*Fr.*)—In strict time.

Execution.—(1) Style, manner of performance. (2) Technical skill.

Exercise.—(1) Technical practice in order to obtain skill. (2) A composition for the development of technical skill. (3) A composition required of candidates for a musical degree at a university.

Exposition.—(1) The first part of a movement in sonata form, in which the themes are announced. (2) The first part of a fugue, in which the several voices for which the fugue is written make their respective entries.

Expressif (*Fr.*)—With expression.

Expression. — The rendering of a composition so as to bring into due prominence its emotional meaning.

Expression stop.—This stop on the harmonium, by closing the waste valve of the bellows, gives a greater control over the wind pressure, and facilitates the production of contrast of light and shade.

Extempore.—Musical improvisation. The art of creating music without premeditation.

Extemporiren (*Ger.*)—To extemporise.

Extended compass.—Notes beyond the usual range of a voice or instrument.

Extended harmony. — (Dispersed harmony.)

Extraneous key.—A key not related to the original key.

Extraneous modulation.— Modulation to an unrelated key.

Extraneous sharps and flats.—Such as do not belong to the key-signature.

Extreme.— (1) *Extreme parts*, the highest and lowest parts in part-writing. (2) *Extreme interval*, one expanded to its utmost limit ; as augmented intervals. (3) *Extreme key*, an unrelated key ; also an old term for a key having more than three sharps or flats. (4) *Extreme sixth*, the name occasionally given to the chord of the augmented sixth.

Extrêmement (*Fr.*)—Extremely.

F.

F.—The name of the fourth degree of the scale of C. As a mark of expression, *f* is the abbreviation of forte ; *ff*, of fortissimo.

Fa.—(1) The fourth of the Aretinian syllables. (2) The name of the note F in Italy, France, etc.

Fa bémol (*Fr.*) ⎰
Fa bemolle (*It.*) ⎱ The note F flat.

Faburden.—One of the early systems of accompanying a "canto fermo"; consisting of a series of thirds and sixths above or below the subject, except in the first and last chords, when the extreme parts had the octave, and the middle voice usually the fifth, of the chord.

Faces d'un accord (*Fr.*)—The positions of a chord.

Facile (*Fr.* and *It.*)—Easy, facile, fluent.

Facilement (*Fr.*)
Facilemente (*It.*) } Fluently, easily.

Facilità (*It.*)—Facility, fluency.

Facilité (*Fr.*)—(1) Made easy. (2) An easy arrangement of a passage, or of a piece.

Facture (*Fr.*)—The design or plan of a composition.

Fa dièse (*Fr.*)
Fa diesis (*It.*) } The note F sharp.

Fagott (*Ger.*)
Fagotto (*It.*) } The bassoon.

Fah.—In Tonic Sol-fa, the syllable for the fourth degree of the scale.

Fall.—A cadence.

Falsa (*Lat.* and *It.*)—False. *Quinta falsa*, a false or diminished fifth.

Falsa musica (*Lat.*)—In the old ecclesiastical musical system false (or "feigned") music contained notes altered by accidentals.

Falsch (*Ger.*)—False, wrong.

Falsche Verbindung (*Ger.*)—False relation.

False cadence.—Another name for an interrupted cadence.

False fifth.—The term applied by some theorists to a diminished fifth.

False intonation.—Singing or playing out of tune.

False relation.—(1) "False relation of the tritone"—so-called, and strictly forbidden by the early school of contrapuntists—arises when the two notes of a scale which form the interval of an augmented fourth (or its inversion a diminished fifth)

occur in adjacent chords, the parts moving by step; as:—

The rule, as expressed by them, read thus:—*Mi contra fa est diabolus in musica*, more generally expressed in abbreviated form, *Mi contra fa*. (2) The term at the present time is applied to the bad effect arising from a note of a chord appearing in the same or following chord chromatically altered, in a different part. (3) An unessential note (*e.g.*, the G♮ in the following example) does not produce the bad effect usually associated with a false relation:—

False string.—One that does not produce a true note.

Falset (*Ger.*)
Falsetto (*It.*) } The highest of the vocal registers. In many instances it is an artificial tone, and is the method of production used by many, if not the majority of, male altos.

Falso, -a (*It.*)—False.

Fandango (*Sp.*)—A lively Spanish dance, in triple time.

Fanfare (*Fr.*)—A flourish of trumpets; a trumpet call.

Fantaisie (*Fr.*)
Fantasia (*It.*)
Fantasie (*Ger.*) } Fantasy, caprice, fancy. (1) The name given to compositions in various styles; to preludes consisting of broken chords, arpeggi and imitative passages; to a *potpourri* of operatic airs, etc. (2) An improvisation.

Fantasia, con (*It.*)—Fancifully; not strictly in time.

Fantastico (*It.*)
Fantastique (*Fr.*)
Fantastisch (*Ger.*) } Fanciful, fantastic, capricious.

Farce
Farsa (*It.*) } A play, or musical work, of a burlesque character.

Fascia (*It.*)—A tie, or bind.

Fausse (*Fr.*)—*Fem.* of Faux (*q.v.*).

Fausse corde (*Fr.*)—False string.

Fausse quinte (*Fr.*)—A diminished fifth.

Faux (*Fr.*)—False, out of tune.

F clef.—The clef which determines the name and absolute pitch of the second line below Middle C. At the present time it is used only to fix the pitch of the fourth line of a staff, which thereby becomes the Bass staff— Formerly, it was used to fix the pitch of the third line, the staff being then the Barytone staff,

F dur (*Ger.*)—F major.

Feierlich (*Ger.*)—Solemn, grave.

Feint, Feinte (*Fr.*)—(Ficta.)

Ferial.—Music for church use on ordinary, not festal, days.

Fermamente }
Fermato } (*It.*)—Firmly.

Fermata (*It.*) }
Fermate (*Ger.*) } A pause.

Fermo (*It.*)—Firm, fixed, unchanged. *Canto fermo*, fixed subject.

Ferne (*Ger.*)—Distance. *Wie aus der Ferne*, as if heard from a distance.

Feroce (*It.*) }
Féroce (*Fr.*) } In a fierce, vehement style ;
Ferocità, con (*It.*) } wildly.

Fertig (*Ger.*)—Quick, dexterous.

Fertigkeit (*Ger.*)—Skill, dexterity.

Fervente } (*It.*)—With fervent,
Fervore, con } passionate feeling.

Fes (*Ger.*)—F♭. *Feses*, F♭♭.

Fest (*Ger.*)—A festival. *Festgesang*, a festival cantata.

Festivo (*It.*) }
Festlich (*Ger.*) } Festive.
Festoso (*It.*) }

Feuer, mit } (*Ger.*) — With fire,
Feuerig } ardour, warmth.

Fiacco (*It.*)– Weak, languishing.

Fiato (*It.*)—Wind, breath. *Stromenti da fiato*, wind instruments. *In un fiato*, in one breath.

Ficta (*Lat.*)—Feigned, false. *Ficta musica.* (Falsa musica.)

Fiddle.—A violin.

Fier, fière (*Fr.*) } Fierce, bold, vigo-
Fiero, -a (*It.*) } rous, spirited.

Fife.—A small octave flute, with six holes and without keys.

Fiffero (*It.*) }
Fifre (*Fr.*) } A fife.

Fifteenth. — (1) The interval of a fifteenth, a double octave. (2) An organ-stop of 2 ft. pitch, the notes sounding two octaves higher than written.

Fifth.—(1) An interval containing five diatonic degrees. (2) The dominant of a key.

Figur (*Ger.*)—(Figure.)

Figura (*Lat.*)—A note.

Figural.—Consisting of figurations (*q.v.*).

Figura muta (*Lat.* and *It.*)—A rest.

Figurations. — Rapid figures or phrases containing ornamental notes.

Figurato (*It.*)—Figured.

Figure.—(1) A pattern of melody, or of accompaniment. (2) A numeral as used in figured bass.

Figuré (*Fr.*)—Figured.

Figured.—(1) Decorated. (2) *Figured bass*, a bass with figures placed above or below the notes, to indicate the chords which are to be added.

Filar la voce (*It.*) } To sustain a
Filer la voix (*Fr.*) } note, gradually increasing and diminishing the tone.

Fin (*Fr.*)—The end.

Fin (*It.*)—(Fino.)

Final.—In the Church modes this term is synonymous with the modern term Tonic.

Finale(*It.*)–The concluding movement of a sonata, symphony, or concerted piece ; the closing section of an opera, or oratorio ; the last item in a programme.

Fine (*It.*)—The end, either of the whole, or portion, of a piece.

Finger-board ⎱ The piece of wood
Fingerbrett (*Ger.*) ⎰ in instruments of the violin and guitar class, against which the strings are pressed by the fingers, *i.e.*, "stopped."

Fingering.—(1) The system of placing the fingers upon the keys, strings, etc., of instruments. (2) The numbers which indicate which fingers are to be used.

Fingersatz ⎱ (*Ger.*)—Fingering.
Fingersetzung ⎰

Fino (*It.*)—Till, as far as.

Finto, -a (*It.*)—False, feigned. *Cadenza finta*, false, or interrupted, cadence.

First.—The highest of any one kind of voice or instrument; as *1st soprano, 1st violin*, etc.

First-movement form.—The name applied by some theorists to sonata form (*q.v.*).

Fis (*Ger.*)—The note F sharp.

Fis dur (*Ger.*)—The key of F sharp major.

Fisis (*Ger.*)—The note F double sharp.

Fis moll (*Ger.*)—The key of F sharp minor.

Fixed Do.—The system of solmisation in which the note C, whatever be the key, or whether the note be C ♮, C ♯, or C ♭, is always called Do, the note D is always Re, and so on.

Flageolet.—A small wooden wind-instrument with a mouthpiece at one end, the air being blown through it after the manner of a whistle. The tone produced is similar to, but softer than, that of the piccolo.

Flageolet tones.—The natural harmonics of stringed instruments, being of a flute-like quality of tone, are sometimes so called.

Flat.—(1) The sign ♭, which lowers the pitch of a note a chromatic semitone. (2) The term used when a singer or instrumentalist produces a note slightly below the true pitch.

Flautando ⎱ (*It.*) — Flute - like. A
Flautato ⎰ direction in violin music to play near the finger-board, in order to obtain a flute-like tone.

Flautino (*It.*)—A small flute. (2) (Flautando.)

Flauto (*It.*)—A flute.

Flauto a becco ⎱ (*It.*)—(Flûte à bec.)
Flauto dolce ⎰

Flauto amabile (*It.*)—A soft-toned organ-stop, usually of 4 ft. pitch.

Flauto piccolo (*It.*)—A small flute; an octave flute, producing notes an octave higher than those written.

Flauto traverso (*It.*)—"Cross flute"; so called because it is held across the mouth, the air being blown through the tube by means of an oval hole near the upper end.

Flebile (*It.*)—Plaintive, mournful.

Flessibile (*It.*)—Flexible, pliant.

Fliessend (*Ger.*)—Flowing, smooth.

Fling.—A Scotch dance, resembling the reel.

Florid. — Embellished with runs, ornaments, etc.

Florid counterpoint. — The fifth species, in which notes of various values are employed, together with syncopations and suspensions.

Flöte (*Ger.*)—A flute.

Flüchtig (*Ger.*) — Light, rapid, nimble, fugitive, hasty.

Flue-pipes.—Those organ pipes (wood or metal) in which the sound is produced by the vibration of a column of air.

Flügel (*Ger.*)—A grand pianoforte, or a harpsichord.

Flute. — An orchestral instrument, usually made of wood, but sometimes of metal. Its form is that of a tube with a cylindrical bore, the air being blown through an oval hole near the end. The compass is about three octaves from Middle C, and the system of fingering having in recent years been much simplified, the instrument is capable of considerable agility.

Flûte-à-bec (*Fr.*)—A flute which has a mouthpiece at one end through which the air is blown.

Flûte à pavillon (*Fr.*)—An organ-stop of 8 ft. pitch.

Flûte harmonique (*Fr.*)—An organ-stop of 4 ft. pitch, its characteristic quality being produced by the pipes being of 8 ft. pitch, and having a hole pierced at half the length.

Flûte traversière (*Fr.*)—(Flauto traverso.)

Flute-work.—The term applied to all those stops on an organ which are of the flute family.

F moll (*Ger.*)—The key of F minor.

Focoso (*It.*)—Fiery, passionate.

Fois (*Fr.*)—Time. *Première fois*, first time.

Folgend (*Ger.*)—Following.

Folk-song.—A song, or simple ballad, whose musical setting is characteristic of its nationality.

Fondamental (*Fr.*) ⎫ Fundamental.
Fondamentale (*It.*) ⎭ The fundamental note of a chord.

Fondamento (*It.*)—Fundamental bass ; also the generator of a chord.

Fonds d'orgue (*Fr.*)—(Foundation-stops.)

Foot.— (1) A metrical division. (2) That part of an organ pipe below the mouth. (3) The measure used to determine the pitch of organ-stops ; 8 ft. pitch implies that the longest pipe produces the note—

, and is approximately

8 ft. long. For a stop of 4 ft. pitch the longest pipe is about 4 ft. in length, producing the note

, and so on. The 8 ft.

octave includes the notes

Forlana (*It.*) ⎫ A lively Italian dance
Forlane (*Fr.*) ⎭ in compound-duple time.

Form.—(1) The presentation of musical ideas in order and shape, based upon certain underlying principles of rhythm, proportion, distribution of keys, etc. (2) The design that a musical work is built upon ; as, sonata form, march form, etc.

Forma (*It.*)—The design or plan of a movement.

Fort (*Fr.*)—Strong. *Temps fort*, the strong beat of a bar.

Forte (*It.*)—Loud, strong ; usually indicated in abbreviated form, *f*.

Fortement (*Fr.*) — Vehemently, vigorous..

Forte-piano (*It.*) — (1) Commencing loudly, and immediately reducing the tone. (2) The pianoforte.

Fortissimo (*It.*)—Very loud (abbreviated, *ff*).

Forza, con (*It.*)—With force, vigorously.

Forzando ⎫ (*It.*)—Forcing the tone ;
Forzato ⎭ usually indicated, *fz.*, *sf.*, or >

Foundation - stops. — The diapasons and other 8 ft. flue-stops on English organs ; the principals on Continental instruments.

Fourniture (*Fr.*)—A mixture stop on an organ.

Fourth.—(1) An interval consisting of four diatonic degrees. (2) The subdominant of the scale.

Française (*Fr.*)—A dance in triple time, after the style of a country dance.

Frase (*It.*)—A phrase.

Free fugue. — One in which the strict rules of fugue writing are more or less disregarded.

Free part.—A supplementary part added to a musical passage in order to strengthen, or complete, the harmony.

Free reed.—(Reed.)

Free style.—A term usually applied to contrapuntal writing in which certain strict rules are not rigidly observed.

Frei (*Ger.*)—Free.

Freie Schreibart (*Ger.*)—Composition in a free style.

French horn.—(Horn.)

French sixth.—One of the forms of the chord of the augmented sixth, consisting of a bass note accompanied with its major third, augmented fourth, and augmented sixth—as, A♭-C-D-F♯

French violin clef.—The G clef placed upon the first line of the stave.

Frets.—Thin strips of wood, metal, or ivory, placed across the fingerboard of the guitar, zither, and similar instruments, in order to facilitate correct stopping.

Fretta (*It.*)—With speed, hastily, hurriedly.

Frettevole
Frettoloso ⎬ (*It.*)—Hasty, hurried.
Frettoso

Frisch (*Ger.*)—Lively, brisk, vigorous.

Fröhlich (*Ger.*) — Joyous, cheerful, gay.

Frosch (*Ger.*)—The nut of a bow.

F Schlüssel (*Ger.*)—The F clef.

Fuga (*Lat.* and *It.*)—A fugue.

Fugara (*It.*)—An organ-stop having metal flue-pipes of 8 or 4 ft. pitch. The tone is sharp and stringy.

Fugato (*It.*)—A composition in the fugal style, but not in strict fugue form.

Fuge (*Ger.*)—A fugue.

Fughetta (*It.*) ⎬ A short fugue.
Fughette (*Ger.*)

Fugue.—A composition in the contrapuntal (polyphonic) style, founded upon a short, pithy theme which is treated and developed by means of various devices, and in accordance with certain laws. A *double-fugue* is one founded upon two subjects.

Führer (*Ger.*) — The subject of a fugue.

Full anthem.—One for the full choir, having no solo or verse parts.

Full cadence, or **Full close.** — A perfect cadence, formed by the progression of the chord of the dominant followed by that of the tonic.

Full score.—A score in which all the parts for voices and instruments are written upon separate staves.

Füllstimmen (*Ger.*)—Additional parts for voices or instruments; not principal parts.

Fundamental.—(1) The root of a chord, the lowest note of a series of thirds. (2) A note which produces a series of harmonics; a generator. *Fundamental position,* when the root of a chord is in the bass.

Funèbre (*Fr.*) ⎫ Funeral, mournful,
Funebre (*It.*) ⎬ dirge-like. *Marche
Funerale (*It.*) ⎭ funèbre,* funeral march.

Fuoco, con ⎱ (*It.*)—With fire, spirit,
Fuocoso ⎰ dash.

Für (*Ger.*)—For. *Für vier Stimmen,* for four voices.

Furia, con (*It.*)⎫
Furibondo (*It.*)⎪ With fury ; wildly,
Furieux (*Fr.*) ⎬ vehemently,
Furioso (*It.*) ⎭ fiercely.

Furlano (*It.*)—A dance. (Forlana.)

Furniture stop.—A mixture stop on an organ.

Furore (*It.*)—Fury, passion. *Con furore,* passionately.

Fuss (*Ger.*)—A foot. (1) The part of an organ pipe below the mouth. (2) The measure of pitch of an organ pipe ; as, 8-füssig,=of 8 ft. pitch.

G.

G.—(1) The fifth degree of the scale of C. (2) The keynote of the scale having one sharp. (3) The lowest string on a violin, the third on the viola and violoncello. (4) The name of the clef which determines the name and absolute pitch of the second line above Middle C.

Gai (*Fr.*)—Gay, merry, lively.

Gaiement (*Fr.*)⎱Gaily, merrily,
Gajamente (*It.*)⎰ lively.

Galant, -e (*Fr.*) } Graceful, pleasing,
Galante (*It.*) } in good taste.

Galliard.—An old dance in triple time, of gay, spirited movement.

Galop
Galopade (*Fr.*)
Galopp (*Ger.*)
Galoppo (*It.*)
} A lively dance in duple time.

Gamba (*It.*) } (1) A *viola de gamba*.
Gambe (*Ger.*) } (2) An organ-stop, the tone being of a stringy, pungent character.

Gamme (*Fr.*)—A scale.

Ganz (*Ger.*)—Whole, quite.

Ganzton (*Ger.*)—A whole tone.

Garbato } (*It.*) Elegantly, grace-
Garbo, con } fully.

Gardez le silence (*Fr.*)—Keep silent.

Gauche (*Fr.*)—Left; *main gauche*, left hand.

Gavot
Gavotta (*It.*)
Gavotte (*Fr. and Ger.*)
} An old, graceful dance of French origin. It is in ¢ time with strong accentuation, and begins upon the weaker half of the bar.

G clef.—The clef which determines the name and absolute pitch of the second line above Middle C. At the present time it is only used upon the second line of the staff.

G dur (*Ger.*)—The key of G major.

Gebet (*Ger.*)—A prayer.

Gebrochener Akkord (*Ger.*) — A broken chord.

Gebunden (*Ger.*) — Slurred, tied, bound, *legato*.

Gedackt, Gedact, or Gedakt (*Ger.*)— Stopped organ pipes.

Gedämpft (*Ger.*)—Damped, muted, muffled.

Gedehnt (*Ger.*)—Lengthened, sustained, prolonged.

Gefährte (*Ger.*)—The answer to a fugue subject.

Gefallen, nach (*Ger.*)—(Ad libitum.)

Gefällig (*Ger.*)—Pleasing, graceful.

Gefühl, mit } (*Ger.*) — With feeling,
Gefühlvoll } expression, soul.

Gegenbewegung (*Ger.*) — Contrary motion.

Gegenpunkt (*Ger.*)—Counterpoint.

Gegensatz (*Ger.*)—Counter-subject.

Gehalten (*Ger.*)—Held, sustained.

Gehämmert (*Ger.*)—Hammered.

Gehaucht (*Ger.*)—To be played very softly.

Gehend (*Ger.*) — Moderately slow. (Andante.)

Geige (*Ger.*)—A violin.

Geigenbogen (*Ger.*)—A bow.

Geigenprinzipal (*Ger.*)—A violin-diapason-stop on the organ.

Geigensaite (*Ger.*)—A violin string.

Gekneipt (*Ger.*)—(Pizzicato.)

Gelassen (*Ger.*)—Calm, placid, tranquil.

Geläufig (*Ger.*)—Fluent, easy.

Geläufigkeit (*Ger.*)—Fluency, velocity.

Geltung (*Ger.*)—Value—as of a note or a rest.

Gemächlich (*Ger.*) — Easy, convenient, comfortable. (Comodo.)

Gemässigt (*Ger.*) — At a moderate speed.

Gemessen (*Ger.*)—Measured, sedately; at a moderate speed.

Gemshorn (*Ger.*)—"Chamois horn." An organ-stop of 8 or 4 ft. pitch on the manuals, and 16 ft. on the pedal organ. The tone is rather thin, but bright.

Gemüt(h), mit (*Ger.*)—With feeling, with emotion.

Genau (*Ger.*)—Exact.

Genera (*Lat.*)—The plural of *genus*, kind. In the ancient Greek system there were three varieties of musical genera: the diatonic, chromatic, and enharmonic.

Generalbass (*Ger.*)—Thorough-bass.

Generalprobe (*Ger.*) — General rehearsal; a final rehearsal.

Générateur (*Fr.*) ⎫ (1) A root, the
Generator ⎬ fundamental
note of a chord. (2) A note which produces a series of upper partial tones or harmonics.

Genere (*It.*) — (1) Manner, style. (2) Kind ; as applied to scales, etc.

Génie (*Fr.*) ⎫ Genius.
Genie (*Ger.*) ⎭

Genre (*Fr.*)—(Genera.)

Gentil, -le (*Fr.*) ⎫
Gentile (*It.*) ⎬ Pretty, tender, with delicacy.
Gentilezza, con (*It.*) ⎭

Geradebewegung (*Ger.*) — Similar motion.

Gerade Takt(art) (*Ger.*)—Duple time.

German flute. — The cross flute ; (Flauto traverso.)

German sixth.—One of the forms of the chord of the augmented sixth, consisting of a bass note accompanied with its major third, perfect fifth, and augmented sixth—as, A♭–C–E♭–F♯.

Ges (*Ger.*)—G♭. *Geses,* G♭♭.

Gesgan (*Ger.*)—Singing ; a song, cantata, hymn, etc.

Gesangartig ⎫
Gesangreich ⎬ (*Ger.*)—In a singing style. (Cantabile.)
Gesangvoll ⎭

Geschleift (*Ger.*)—Slurred ; legato.

Geschmackvoll (*Ger.*)—Tastefully.

Geschwind (*Ger.*)—Quick, swift, rapid.

Geschwindmarsch (*Ger.*)—A quick march.

Ges dur (*Ger.*)—The key of G flat major.

Gesteigert (*Ger.*)—Intensified ; with increase of tone.

Gestossen (*Ger.*)—(Staccato.)

Get(h)eilt (*Ger.*)—Divided. *Getheilte Violinen,* divided violins.

Getragen (*Ger.*)—Sustained. (Sostenuto.)

Gewichtig (*Ger.*)—Heavily, gravely.

Giga (*It.*) ⎫ A jig. A lively old
Gigue (*Fr.*) ⎭ dance, usually written in compound duple or quadruple time, and rapid tempo. In the suite, the gigue is generally the last movement.

Giochevole (*It.*)—Merry, jocose.

Gioco, con ⎫ (*It.*) — In a sportive,
Giocondo, -a ⎭ playful style.

Gioсoso, -a (*It.*)—Jocose, gay, merry.

Gioja, con ⎫
Giojante ⎬ (*It.*)—With mirth ; joyfully, merrily.
Giojoso ⎭

Gioviale (*It.*)—Jovial, cheerful, pleasant.

Giovialità, con (*It.*)—With joviality, cheerfully.

Gis (*Ger.*)— The note G sharp.

Gisis (*Ger.*)—The note G double sharp.

Giubilante ⎫ (*It.*)—Jubilant ; joyful.
Giubiloso ⎭

Giustamente ⎫ (*It.*) — Strictly, accurately.
Giustezza ⎭

Giusto (*It.*)—Just, appropriate. Often interpreted "exact."

Glänzend (*Ger.*)—Brilliant, sparkling.

Glee.—A secular composition, peculiar to England, for three or more unaccompanied solo voices. It usually contains two or more contrasted movements, and may be either gay or serious in character.

Gleich (*Ger.*)—Equal ; similar.

Gleichebewegung (*Ger.*) — Similar motion.

Gleichsam (*Ger.*)—As if.

Gleichschwebende Temperatur (*Ger.*) —Equal temperament.

Gleitend (*Ger.*)—Gliding.

Gli (*It.*)—The (*mas. plural*). *Gli stromenti,* the instruments.

Glissando ⎫ (*It.*)—The execution of
Glissato ⎪ a rapid scale-passage
Glissicando ⎬ by gliding the tip of the thumb, or of a finger,
Glissicato ⎭ along the keys. (2) A portamento effect on the violin, etc.

Glisser (*Fr.*)—To slide. (Glissando.) *Glissant,* gliding.

Glocke (*Ger.*)—A bell.

Glockenspiel (*Ger.*)–(1) *See* Carillon 1. (2) An instrument consisting of a set of bells, or of a set of steel bars, which are played upon by being struck with hammers, or by levers which are acted upon by a keyboard. (3) An organ-stop.

Gloria (*Lat.*) — A movement of the Mass.

Glottis.—The aperture between the vocal chords.

Gnaccare (*It.*)—Castanets.

Gondeliera (*It.*) } A barcarole.
Gondellied (*Ger.*) }

Grace.—A melodic ornament or embellishment.

Grace-note. — A note of embellishment, such as an appoggiatura, a turn, shake, etc.

Gracieu-x, -se (*Fr.*)—Graceful.

Grad (*Ger.*)—Degree.

Gradatamente (*It.*) — By degrees, gradually.

Gradevole (*It.*)—Pleasing, grateful.

Grado (*It.*)—A degree, step. *Digrado*, by conjunct movement.

Graduale (*Lat.*) — (1) The response sung between the reading of the Epistle and Gospel in the Roman Church. (2) A book containing the graduals, introits, etc., of the Mass.

Graduellement (*Fr.*)—Gradually. *Graduellement plus doux*, softer by degrees.

Gran (*It.*)—Large, great, complete.

Gran cassa (*It.*)—The big, or bass, drum.

Grand, -e (*Fr.*)—Large, great; full. *Grand bourdon*, double bourdon. *Grand chœur*, full organ. *Grand jeu*, (*a*) full organ; (*b*) a stop on the harmonium which brings into play the full power of the instrument. *Grand orgue* (*a*) full organ; (*b*) Great organ.

Grande mesure à deux temps (*Fr.*) —A measure having two beats.

Grandezza, con } (*It.*)—With gran-
Grandioso } deur; in a lofty, pompous style.

Grandisonante (*It.*)—Loud, sonorous.

Grappa (*It.*)—The brace connecting two or more staves.

Grave.—Low in pitch.

Grave (*It.* and *Fr.*)—(1) Low in pitch. (2) Slow, ponderous in movement. (3) Serious in expression.

Gravecembalo }
Gravicembalo } (*It.*)—A harpsichord.

Gravità, con (*It.*)—With dignity, seriousness, gravity.

Grazia, con } (*It.*)—In a graceful,
Grazioso, -a } elegant style.

Greater.—Belonging to the major scale, *i.e.*, suggesting the greater third—the major third. The earlier composers made use of the term to indicate the mode of a key; as, "The key of C with the greater third," the key of C major; "C with the lesser third," the key of C minor.

Great octave.—The notes—

Great organ.—The manual (or keyboard) on the organ which controls the flue pipes of largest scale, and the most powerful reeds. On an organ having two manuals, it is the lower row of keys; where there are more than two, it is the lowest but one.

Gregorian Chant.—The revised ancient Plain-song as established by Pope Gregory in the sixth century. It is entirely in unison, strictly diatonic, and the time is free.

Griffbrett (*Ger.*)—The finger-board of a stringed instrument.

Grille (*Ger.*)—A caprice, or whim.

Gross (*Ger.*)—(1) Great, large. (2) Major, as *Grosse Terz*, a major third. *Grösster*, greatest.

Grossartig (*Ger.*)—Grandly, magnificent.

Grosse caisse (*Fr.*) } The big, or
Grosse Trommel (*Ger.*) } bass, drum.

Grosso (*It.*)—Large, great, grand. *Concerti grossi*, grand concertos.

Grottesco (*It.*) ⎱ Grotesque, humor-
Grotesk (*Ger.*) ⎰ ous.

Ground bass.—A short bass passage, which is repeated several times, each repetition receiving varied treatment.

Group.—(1) Two or more notes, the stems of which are joined together. (2) A section of the orchestra, embracing instruments of one class.

Grundakkord (*Ger.*)—A chord in root position.

Grundbass (*Ger.*)—A fundamental bass.

Grundstimme (*Ger.*)—The bass part.

Grundton (*Ger.*)—(1) The fundamental note of a chord. (2) The tonic of a scale, also of the principal key in a composition.

Gruppetto ⎱ (*It.*)—A turn.
Gruppo   ⎰

G Schlüssel (*Ger.*)—The G clef.

G string. — On the violin, the 4th ; on the viola and 'cello, the 3rd ; on the double bass, the 1st.

Guaracha (*Sp.*)—A lively Spanish dance in triple time.

Guerriero (*It.*)—Martial, warlike.

Guida (*It.*) ⎱ The subject of a fugue,
Guide (*Fr.*) ⎰ and antecedent of a canon.

Guidon (*Fr.*)—A direct (*q.v.*).

G u i d o n i a n syllables.—(Aretinian syllables.)

G u i t a r.—A stringed instrument, played by the strings being plucked with the right hand, the notes being " stopped " with the left. It usually has six strings.

Guitare (*Fr.*) ⎱
Guitarra (*Sp.*) ⎰ A guitar.
Guitarre (*Ger.*)⎰

Gusto (*It.*)—Taste. *Con gusto*, with taste and expression.

Gut (*Ger.*)—Good, well.

Guter Taktt(h)eil (*Ger.*)—The accented part of a bar.

Guttural.—A throaty production of tone.

H.

H.—The abbreviation used for *Horn* in an orchestral score, and for *Hand* in music for the pianoforte, etc.

H (*Ger.*)—The note B natural, the letter B always indicating B flat.

Halb (*Ger.*)—Half.

Halbe Note (*Ger.*)—A half-note ; a minim.

Halbe Pause (*Ger.*)—A half-note rest ; a minim rest.

Halbschluss (*Ger.*) — A half or imperfect cadence.

Halb stark (*Ger.*) — *lit.*, half loud. Moderately loud.

Halbton (*Ger.*)—A semitone.

Half cadence.—(See Cadence (3)).

Half close.—(Half cadence.)

Half note.—A minim.

Half shift.—A position of the hand in playing on a stringed instrument. The term is synonymous with what is known as the second position.

Half step.—A semitone.

Hallelujah.—The same as Alleluia.

Hals (*Ger.*)—The neck of stringed instruments, such as the violin, guitar, etc.

Hammer.—That portion of the action of a pianoforte which strikes the strings, causing them to vibrate, thus producing sound.

Hammerclavier (*Ger.*)—The pianoforte.

Hand-horn.—A horn without valves or pistons.

Hand - note. — A stopped note on the horn, produced by the hand being inserted in the bell of the instrument.

Handstücke (*Ger.*)—Technical exercises.

Hand übersetzen (*Ger.*)—To pass one hand over another.

Hardiment (*Fr.*)—Boldly.

Harfe (*Ger.*)—A harp.

Harmonia (*Gk.*, *Lat.* and *It.*)—Harmony.

Harmonica.—(1) An instrument, the tones of which are obtained from plates of glass or of metal, by striking them with a hammer held in the hand of the performer, or acted upon through the medium of a keyboard. (2) The name sometimes given to a mixture stop on foreign organs.

Harmonichord.—A keyboard stringed instrument, the tones of which are produced by a revolving cylinder, which, by the depression of a key, is brought into contact with the strings, thus causing them to vibrate.

Harmonic mark.—The sign ° placed over notes for instruments of the violin family, indicating that such notes are to be produced as harmonics.

Harmonics.—(1) Sounds (also called *Partial tones*, or *Overtones*) given out by a vibrating string, or column of air, in addition to its *fundamental tone, prime,* or *generator.* This arises from the fact that if, for instance, a string be set in motion, it vibrates, not only as a whole, but also simultaneously in fractional parts. The vibration of the full length gives the fundamental tone; one-half—vibrating at twice the speed —the octave above the fundamental; one third—vibrating at three times the speed—the twelfth above the fundamental, and so on. Thus, what strikes the ear as one sound is in reality an aggregation of sounds, forming what is termed a "Compound tone." A fundamental without any overtones—a very rare occurrence—is termed a "Simple tone."

The following diagram illustrates the harmonics of the note C up to the 10th of the series, the note B♭ being only approximately correct as representing the 7th harmonic :—

(2) Tones produced on stringed instruments by lightly touching the strings at certain points, instead of "stopping" the strings in the usual way.

Harmonic stops.—Organ-stops, both flue and reed, having pipes twice the length necessary for producing the required pitch, but pierced with a small hole in the middle. Thus, an 8 ft. pipe will produce what is known as 4 ft. tone.

Harmonie (*Ger.*)—(1) Harmony. (2) Music for wind instruments. (3) The wind instruments of an orchestra.

Harmoniemusik (*Ger.*)—Music for wind instruments.

Harmonieu-x, -se (*Fr.*) ⎱ Harmon-
Harmonisch (*Ger.*) ⎰ ious.

Harmonique (*Fr.*)—Harmonic.

Harmonium.—A keyboard wind instrument, the tones of which are produced by means of free reeds, made to vibrate by air being forced through the apertures over which they are placed. The larger instruments have several sets of reeds, differing in pitch and quality of tone.

Harmony.—(1) A combination of musical sounds, producing a chord either consonant or dissonant. (2) The word used in describing the number of parts employed, as, 2-part, 3-part, or 4-part, harmony. (3) The study of the combination of musical sounds.

Harp.—One of the most ancient of stringed instruments, the tone being produced by plucking the strings with the fingers. There are several types of instruments, the most modern being the "double action pedal harp" invented by Erard. It is fitted with seven pedals, by means of which the pitch of each string can be raised either a semitone or a tone, making the complete chromatic scale available. Its normal key is C♭, and it has a compass of just over 6½ octaves, from

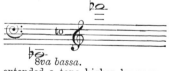

extended a tone higher by means of the pedals.

Harpe (*Fr.*)—A harp.

Harpicordo (*It.*)—A harpsichord.

Harpsichord.—A keyboard stringed instrument somewhat resembling a modern grand pianoforte in shape. It was one of the types of instrument which preceded the pianoforte, and the tone was produced by the strings being plucked by quills or pieces of hard leather. Some harpsichords were constructed with two keyboards, one for producing loud, the other soft, tones ; others had stops, by means of which the tone could be varied.

Hastig (*Ger.*)—Quick.

H a u p t (*Ger.*)—Chief, principal. *Hauptsatz*, principal theme.

Hauptgesang ⎱ (*Ger.*)—The princi-
Hauptmelodie ⎰ pal melody.

Hauptmanual (*Ger.*) — The great organ.

Hauptnote (*Ger.*)—(1) An essential note. (2) An accented note.

Hauptpartie (*Ger.*)—A principal part.

Hauptsatz (*Ger.*) — The principal theme of a movement; the first theme of a double fugue.

Hauptschluss (*Ger.*)—A full close; a perfect cadence.

Hauptstimme (*Ger.*)—The principal part.

Hauptton (*Ger.*)—The key-note.

Hauptwerk (*Ger.*)—The great organ.

Hausse d'archet (*Fr.*)—The nut of a bow.

Haut (*Fr.*)—High, acute, loud.

Hautbois (*Fr.*)—(Oboe.)

Hautbois d'amour (*Fr.*)—An obsolete species of oboe.

Hautboy.—(Oboe.)

Haut-dessus (*Fr.*)—A high soprano.

Haute-contre (*Fr.*)—The alto part.

Haute-taille (*Fr.*)—First, or higher, tenor.

H dur (*Ger.*)—The key of B major.

Head-voice.—The term used by some authorities to describe the higher register of the human voice.

Heftig (*Ger.*)—Fervent, impetuous, passionate, vehement.

Heiter (*Ger.*)—Calm, serene, cheerful.

Helicon.—A brass wind instrument used in military bands as a bass. It is circular in form, and is carried over the shoulder.

Hemidemisemiquaver.—A note half the value of demisemiquaver; a *sixty-fourth note.*

Heptachord.—(1) The interval of a seventh. (2) A series of seven diatonic notes. (3) An instrument having seven strings.

Herabstrich (*Ger.*)—The down stroke of the bow in playing the violin or viola.

Héroïque (*Fr.*) ⎱
Heroisch (*Ger.*) ⎰ Heroic.

Herstrich (*Ger.*)—The stroke of the bow from heel to point, as in playing the violoncello and instruments held in a similar position. It corresponds to the down stroke of the bow in violin playing.

Herunterstrich(*Ger.*)—(Herabstrich.)

Hervorragend (*Ger.*)—Prominently.

H e r z i g (*Ger.*)—With heartiness ; tenderly.

Hexachord.—A series of six diatonic notes : *e.g.*, ut, re, mi, fa, sol, la.

Hidden fifths and **Hidden octaves.**
—Harmonic progressions which are, under certain conditions, forbidden in strict part - writing. Hidden fifths occur when the *second* of two intervals formed between any two parts is a perfect fifth, and is approached in similar motion ; hidden octaves, when, under similar conditions, the second interval is a perfect octave. The reason for the use of the term " hidden " is explained by some by taking as an illustration the two-part progression as at (a) which, if altered by the addition of passing notes, as at (b), would result in direct consecutives :—

Hilfslinie (*Ger.*)—Leger line.

Hinaufstrich (*Ger.*)—An up stroke of the bow in playing the violin and any instrument held in a similar position.

Hinstrich (*Ger.*)—The stroke of the bow from the point to the heel, as in playing the violoncello and any instrument held in a similar position.

His (*Ger.*)—The note B sharp.

H moll (*Ger.*)—The key of B minor.

Hoboe (*Ger.*)—An oboe.

Hoch (*Ger.*)—High. *Höher*, higher.

Höchste Stimme (*Ger.*)—The highest part.

Höhe (*Ger.*)—Height, elevation.

Hohl Flöte (*Ger.*)—Hollow-toned flute. An organ-stop of hollow, mellow quality of tone, usually of 8 or 4 ft. pitch.

Hold.—An old English name for the sign indicating a pause. It is now obsolete.

Holding note.—A note sustained in one part while the other parts are moving.

Holzbläser (*Ger.*)—One or more performers on wood-wind instruments.

Holzblasinstrument (*Ger.*)—A wood-wind instrument.

Homophonic. — (1) Alike in sound and pitch, *i.e.*, music in unison as opposed to music in harmony. (2) The style of music in which one part sustains the melodic interest, the other parts forming an accompaniment, as opposed to the polyphonic or contrapuntal style, in which all the parts are of equal importance.

Homophony.—Music in the homophonic style.

Horn.—A brass wind instrument, formed of a long twisted tube, to one end of which the mouthpiece is fixed, the other end gradually expanding to a rather large bell-shaped opening. Horns are of two kinds, the natural or French horn, and the valve horn. The notes produced without the aid of valves are those of the harmonic series; the difference of pitch being obtained by varying the position of the lips, and varying also the amount of wind pressure. The notes so produced are termed " Open " notes. The capabilities of the natural horn are very limited, inasmuch as if any notes other than open notes be required, they have to be produced by inserting the hand in the bell of the instrument, by which means the open notes may be more or less flattened. Such notes are termed " Closed " notes. By means of crooks, which alter the length of the tube, the horn can be tuned in different keys ; those most generally used being C, D, E flat, E, and F. The horn is a transposing instrument, which means that the notes sounded differ from those written ; the notes on the horn in C sounding an octave lower, in D a minor seventh lower, in E flat a major sixth lower, and so on. The valve horn is similar to the natural horn, inasmuch as the same series of open notes is produced ; but, by means of valves which alter the length of the tube, the complete chromatic scale becomes available. At the present day the valve horn is exclusively used, and practically always in the key of F.

Hörner (*Ger.*)—Horns.

Hornpipe.—(1) An old wind instrument of the shawm character. (2) An old, lively, English dance ; originally in 3-2 time, later in 4-4 time.

Huitième de soupir (*Fr.*) A demi-semiquaver rest.

Huit pieds (*Fr.*)—An organ in which the largest pipes are of 8 ft. pitch.

Hülfslinien (*Ger.*)—Leger lines.

Hülfsnote (*Ger.*)—An auxiliary note.

Humor (*Ger.*)—Humour.

Humoreske (*Ger.*)—A piece of a humorous character.

Hurdy-gurdy.—An ancient instrument, having a body shaped somewhat like that of a violin, a neck furnished with keys, four gut strings, two of which, acted upon by the keys, serve for playing the melody, the other two forming a drone bass. By means of a crank a rosined wheel revolves, setting the strings in vibration.

Hurtig (*Ger.*)—Nimble, quick, agile.

Hymn.—A sacred metrical poem set to music, and forming part of a religious service.

Hyper (*Gk.*)—Above. As a prefix to the names of intervals it means "super," or "upper."

Hypo (*Gk.*)—Below. As a prefix to the names of intervals it means "sub," or "lower." As a prefix to the names of Ecclesiastical modes it signifies a mode produced by beginning a 4th below any Authentic mode(*e.g.*,Hypo-Dorian), and is termed Plagal.

I.

I (*It.*)—The (*mas. plural*).

Iambic.—Metre composed of a succession of alternate short and long syllables : ‿ —, ‿ —, etc.

Iambus.—A metrical foot consisting of a short and a long syllable : ‿ —

Iastian.—One of the Greek modes, the same as the Ionian.

Idillio (*It.*)—An idyl.

Idyl.—A composition of a pastoral, romantic character.

Idylle (*Fr.* and *Ger.*)—An idyl.

Il (*It.*)—The (*mas. sing.*).

Il doppio movimento (*It.*)—The speed of the movement to be doubled ; twice as fast.

Il fine (*It.*)—The end.

Il più (*It.*)—The most. *Il più presto possibile*, as quick as possible.

Im (*Ger.*)—In the. *Im tempo*, to resume the regular speed (*a tempo*).

Imboccatura (*It.*)— The mouthpiece of a wind instrument, such as the horn, etc.

Imitando (*It.*)—Imitating.

Imitation.—The repetition of a figure, or of a phrase, by another part. The part which proposes the theme is the *Antecedent*, the imitative part, the *Consequent*. When the consequent is an exact reproduction of the antecedent, the imitation is said to be *strict* or *canonic;* if only the general outline be followed, the imitation is *free.*

Imitazione (*It.*)—Imitation.

Im lebhaftesten Zeitmasse (*Ger.*)—In the quickest time possible.

Immer (*Ger.*)—Always; continuously. *Immer langsam*, slow throughout.

Imperfect cadence.—Half close. (See Cadence (3)).

Imperfect concords, or consonances.- A term applied to the major and minor thirds and sixths, in the classification of intervals.

Imperfect intervals.—A term occasionally applied to intervals which are a chromatic semitone less than perfect.

Imperioso (*It.*)—Imperious, lofty.

Impeto, con
Impetuosita, con⎱ (*It.*) Impetuously,
Impetuoso   ⎰   vehemently.

Impétueux (*Fr.*) — In a boisterous manner ; impetuously.

Implied intervals. — Intervals not expressed in a figured bass, but understood to be a component part of any chord.

Impresario (*It.*)—The manager of a theatre or concert.

Impromptu.—(1) A musical performance without previous preparation. (2) A piece of music partaking of the nature of an improvisation. (3) A term used by some composers, notably Chopin, to express a piece of music of a lyrical nature.

Improvisateur (*mas.*) ⎱ *Fr.* One who
Improvisatrice (*fem.*) ⎰ improvises.

Improvisation.—An impromptu performance ; an extemporization.

Improviser (*Fr.*) ⎱
Improvvisare (*It.*) ⎰ To improvise.

Improvvisata (*It.*)—An impromptu. An improvisation.

Improvvisatore (*It.*)—An improviser.

Im Stile einer . . . . (*Ger.*)—In the style of a . . .

Im Zeitmass (Ger.)—In time.

In alt (*It.*)—The notes G to F in the

octave above

In altissimo (*It.*)—The notes G to F

in the octave above

Incalzando(*It.*)—Increasing or working up the speed and tone.

Incidental music. — Music written with a view to enhancing and supplementing the effect of a drama.

Inciso (*It.*) — Incisive; with clear articulation.

Incomplete stop.—A half stop on the organ.

Indeciso (*It.*) — In an undecided manner.

Indifferente   ⎱(*It.*) With indifferIndifferenza, con⎰ ence, or unconcern.

In distanza (*It.*) — A passage performed as if the sound came from a distance.

In Eile (*Ger.*)—In haste.

Infinite canon.—A canon without cadential ending; an endless, or perpetual, canon.

Infino (*It.*)—Up to, as far as.

Inflection.—The notes which follow the reciting note in a chant.

In fretta (*It.*)—In haste; hurriedly.

Inganno (*It.*) — *lit.*, deception. *Cadenza d'inganno*, a deceptive cadence. (Interrupted cadence.)

In gehender Bewegung (*Ger.*)— Rather quicker than *Andante*, = *Andante con moto.*

Inhalt (*Ger.*)—Contents.

Iniziale (*It.*)—Initial; the first.

Inner parts.—The parts in harmony which lie between the "extreme" (*i.e.*, the highest and lowest) parts.

Inner pedal.—A sustained, or held, note in an inner part.

Innig (*Ger.*) — Deep, heartfelt, genuine, intense, fervent.

Innigkeit, mit ⎱(*Ger.*)—With deep Inniglich   ⎰ emotion, fervently.

Innocenza, con (*It.*)—Innocently; in a simple manner.

In partito (*It.*)—In score.

Inquiet (*Fr.*) ⎱ Restless, agitated. Inquieto (*It.*) ⎰

Insensibile (*It.*)—Imperceptible.

Insistendo   ⎱ (*It.*)—Urgently. Insistenza, con ⎰

Inständig (*Ger.*)⎱ Urgent, pressing. Instante (*It.*)   ⎰

Instrument à archet (*Fr.*)—An instrument played with a bow.

Instrument à cordes (*Fr.*)—A stringed instrument.

Instrument à percussion (*Fr.*)—An instrument of percussion, such as the drum, etc.

Instrument à vent (*Fr.*)—A wind instrument.

Instrumentation.—The art of composing, or adapting, music for a number of instruments of different kinds ; *e.g.*, for an orchestra, a military band, etc.

Instrumenti (*It.*)—The plural of *instrumento* (*q.v.*).

Instrumentirung (*Ger.*)—Instrumentation.

Instrumento (*It.*)—An instrument.

Instrumento da fiato (*It.*)—A woodwind instrument.

Intavolatura (*It.*)—(Tablature.)

In tempo (*It.*)—(A tempo.)

Interlude   ⎱(1) Music perInterludium (*Lat.*)⎰ formed between the acts of a play or of an opera. (2) The music played between the verses of a hymn or other portion of a Church service.

Intermède (*Fr.*)⎫(1) Music performed Intermedio (*It.*)⎬ between the acts Intermezzo (*It.*)⎭ of a play or of an opera.   (2) The name applied to many instrumental compositions which possess no very characteristic feature.

Interrupted cadence. — When the dominant chord is followed by some chord other than the tonic. (See Cadence (4)).

Interval.—The distance from one note to another ; the difference in pitch between two sounds.

Intervall (*Ger.*) }
Intervalle (*Fr.*) } An interval.
Intervallo (*It.* }

Intimo (*It.*)—Heartfelt, fervent. *Con intimo sentimento*, with inward emotion.

Intonare (*It.*)—To tune ; to sing ; to intone.

Intonation.—(1) The production of either instrumental or vocal tone. (2) Playing or singing in tune. (3) The method of chanting employed in Plain Chant. (4) The notes leading up the reciting note in a Gregorian chant.

Intonatura }
Intonazione } (*It.*)—Intonation.

Intoning.—The chanting in monotone by the minister, or choir, of certain portions of the Church service.

Intrada (*It.*)—An interlude, a prelude.

Intrepidezza, con (*It.*)—Boldly, dashingly.

Intrepido, -a (*It.*)—Intrepid, bold.

Introduction.—A musical "preface" to a movement or series of movements. An introduction generally ends with a chord which leads directly into what follows, and is free in style, structure, and length.

Introduzione (*It.*)—An introduction.

Introit }
Introito (*It.*) } (1) An antiphon sung while the priest proceeds to the altar to celebrate the Mass. (2) In the Anglican Church, a short anthem, hymn, or psalm, sung at the commencement of the Communion Service.
Introitus (*Lat.*) }

Invention.—A short piece in the contrapuntal style. The title was given by I. S. Bach to 30 short pieces of his own.

Invenzione (*It.*)—Invention.

Inversion.—(1) An interval is inverted when the relative position of the two notes is changed ; the lower becoming the higher, and *vice versâ*. (2) A chord is inverted when some note other than the root is in the bass. (3) A theme is inverted when the movement is in contrary motion to that of the original—that is, ascending intervals becoming descending, and *vice versâ*. (4) Two themes are inverted when the higher is placed below the lower, or *vice versâ*. This constitutes "double counterpoint," and the inversion may be at different intervals, such as the octave, tenth, etc. (5) A pedal-point is inverted when the sustained note is in some part other than the bass.

Invocazione (*It.*)—An invocation, a prayer.

Ionian mode. — The Ecclesiastical mode commencing on C.

Ira, con }
Irato } (*It.*)—Passionately ; with anger.

Irresoluto (*It.*)—Uncertain ; in an undecided manner.

Islancio, con (*It.*) — Impetuously ; with dash.

Istesso (*It.*)—The same ; as *l'istesso tempo*, the same speed.

Istrumentazione (*It.*) — Instrumentation.

Italian sixth.—One of the forms of the chord of the augmented sixth, consisting of a bass note with its doubled major third, and augmented sixth—as, A♭–C–F♯–C.

Italiano, -a (*It.*)—Italian.

J.

Jack.—(1) In the harpsichord an upright piece of wood fixed at the end of the lever, to which is attached a piece of crow-quill or hard leather, which plucks the string. (2) In the pianoforte, the escapement lever, also called the "hopper."

Jagdhorn (*Ger.*)—A hunting horn.

Jagdstück (*Ger.*)—A hunting piece.

Jägerchor (*Ger.*)—A hunting chorus.

Jägerhorn (*Ger.*)—(Jagdhorn.)

Jeu (*Fr.*)—(1) Style of playing. (2) A stop on an organ, harmonium, etc. *Grand jeu*, full organ, or full power ; *Demi jeu*, half power.

Jeux (*Fr.*)—Plural of *jeu*.

Jeux doux (*Fr.*)—Sweet, soft stops.

Jeux forts (*Fr.*)—Loud stops.

Jew's-harp.—A small instrument with an iron frame and a thin metal tongue, which at the end is bent at a right angle. The frame is held between the teeth and the tongue twanged with the finger, the pitch of the notes being regulated by varying the cavity of the mouth.

Jig.—(Gigue.)

Jingles.—Discs of tin or other metal, fastened at intervals round a tambourine.

Jodeln ⎫ (*Ger.*)—A method of singing as
Jodl ⎬ practised by the Swiss and Tyrolese, characterized by
Jodler ⎭ the rapid alternation of the natural and the falsetto voices.

Jota.—A Spanish dance.

Joyeusement ⎫ (*Fr.*)—Joyously.
Joyeux ⎭

Jusqu' à (*Fr.*)—Until.

Just intonation.—The production of notes in singing or playing absolutely true in pitch, *i.e.*, each note having its true number, and each interval its true ratio, of vibrations. Just intonation is opposed to tempered intonation. (See Equal temperament.)

Juste (*Fr.*)—Appropriate, exact, in tune.

Justesse (*Fr.*)—Equality, purity, and correctness of intonation.

K.

Kadenz (*Ger.*)—A cadence.

K a m m e r (*Ger.*)—" Chamber " ; " court " ; as, *Kammercantate*, chamber cantata ; *Kammerconcert*, a chamber concerto, or a chamber concert ; *Kammermusik*, chamber music ; *Kammer Sonate*, a chamber sonata ; *Kammerton*, concert pitch.

Kanon (*Ger.*)—A canon.

Kanonik (*Ger.*)—Canonic.

Kantate (*Ger.*)—A cantata.

Kapelle (*Ger.*)—(1) A chapel. (2) A term formerly applied to a body of instrumentalists or a choir. (3) An orchestra.

Kapellmeister (*Ger.*)—(1) A choir-master. (2) The leader or director of an orchestra.

Kavatine (*Ger.*)—(Cavatina.)

Keckheit, mit (*Ger.*)—With boldness; pertness ; confidently.

Keraulophon.—An 8 ft. stop on an organ, with a soft and rather "reedy" quality of tone.

Kesselpauke (*Ger.*)—A kettle-drum.

Kettentriller (*Ger.*)—A succession or chain of trills.

Kettle-drum.—The orchestral drum. It is constructed of a metal shell, hemispherical in shape, the top being covered with stretched vellum. By means of a set of screws the tension of the vellum may be regulated, and the pitch altered. Generally speaking, an orchestra contains two kettle-drums, though in modern scores three are frequently used. Each has a compass of a perfect fifth, the lower from and the higher from

Key.—(1) The series of sounds which, taken together, form some particular scale, major or minor, each note having a certain relationship to one sound, called the key-note or tonic. (2) The name formerly applied to what is now called a clef. (3) Part of the mechanism of many musical instruments. In the pianoforte, organ, or harmonium, the key is a lever, which at the further end is connected with the internal mechanism of the instrument which it sets in motion, causing a hammer to strike the strings in the pianoforte and a valve to open in the organ or harmonium. (4) An implement used for tuning instruments, such as the pianoforte or harp.

Keyboard.—The set of keys on the pianoforte, organ, etc.

Key-chord.—The common chord on the tonic of a key.

Key-note.—The first note or tonic of a key or scale.

Key-signature.—The sharps or flats placed at the commencement of a composition, or of some portion thereof, to indicate the key of the piece.

Key-trumpet.—A trumpet provided with keys.

Kindlich (*Ger.*)—Simple, artless.

Kirche (*Ger.*) — Church. *Kirchenmusik*, Church music.

Kirchenstil (*Ger.*)—In the style of Church music.

Kithara (*Gk.*)—A species of lyre.

Klagend (*Ger.*)—Mournful, plaintive, wailing, complaining.

Klang (*Ger.*)—Sound ; quality of a note.

Klangboden (*Ger.*) — Soundboard ; resonance-box.

Klangfarbe (*Ger.*) — Quality of a sound ; *timbre*.

Klappe (*Ger.*)—The key of a wind instrument.

Klappenflügelhorn ⎱ (*Ger.*) — A keyed
Klappenhorn ⎰ bugle.

Klappentrompete (*Ger.*) — A keyed trumpet.

Klarinette (*Ger.*)—A clarinet.

Klavier (*Ger.*)—(1) A keyboard.   (2) A keyboard stringed instrument.

Klavierauszug (*Ger.*)—A pianoforte score.

Klein (*Ger.*)—(1) Small, as *kleiner Bass*, or *kleine Bassgeige*, a violoncello.   (2) Minor, as *kleiner Halbton*, a minor semitone.

Kleine Flöte (*Ger.*)—A small flute-stop on the organ, of 4 ft. or 2 ft. pitch.

Klingel (*Ger.*)—A small bell.

Knee-stop.—A mechanical contrivance fitted under the keyboard of the harmonium, by means of which a crescendo and diminuendo can be produced.

Knell.—The tolling of a bell on the occasion of a death, or at a funeral.

Kniegeige (*Ger.*)—A viol da gamba.

Kokett (*Ger.*)—Coquettishly.

Komponiren (*Ger.*) — To compose. *Komponirt*, composed.

Konzert (*Ger.*)—(1) Concert.   (2) Concerto.

Konzertmeister (*Ger.*)—The leader of an orchestra.

Konzertstück (*Ger.*)—(1) A concert piece.   (2) A short concerto in one movement.

Kopfstimme (*Ger.*)—Head voice.

Kraft, mit ⎱ (*Ger.*) — With strength,
Kräftig ⎰ vigour ; energetically.

Krebsgängig (*Ger.*)—Retrograde motion.

Kreuz (*Ger.*)—A sharp.

Kriegerisch (*Ger.*)—Martial, warlike.

Kriegsgesang ⎱ (*Ger.*)—A battle-
Kriegslied ⎰ song.

Krome (*Ger.*)—A quaver, ♪.

Krummbogen (*Ger.*)—A crook for altering the pitch of a horn or trumpet.

Krummhorn (*Ger.*)—(1) An obsolete wind instrument.   (2) An organ-stop of 8 ft. pitch.

Krustische Instrumente (*Ger.*)—Instruments of percussion.

Kunstfuge (*Ger.*)—A fugue in which all the devices peculiar to this style of writing are employed.

Kurz (*Ger.*)—Short.

Kurzer Mordent.—A short mordent.

Kurzer Vorschlag (*Ger.*)—A short appoggiatura.

L.

L.—Used as the abbreviation for "left," in the direction *l.h.* (left hand).

La.—(1) The name of the sixth of the Aretinian syllables used in solmisation.   (2) The name of the note A in French and Italian.   (3) The (*Fr., fem.*).

La bémol (*Fr.*)—The note A flat.

La bémol majeur (*Fr.*)—The key of A flat major.

La bémol mineur (*Fr.*)—The key of A flat minor.

La bemolle (*It.*)—The note A flat.

La bemolle maggiore (*It.*)—The key of A flat major.

La bemolle minore (*It.*)—The key of A flat minor.

Labialpfeife (*Ger.*)—A flue-pipe in the organ.

Labialstimme (*Ger.*)—A flue-stop in the organ.

L'accord de septième (*Fr.*)— The chord of the seventh.

Lacrimoso (*It.*)—Tearful, sad.

La destra (*It.*)—The right hand.

La dièse (*Fr.*)—The note A sharp.

La dièse mineur (*Fr.*)—The key of A sharp minor.

La diesis (*It.*)—The note A sharp.

La diesis minore (*It.*)—The key of A sharp minor.

Lagrimoso (*It.*)—Lamenting, complaining.

Lah.—The Tonic Sol-fa name for the sixth degree of the scale.

La maggiore (*It.*) ⎱ The key of
La majeur (*Fr.*) ⎰   A major.

Lamentabile ⎫
Lamentando ⎬ (*It.*) — Lamenting,
Lamentavole ⎪   mournful, doleful.
Lamentoso ⎭

Lancers.—A special set of dances.

Ländler (*Ger.*)—A kind of slow waltz peculiar to South Germany.

Ländlich (*Ger.*)—Rustic.

Lang (*Ger.*)—Long. *Lange Pause,* a long pause.

Langoureusement (*Fr.*)—Languidly.

Langsam (*Ger.*)—Slow. *Langsamer,* slower. *Langsam und getragen,* slow and sustained.

Language.—Part of an organ pipe.

Languendo (*It.*) ⎫
Languente (*It.*) ⎬ Languishing,
Languissant (*Fr.*)⎭ plaintive.

Languido ⎫(*It.*)—Languid, faint.
Languore⎭

Largamente (*It.*)—Broadly, largely.

Large.—The longest note used in the ancient notation. It is the equivalent of two " longs " (*q.v.*).

Large (*Fr.*)—Broadly.

Largement (*Fr.*)—(Largamente.)

Larghetto (*It.*)—At a slow rate of speed, but not so slow as *Largo,* of which *Larghetto* is the diminutive.

Larghezza, con (*It.*)—(Largamente.)

Largo (*It.*)—Large, broad. The term indicates an extremely slow and stately movement.

Largo assai ⎱ (*It.*)—Terms which
Largo di molto⎰ intensify the meaning of Largo.

Largo ma non troppo (*It.*)—Slow and stately, but not too much so.

Larigot (*Fr.*)—Originally, a species of flageolet ; now, an organ-stop of 1⅓ ft. pitch, sounding a note two octaves and a fifth above that produced by an 8 ft. stop.

Larynx.—The organ in the throat by means of which vocal tone is generated.

Laut (*Ger.*)—Loud.

Laute (*Ger.*)—A lute.

Lay.—A song ; a melody or tune.

Le (*Fr., mas.,* and *It.*)—The.

Lead.—(1) A point or passage given out, or commenced, by one particular part. (2) A cue.

Leader.—(1) A conductor, director. (2) The principal first violinist in an orchestra ; the first clarinettist in a military band.

Leading note.—The note which lies a semitone below the tonic (keynote) of a scale, and has a tendency to progress upwards to—to *lead* to—the tonic ; hence its name.

Leaning note.—A term sometimes used to describe the appoggiatura.

Lebendig (*Ger.*)—Lively, animated, vivacious, brisk.

Lebe wohl! (*Ger.*)–Farewell ! adieu !

Lebewohl, das (*Ger.*)—The farewell.

Lebhaft (*Ger.*)—(Lebendig.) *Lebhaft, aber nicht zu sehr,* lively, but not too much so.

Lebhafter (*Ger.*)—More lively. *Im lebhaftesten Tempo*, in very animated time.

Lebhaftigkeit, mit (*Ger.*) — With animation.

Leçon (*Fr.*)—A lesson, a study.

Ledger lines.—(Leger lines.)

Leere Saiten (*Ger.*)—Open strings.

Legabile ⎱ (*It.*)—Tied, connected ;
Legando ⎰ indicating a legato style of performance, the slurring of one note to the next.

Legatissimo (*It.*)—The superlative of *legato*. The tones to be so closely connected that they slightly overlap.

Legato (*It.*) — Bound, smooth ; a direction to render a passage so that the tones are well connected, and have no break between them. *Legato* is usually indicated by a curved line drawn under or over two or more notes.

Legatobogen (*Ger.*)—A slur.

Legatura (*It.*)—A slur, tie, or brace.

Legatura di voce (*It.*) — A vocal passage executed smoothly in one breath.

Legend ⎫
Legende (*Ger.*) ⎬ A composition of a lyrical character.
Légende (*Fr.*) ⎭

Léger (*Fr.*)—Light, nimble. *Légèrement*, lightly.

Leger lines.—The short auxiliary lines which are used to indicate the pitch of notes which exceed the compass of the staff, above or below.

Légèreté (*Fr.*) ⎱ Lightness,
Leggerezza (*It.*) ⎰ rapidity.

Leggero (*It.*)—(Leggiero.)

Leggiere ⎱ (*It.*) — Light, nimble,
Leggiero ⎰ rapid.

Legno, col (*It.*)—With the stick of the bow.

Leicht (*Ger.*)—Easy, light, nimble. *Leicht und luftig*, light and airy.

Leidenschaft, mit ⎫ (*Ger.*) With pas-
Leidenschaftlich ⎬ sion, passion-
⎭ ately.

Leidvoll (*Ger.*) — Sorrowful, mournful.

Leise (*Ger.*)—Soft, low ; *piano*.

Leiser (*Ger.*)—Softer ; *immer leiser*, softer and softer.

Leitakkord (*Ger.*)—A chord requiring resolution.

Leiter (*Ger.*)—A leader.

Leitmotiv (*Ger.*)—A leading motive. A theme which illustrates, or depicts, a certain character, idea, or situation in a drama or opera.

Leitton (*Ger.*)—The leading note.

Le même (*Fr.*)—The same.

Leno (*It.*) — Faint, weak, gentle, quiet.

Lent (*Fr.*)—Slow.

Lentando . (*It.*)—Getting slower by degrees. (Ritardando.)

Lentement (*Fr.*) ⎫
Lentemente (*It.*) ⎬ Slowly.
Lenteur, avec (*Fr.*) ⎪
Lentezza, con (*It.*) ⎭

Lento (*It.*)—Slow. Opinions differ as to the exact degree of slowness this term indicates ; but it may be taken to lie approximately between *largo* and *andante*. *Lento assai*, and *lento di molto*, extremely slow.

Lesser.—An expression formerly used to indicate minor. For example :— " The key of C with the lesser third " meant the key of C minor.

Lesto (*It.*)—Lively, nimble, quick.

Levé (*Fr.*)—The unaccented beat of a bar ; the up-beat.

Liaison (*Fr.*)—A tie or bind ; a syncopation.

Liberamente (*It.*) ⎱ Freely.
Librement (*Fr.*) ⎰

Libitum (*Lat.*)—(Ad libitum.)

Libretto.—The book of words of an opera or other musical work.

Licence.—A departure from rule in musical writing.

Licenza (*It.*)—Licence, freedom. *Con alcuna licenza*, with a certain amount of freedom.

Lié (*Fr.*)—Slurred, tied.

Lieblich (*Ger.*)—Lovely, sweet toned. The word is used to describe the tone of certain organ-stops, as *Lieblich-Gedackt.*

Lied (*Ger.*)—A song. *Lieder*, the plural of Lied.

Liedchen (*Ger.*)—A little song or tune.

Lieder ohne Worte (*Ger.*)—Songs without words.

Liederspiel (*Ger.*)—A play interspersed with songs of a light, popular character.

Liedform (*Ger.*)—Song-form.

Ligatur (*Ger.*) ⎫ (1) A system of connecting notes together in ancient music. (2) In modern music a succession of notes sung to one syllable, or played with one bow. (3) A tie ; a syncopation.
Ligatura (*Lat.*) ⎬
Ligature ⎭

Ligne (*Fr.*)—A line. *Ligne ajoutée*, leger line.

Lilt.—(1) To sing or play cheerfully. (2) A merry tune.

Linea (*It.*) ⎫ A line. *Linea aggiunto*, (*It.*) A leger line.
Linie (*Ger.*) ⎭

Liniensystem (*Ger.*)—The staff.

Linke Hand (*Ger.*)—The left hand.

Lip.—The flat surfaces above and below the mouth of an organ pipe. Lipping = the art of adjusting the lips so as to produce the proper tone upon wind instruments.

Lira (*It.*) ⎫ A lyre.
Lyre (*Fr.*) ⎭

L'istesso (*It.*)—The same. *L'istesso tempo.* the same time ; an indication that the rate of pulsation is to remain the same.

Litany.—A portion of the Church service, in which the supplications of the priest are responded to by the congregation.

Liuto (*It.*)—A lute.

Livre ouvert (*Fr.*)—*À livre ouvert*, at first sight.

Livret (*Fr.*)—(Libretto.)

Lobgesang (*Ger.*)—A hymn of praise.

Loco (*It.*)—Place. An indication that the notes are to be played at the normal pitch after having been marked 8*va* (an octave higher or lower).

Long (*Fr.*)—Long.

Long ⎫ The second longest note of the ancient musical characters, and equal to two, sometimes to three, breves.
Longa (*Lat.*) ⎭

Lontano (*It.*)—Distant.

Lourd (*Fr.*)—Heavy.

Loure (*Fr.*) — An ancient French dance, usually in 6–4, but sometimes in 3–4, time.

Luftig (*Ger.*)—Light, airy.

Lugubre (*Fr.* and *It.*) — Doleful, mournful.

Lunga (*It.*)—Long. *Lunga pausa*, a long pause, or rest.

Lusingando ⎫
Lusingante ⎬ (*It.*)—Coaxing, caressing.
Lusinghevole ⎪
Lusinghiero ⎭

Lustig (*Ger.*)—Merry, cheerful.

Lute.—An obsolete stringed instrument, in shape resembling the mandoline. The strings were arranged in pairs, each pair being in unison, or an octave apart.

Lute (*Fr.*)—A lute.

Lydian.—The name of the ancient Ecclesiastical mode beginning on the note F.

Lyre.—An ancient stringed instrument of the Greeks. It varied as to size, shape, and the number of strings, and the tone was produced by the strings being acted upon by a plectrum.

Lyric, or Lyrical.—A term derived from the lyre, which was the instrument employed for accompanying the musical settings of the ancient Greek poems. It is generally associated with poetry which expresses some individual emotion, and which, though not necessarily set to music, would be suitable for such treatment. Regarded from this standpoint it is, in a sense, to be distinguished from that which is dramatic, *i.e.*, accompanied by action.

M.

M.—The abbreviation of *mezzo, mano, main, manual.* M.M. is the abbreviation for Maelzel's metronome.

Ma (*It.*) — But. *Allegro ma non troppo*, quickly, but not too much so.

Madrigal.—(1) A short lyrical poem. (2) A vocal composition in from three to eight parts, but more generally in four or five. It is contrapuntal in style, and usually for unaccompanied voices. It originated in Italy in the 16th century, and became a prominent feature in most European countries. It flourished in England in the Elizabethan period.

Madrigale (*It.*)—A madrigal.

Maesta, con ⎫
Maestade, con ⎬ (*It.*)—With dignity,
Maestevole ⎪   majestically.
Maestoso ⎭

Maestrale (*It.*)—The term applied to a " stretto " in a fugue in which all the voices take part, and in which the subject is heard complete in each voice.

Maestri (*It.*)—The plural of *maestro* (*q.v.*).

Maestria (*It.*)—Skill, authority.

Maestro (*It.*)—A master. *Maestro di capella*, a choir-master, a conductor.

Maggiore (*It.*)—Major.

Main (*Fr.*)—Hand. *Main droite*, right hand ; *main gauche*, left hand.

Mais (*Fr.*)—But.

Maître (*Fr.*)—Master.

Maître de musique (*Fr.*)—A conductor, a music master.

Majestätisch (*Ger.*) ⎫ Majes-
Majestueusement (*Fr.*) ⎬ tically.

Majeur (*Fr.*)—Major.

Major.—" Greater," as opposed to *minor*, " lesser." This term is applied to keys, intervals, and scales.

Malinconia, con ⎫
Malinconico ⎪ (*It.*)—In a melan-
Malinconioso ⎬ choly, dejected,
Malinconoso ⎪ gloomy style.
  ⎭

Mancando (*It.*)—Decreasing in tone, dying away.

Manche (*Fr.*)—The neck of a violin, guitar, etc.

Mandoline ⎫ A small species of
Mandolino (*It.*) ⎬ lute. The strings are of wire, tuned in pairs, and the tone is produced by means of a plectrum.

Manica (*It.*)—Fingering.

Manico (*It.*)—The neck of a violin, guitar, etc.

Manier (*Ger.*)—(1) Manner ; (2) An ornament.

Maniera (*It.*) ⎫ Manner, style.
Manière (*Fr.*) ⎭

Männerstimmen (*Ger.*) — Men's voices.

Mano (*It.*)—Hand. *Mano destra*, right hand ; *mano sinistra*, left hand.

Manual.—A keyboard played upon by the hands, as distinguished from the *pedals* played upon with the feet.

Manualcoppel (*Ger.*)—A manual coupler.

Manuale (*It.*)—A manual.

Marcando (*It.*)—Marking, accentuating.

Marcatissimo (*It.*)—Very marked.

Marcato (*It.*)—Marked, accented.

March.—A composition usually written in 4-4 time, and having a strongly marked rhythm. Marches are of three kinds : the quick march, or quick step ; the slow, processional, march (the latter being of a much more dignified character than the former), and the funeral march.

Marche (*Fr.*)—A march.

Marche harmonique (*Fr.*) — A sequence.

Marche triomphale (*Fr.*)—A triumphal march.

Marcia (*It.*)—A march.

Markirt (*Ger.*) ⎱
Marqué (*Fr.*) ⎰ Marked, accented.

Marsch (*Ger.*)—A march.

Marschmässig (*Ger.*)—In march style.

Marseillaise (*Fr.*)—A French national song.

Martelé (*Fr.*) ⎱ " Hammered " ; an
Martellato (*It.*) ⎰ indication that the notes are to be played in a sharp, incisive manner.

Marziale (*It.*)—Martial, warlike.

Masque.—A dramatic entertainment of the 16th and 17th centuries, consisting of poetry, with vocal and instrumental music, and usually founded upon some legendary or mythological subject.

Mass.—The musical service of the celebration of the Holy Eucharist in the Roman Catholic Church. The principal divisions are the Kyrie, Gloria, Credo, Sanctus, Benedictus, and the Agnus Dei.

Mässig (*Ger.*)—Moderate. *Mässig langsam*, moderately slow.

Masur ⎫
Masurek ⎬(*Ger.*)—A mazurka (*q.v.*).
Masurka ⎭

Matinée musicale (*Fr.*)—A morning concert.

Matins.—(1) Morning prayer. (2) The first of the canonical hours.

Maxima (*Lat.*)—The longest note of the ancient mensurable music.

Mazourk (*Ger.*)⎱ A national Polish
Mazurka ⎰ dance in triple time, and having a certain accentuation on the weaker beats of the bar.

Me.—The Tonic Sol-fa name for the third degree of the scale.

Measure.—(1) A stately dance. (2) The music contained between two bar-lines, more generally spoken of as a bar.

Mechanism.—(1) That portion of an instrument which connects the act of the performer with the sound-producing medium. (2) The physical, as distinguished from the intellectual, act of a performer upon any instrument.

Mediant ⎫ The third
Mediante (*It.*) and (*Ger.*) ⎬ degree of
Médiante (*Fr.*) ⎭ the scale.

Mehr (*Ger.*)—More. *Mehrere*, several.

Mehrfach (*Ger.*)—Manifold. *Mehrfache Intervalle*, compound intervals.

Mehrstimmig (*Ger.*) — In several parts : polyphonic.

Meister (*Ger.*)—A master.

Meisterfuge (*Ger.*)—A master-fugue ; one containing all the possible fugal devices.

Meistersinger (*Ger.*) — Mastersingers ; the successors in Germany of the more ancient Troubadors. They flourished in the 14th, 15th, and 16th centuries.

Melancolia (*It.*) ⎱ (Malinconia.)
Mélancolie (*Fr.*) ⎰

Melodia.—An organ-stop resembling the clarabella.

Melodia (*It.*)—Melody, air.

Melodic. — (1) In the style of a melody ; the progression of a single part. (2) Vocal, singable.

Melodioso (*It.*)—Melodious.

Mélodie (*Fr.*) ⎱ Melody, air.
Melodie (*Ger.*) ⎰

Melodrama ⎫ (1) Originally a
⎪ musical drama.
Melodrame (*Fr.*) ⎬ (2) Spoken drama
Melodramma (*It.*) ⎭ accompanied by instrumental music. (3) A play of a romantic and sensational character, in which music plays a subordinate part.

Melody.—(1) A well-ordered succession of single sounds. (2) The principal part, usually the highest. (3) An air or tune.

Même (*Fr.*) — The same. *Même mouvement*, at the same speed.

Men } (*It.*)—Less. *Meno mosso*, not
Meno } so fast.

Menschliche Stimme (*Ger.*) — The human voice.

Mensur (*Ger.*) } (1) Measure. (2) The
Mensura (*Lat.*) } scale of organ pipes.

Mensurable music } Measured
Mensuralgesang (*Ger.*) } music, *i.e.*, music written with notes having proportionate time-values, as distinguished from Plain-song, in which the rhythm was free.

Menuet (*Fr.*) } A minuet (*q.v.*).
Menuetto (*It.*) }

Messa (*It.*) } A Mass.
Messe (*Fr.* and *Ger.*) }

Messa di voce (*It.*)—The execution of a sustained note in singing by beginning softly, with a gradual increase to *forte*, and dying away to *piano* again.

Mesto (*It.*)—Sad, pensive, melancholy.

Mesure (*Fr.*)—Measure; time; a bar.

Méthode (*Fr.*) } Method; a system of
Metodo (*It.*) } teaching.

Metre.—The rhythmic element in music and poetry. In the former metre is measured by beats and bars; in the latter, by syllables and feet.

Metro (*It.*) } Metre.
Metrum (*Lat.*) }

Metronom (*Ger.*) } A mechanical in-
Metronome } strument, by
Métronome (*Fr.*) } means of which the exact speed
Metronomo (*It.*) } of a movement can be determined. It consists of a clockwork action which sets a pendulum in motion, the speed being regulated by means of a sliding weight. A graduated series of numbers gives the number of beats per minute.

Mezza (*It.*)—(Mezzo.)

Mezza voce (*It.*)—Half the power of the voice.

Mezzo, -a (*It.*) — Half, medium. *Mezza manica*, half shift; *mezzo forte*, moderately loud; *mezzo piano*, moderately soft; *mezzo-soprano*, a voice having a compass between that of a soprano and a contralto; *mezzo staccato*, half staccato.

Mezzo-soprano clef.—The C clef upon the second line of the staff.

Mi.—The third of the Aretinian syllables; the name of the note E in France, Italy, etc.

Mi bémol (*Fr.*) } The note E flat.
Mi bemolle (*It.*) }

Mi bémol majeur (*Fr.*) } The key
Mi bemolle maggiore (*It.*) } of E flat major.

Mi bémol mineur (*Fr.*) } The key of E
Mi bemolle minore (*It.*) } flat minor.

Mi contra fa (*Lat.*) — The term applied by the old contrapuntists to the false relation of the tritone.

Middle C.—The name of the middle line of the Great Staff. It is the note upon the first leger line below the treble staff, or the first leger line above the bass staff.

Mi dièse (*Fr.*) } The note of E sharp.
Mi diesis (*It.*) }

Mi fort (*Fr.*)—Moderately loud.

Militairement (*Fr.*) } In a military
Militarmente (*It.*) } style.

Mineur (*Fr.*)—Minor.

Minim.—A half-note. A time character in music equal to one-half of a semibreve, and twice the value of a crotchet.

Minima *It.* and *Lat.*)—A minim.

Minor.—Less, smaller. The term is applied to intervals, scales, keys, and chords.

Minore (*It.*)—Minor.

Minuet.—A dance of French origin, in triple time, and slow, stately movement. A Minuet is usually followed by a second called a Trio, after which the first Minuet is played over again.

Minuetto (*It.*).—A minuet.

Miracle-Plays.—A form of sacred play founded upon certain apocryphal legends connected with the Saints and the Virgin.

Mise de voix (*Fr.*)—(Messa di voce.)

Miserere (*Lat.*)—The opening words of the 51st Psalm ; the name applied to musical settings of this Psalm.

Missa (*Lat.*)—The Mass.

Missa brevis (*Lat.*)—A short Mass.

Missa pro defunctis (*Lat.*)—A Requiem Mass.

Missa solemnis (*Lat.*)—High Mass.

Misshällig ⎫ (*Ger.*)—Dissonant.
Misshellig ⎭

Missklang (*Ger.*) — Discord, cacophony.

Misterieu-x, -se (*Fr.*) ⎫
Misterioso (*It.*)   ⎬Mysterious.
Mistero, con (*It.*)   ⎭

Misura (*It.*)—A measure, a bar. *Alla misura*, in strict time.

Misurato (*It.*)—Measured ; in strict time.

Mit (*Ger.*)—With. *Mit Ausdruck*, with expression. *Mit Bewegung*, with animation. *Mit dem, mit der*, with the. *Mit Empfindung*, with emotion. *Mit halber Stimme*=mezza voce. *Mit Humor*, whimsically. *Mit Gefühl*, with soul. *Mit innigster Empfindung*, with deepest emotion. *Mit Kraft*, with force.

Mit dem solo Part (*Ger.*)—With the solo part.

Mit der linken Hand (*Ger.*)—With the left hand.

Mit der rechten Hand (*Ger.*)—With the right hand.

Mit der Singstimme (*Ger.*)—With the voice.

Mitklang (*Ger.*)—Resonance.

Mitklingende Töne (*Ger.*)—Upper partial tones, overtones.

Mit Verschiebung (*Ger.*)—With the soft pedal.

Mixed cadence.—An old name for a cadence formed with the subdominant, dominant, and tonic chords.

Mixolydian.—(1) The ancient Greek scale consisting of the notes B C D E F G. (2) The Ecclesiastical mode, commencing on G.

Mixture.—An organ-stop having two or more ranks of pipes, *i.e.*, two or more pipes to each note. They are tuned to different notes of the harmonic series.

Mode.—(1) In the ancient Greek and Ecclesiastical systems, a scale beginning upon any note, and extending to the octave above or below such note. (2) In the modern system the term is applied to the major or minor form of a scale, also to a major or minor key.

Moderato (*It.*)—Moderate. An indication of the speed of a movement which is approximately between *andante* and *allegro*.

Mode relatif (*Fr.*)—Relative key.

Modéré (*Fr.*)—Moderately fast.

Moderno, -a (*It.*)—Modern.

Modo (*It.*)—Mode.

Modulate.—(1) To pass from one key to another. (2) To grade the tone.

Modulation.—A change of key.

Moduler (*Fr.*)   ⎫
Modulieren (*Ger*) ⎬To modulate.
                                ⎭

Modus (*Lat.*)—Mode.

Möglich (*Ger.*)—Possible. *So rasch wie möglich*, as fast as possible.

Moins(*Fr.*)—Less ; *Moins vite*, slower.

Moll (*Ger.*)—Minor.

Mollakkord (*Ger.*)—A minor chord.

Molltonart (*Ger.*)—A minor key.

Molltonleiter (*Ger.*)—A minor scale.

Molto (*It.*)—Much, very, extremely. *Molto adagio*, very slow. *Molto allegro*, very quick.

Monochord.—An instrument consisting of a single string and a movable bridge, used for measuring intervals.

Monody.—The style of composition having the interest centred in one part, the other parts forming the accompaniment.

Monotone.—(1) Of one tone. (2) Intoning or chanting on one note.

Morceau (*Fr.*)—A piece ; a composition of an unpretentious character.

Mordant (*Fr.*)—A mordent.

Mordent (*Ger.*)—An ornament consisting of the principal note, the upper auxiliary, and the principal note. This is the application of the term which prevails in England ; the Germans, however, use the term *Pralltriller* for the above rendering, the mordent embracing the *lower* instead of the upper auxiliary note.

Mordente (*It.*)—A mordent.

Morendo (*It.*)—Dying away ; decreasing in tone.

Mormorando ⎫
Mormorevole ⎬ (*It.*)—Murmuring ; in
Mormoroso ⎭ a subdued tone.

Morris-dance.—A rustic dance, said to be derived from the Moors.

Mosso (*It.*)—Moved. *Più mosso*, with more movement, rather faster.

Motet.—A sacred vocal composition in several parts, usually without accompaniment.

Motet (*Fr.*) ⎫
           ⎬ A motet.
Motette (*Ger.*) ⎭

Motif (*Fr.*)—A motive.

Motion.—(1) The progression of a single part ; *conjunct motion* is the progression of a part by step, *disjunct motion*, progression by skip. (2) The movement of two parts in relation to one another ; *contrary motion*, when one part ascends and the other descends ; *oblique motion*, when one part remains stationary and the other moves ; *parallel motion*, when both parts move in the same direction by the same interval ; *similar motion*, when both parts move in the same direction, but by dissimilar intervals.

Motiv (*Ger.*) ⎫ (1) A musical figure ;
Motive   ⎬ the smallest portion
Motivo (*It.*) ⎭ of a phrase. (2) A
subject of more or less extent. (3) A leading theme.

Moto (*It.*) — Motion ; movement. *Con moto*, with animated movement.

Moto contrario (*It.*) — Contrary motion.

Motoobbliquo (*It.*)—Oblique motion.

Moto perpetuo (*It.*) — Perpetual motion.

Moto precedente (*It.*)—At the preceding speed.

Moto retto (*It.*)—Similar motion.

Mottetto (*It.*)—A motet.

Mounted cornet.—A solo-stop found in old organs, consisting of a stopped diapason, principal, twelfth, fifteenth, and tierce, placed on a separate sound-board, and mounted above the ordinary level.

Mouth.—The speaking part of an organ pipe.

Mouthpiece.—The part of a wind instrument which the performer places against, or between, the lips.

Mouvement (*Fr.*)—Movement.

Mouvement contraire (*Fr.*)—Contrary motion. *Mouvement oblique*, oblique motion. *Mouvement similaire*, or *Mouvement pareil*, similar motion.

Mouvement précédent (*Fr.*) — The resumption of the preceding speed.

Movement.—(1) Motion. (2) Degree of speed. (3) A division, or part, of a composition.

Movendo il tempo (*It.*)—Getting faster.

Movimento (*It.*)—Movement, time.

Movimento in unaccentato (*It.*)—An unaccented beat.

Müde (*Ger.*)—Languid.

Mund (*Ger.*)—Mouth.

Mundstück (*Ger.*)—Mouthpiece.

Murmurant (*Fr.*)—Whispering.

Musette (*Fr.*)—(1) A species of small oboe. (2) A kind of bagpipe. (3) A short piece of a pastoral character, with a drone bass. (4) A reed-stop on the organ.

Musica (*It.* and *Lat.*)—Music.

Musikdirektor (*Ger.*) — A musical conductor.

Musikschule (*Ger.*)—A school of music.

Muta (*It.*)—" Change." A direction to a player on the horn, trumpet, etc., that he is to change the key of his instrument, as, *muta in B*, etc.

Mutation.—(1) In the early system of solmisation, the change that had to be made in the syllables in order that the semitone should always occur between *mi* and *fa*. (2) Change of voice. (3) The change of position on the violin, commonly known as a "shift."

Mutation (*Fr.*)—Change.

Mutation-stop.—Any stop on an organ (other than the mixture) the pipes of which do not produce a note in unison or octaves with the key pressed down. Such stops are the tierce, quint, etc.

Mutazione (*It.*)—Change.

Mute.—An appliance for deadening the tone of musical instruments. The most important are : (1) a piece of metal, wood, etc., placed upon the bridge of stringed instruments, such as the violin, etc. ; (2) a leather-covered pad inserted in the bell of the horn or trumpet.

Mut(h) (*Ger.*)—Spirit, courage.

Mut(h)ig (*Ger.*)—Spirited, bold.

Mysteriös (*Ger.*)—Mysterious.

N.

Nach (*Ger.*)—After ; according to.

Nachahmung (*Ger.*)—Imitation.

Nach Belieben (*Ger.*)—At pleasure. (Ad libitum.)

Nachdrücklich ⎫ (*Ger.*)—With em-
Nachdruck, mit ⎭ phasis, accented.

Nachschlag (*Ger.*) — An ornament consisting of one or two notes *after* the principal note. Also the two notes added at the end of a shake, which, together with the two last notes of the shake, form a turn.

Nachspiel (*Ger.*)—A postlude.

Nächstverwandte Töne (*Ger.*)—The nearest related keys.

Nachtstück (*Ger.*)—A night piece.

Nach und nach (*Ger.*) — Little by little, gradually. *Nach und nach schneller*, getting quicker by degrees.

Naï-f, -ve (*Fr.*)⎫ Unaffected, simple.
Naïv (*Ger.*) ⎭

Naïvement (*Fr.*) — Unaffectedly, simply.

Naked fifth.—The interval of a fifth without a third.

Narrante (*It.*) — As if narrating. Indicates that the words are to be distinctly declaimed.

Nasard (*Fr.*) ⎫ A mutation-stop on
Nasat (*Ger.*) ⎭ the organ, It varies in pitch, being 2⅔ (the Twelfth), 5⅓, and 10⅔ ft. (the Quint), the last usually being found on the pedals.

Nason flute.—An organ-stop having stopped pipes of 4 ft. pitch. The quality of tone is soft and delicate.

Natural.—(1) The sign (♮), which contradicts an accidental sharp or flat. (2) A white key on the keyboard. *Natural harmonics*, those produced upon an open string. *Natural horn*, the French horn without valves. Natural key, the key of C major. *Natural interval*, an interval in a key, unaltered by an accidental.

Naturale (*It.*)⎫ Natural.
Naturel (*Fr.*)⎭

Naturhorn (*Ger.*)—The natural horn, the horn having no valves.

Naturtöne (*Ger.*)—Natural, or open, notes.

Naturtrompete (*Ger.*)—The natural trumpet, without valves.

Nazard.—(Nasard.)

Neapolitan sixth.—The name of a chord of the sixth found upon the subdominant of a key, most frequently met with in the minor mode. In the key of C major or minor it would consist of the notes—F, A flat, and D flat.

Nebengedanken (*Ger.*) — Accessory ideas, or secondary subjects.

Nebenlinien (*Ger.*)—Leger lines.

Nebennoten (*Ger.*)—Auxiliary notes.

Nebenstimmen (*Ger.*)—Accessory parts.

Neck.—That part of stringed instruments, such as the violin, violoncello, etc., which lies between the body of the instrument and the tuning pegs.

Nei, nel, nell', nella, nelle, nello (*It.*)—In the. *Nel battere*, at the downbeat. *Nel stilo antico*, in the ancient style. *Nel tempo*, in time, or in the previous time.

Nero (*It.*)—A crotchet, a black note as opposed to the minim (bianca), a white note.

Netto, -a (*It.*)—Neat, clear, distinct.

Neumes.—Signs used in one of the early mediæval systems of musical notation.

Neuvième (*Fr.*)—The interval of the ninth.

Nicht (*Ger.*)—Not. *Nicht zu langsam*, not too slow ; *Nicht zu sehr*, not very.

Nicht schleppend (*Ger.*)—Without dragging.

Niente (*It.*)—Nothing. *Quasi niente*, almost nothing (*i.e.*, barely audible).

Nineteenth.—(1) An interval containing two octaves and a fifth. (2) An organ-stop. (Larigot.)

Ninna-nanna (*It.*)—A cradle song.

Ninth.—(1) The *interval of the ninth* is formed of the interval of an octave, plus a second. (2) The *chord of the ninth* is formed by the addition of a third to a chord of the seventh. (3) The *suspended ninth* is formed by the delaying of the root of a chord by prolonging from a previous chord the note alphabetically next above it ; *e.g.*,

Nobile (*It.*)—Noble.

Nobilità, con⎫ (*It.*) Nobly; in a lofty,
Nobilmente ⎭ dignified style.

N o c h (*Ger.*)—Still, yet. *Noch schneller*, still faster.

Nocturne (*Fr.*)—A night piece. A composition of a dreamy, romantic character.

Node.—A point or line in a vibrating string, sound-board, pipe, etc., which remains at rest while vibration continues in the adjacent parts of the same body.

Noël (*Fr.*)—A Christmas carol.

Noire (*Fr.*)—A crotchet.

Nomenclature.—The terms applied in music to the various signs used to represent time, pitch, the duration of sounds, etc.

Non (*It.*)—Not ; as *non troppo*, not too much ; *non tanto*, not so much.

Nona (*It.*) ⎫ The interval of a
None (*Ger.*)⎭ ninth.

Nonenakkord (*Ger.*)—The chord of the ninth.

Nonet.—A composition for nine voices or instruments.

Nonett (*Ger.*) ⎫
Nonetto (*It.*) ⎭ A nonet.

Nonuplet.—An irregular group of nine equal notes, executed in the time of a normal group of six or eight notes of the same value.

Normal.—The term sometimes applied to the scales of C major and A minor, as forming the model upon which all the other major and minor scales are constructed.

Nota (*Lat.* and *It.*)—A note.

Nota accentata (*It.*)—Accented note.

Nota bianca (*It.*)—A minim.

Nota cambiata (*It.*) — A changing note.

Nota caratteristica (*It.*) — Leading note.

Nota d'abbellimento (*It.*)—A grace note.

Nota di passaggio (*It.*)—A passing note.

Nota inaccentato (*It.*)—Unaccented note.

Nota principale (*It.*)—An essential note.

Nota sensibile (*It.*) — The leading note.

Notation.—The various signs used to represent musical sounds, with their several modifications as to pitch, duration, etc.

Note.—A character, of which there are several varieties, used to represent the relative duration of musical sounds.

Note (*Fr.* and *Ger.*)—A note.

Note d'agrément (*Fr.*) — A grace note.

Note intégrant (*Fr.*) — An essential note.

Note sensible (*Fr.*) — The leading note.

Notturno (*It.*)—A nocturne (*q.v.*).

Novellette (*Ger.*)—An instrumental piece of romantic character, usually containing a variety of contrasted themes.

Nuance (*Fr.*)—Shading, gradation; change of musical colour.

Number.—(1) A sub-division or portion of a musical work, such as a song, chorus, etc., in an opera or cantata. (2) Any single item on a programme.

Nuovo, di (*It.*)—Again.

Nut.—(1) The ridge over which the strings pass at the end of the finger-board near the head of the violin, etc. (2) The portion of a violin bow near its heel, to which the hairs are attached and by means of which they may be tightened or loosened.

O.

O.—On instruments of the violin family a small circle (o) indicates (*a*) an open string; (*b*) the harmonic of the note over which it is placed.

O (*It.*)—Or; *flauto o violino*, flute or violin.

Obbligato (*It.*)—Required, indispensable. A form of instrumental accompaniment (to a song, etc.) possessing a degree of musical importance and independence of its own.

Obbliquo (*It.*)—Oblique.

Ober (*Ger.*) — Over, upper, above. *Oberstimme*, the highest part.

Obligat (*Ger.*) ⎫
Obligato (*It.*) ⎬ (Obbligato.)
Obligé (*Fr.*) ⎭

Oblique.—The term applied to the progression of two parts, one of which moves while the other remains stationary.

Oboe.—(1) An orchestral wood-wind instrument, having a double reed. It has a compass of about two octaves and a fifth upwards from B (or occasionally B ♭) below the treble staff, with the intervening semitones. (2) A reed-stop on the organ, of 8 ft. pitch.

Ocarina (*It.*)—An instrument usually made of terra cotta and pierced with finger holes. The tone is produced by air being blown through a kind of whistle-mouth-piece.

Octave.—(1) The interval of an eighth. (2) The reproduction of any given sound at a higher or lower pitch. (3) The sounds contained between any note and its reproduction, and including both. (4) Another name for an organ-stop of 4 ft. pitch, more generally known as the *Principal*. (5) The eight days following any great festival of the Church.

Octave-coupler.—That portion of the mechanism of an organ which connects any sound played upon one manual with that an octave higher. This latter sound may be upon the same, or another, manual.

Octave flute.—(1) The piccolo, a small flute whose pitch is an octave higher than that of the ordinary orchestral flute. (2) An organ-stop of 4 ft. pitch.

Octet.—A composition for eight voices or instruments.

Octuor (*Fr.*)—An octet.

Octuplet.—A group of eight equal notes played in the time (usually) of six of the same time-value.

Ode.—(1) A lyric poem of a lofty character. (2) The musical setting of such a poem.

Oder (*Ger.*)—Or; or else.

Œuvre (*Fr.*)—A work. *Chef d'œuvre*, a masterpiece.

Offen (*Ger.*)—Open. *Offenflöte*, an open flute on the organ.

Offertoire (*Fr.*) ⎫ The music per-
Offertorio (*It.*) ⎬ formed during
Offertorium (*Lat.*) ⎭ the collection
of alms, which
in the Roman Catholic Mass takes
place between the *Credo* and the
Sanctus.

Oficleide (*It.*)—An ophicleide (*q.v.*).

Ohne (*Ger.*)—Without ; *Ohne Pedale*,
without pedal.

Ohne Verschiebung (*Ger.*)—Without
the soft pedal.

Oktavflöte (*Ger.*)—An octave flute.

Oktett (*Ger.*)—An octet.

Omnes (*Lat.*)—All. The same as
tutti.

Once-accented octave.—The notes

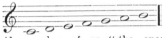

Also spoken of as " the once
marked octave," indicated thus :
c′, d′, e′, etc.

Ondeggiamento (*It.*) ⎫ With an undu-
Ondeggiante (*It.*) ⎬ lating, waving
Ondulé (*Fr.*) ⎭ effect.

Open diapason.—The most important
open foundation stop on an organ.
It is usually of 8 ft. or 16 ft. pitch,
and the pipes are made either of
wood or metal.

Open harmony.—When the parts are
distributed at approximately equal
distances from one another.

Open notes.—On stringed instruments, the notes produced by the
vibration of the full length of the
string. On the horn, trumpet, etc.,
the term is used to express the
notes of the harmonic series produced without the aid of pistons,
slide, etc.

Open pipes.—Organ pipes open at
the upper end, not closed as are
those of stopped pipes.

Open score.—When each part of the
harmony is written upon a separate
staff.

Open strings.—The strings of the
violin and kindred instruments,
when not stopped by the pressure
of the finger, thus vibrating in
their whole length.

Oper (*Ger.*)—Opera.

Opera.—Musical drama, of Italian
origin, dating from about the year
1600. Apart from the overture and
the introductions to the various
acts, the constituent parts of the
opera in the hands of such composers as Mozart, Weber, Rossini,
etc., were the following : recitatives, arias, duets, trios, and other
concerted vocal pieces, accompanied by the orchestra. In the
operas (or, more correctly speaking,
the music-dramas) of Wagner,
there is little or no division into
set pieces, such as the above ; the
chief musical interest is often to be
found in the orchestra, which
supplies a commentary upon the
action. The vocal writing is chiefly
a species of declamation, ranging
in character from recitative to impassioned song.

Opéra bouffe (*Fr.*) ⎫ A comic opera.
Opera buffa (*It.*) ⎭

Opéra comique (*Fr.*)—Comedy opera
An opera with spoken dialogue.

Opera seria (*It.*) — Serious (grand,
tragic) opera.

Operetta (*It.*) ⎫
Opérette (*Fr.*) ⎬ A short, light,
Operette (*Ger.*) ⎭ opera.

C phicleide.—A keyed wind instrument made of brass. The one most
commonly used was in the key of C,
and had a compass of three octaves
and a note upwards from B below
the bass staff. There were also
alto ophicleides in E flat and F,
and contra-bass ophicleides an octave below the alto. This instrument is now entirely superseded by
the bass-tuba.

Opus (*Lat.*)—A work. The word is
usually met with in its abbreviated
form, *Op.* Op. 1 would therefore
mean *first work*, usually referring
to order of publication.

Orageux (*Fr.*)—Tempestuously.

Oratorio.—An extended composition,
usually founded upon some Biblical
subject, for voices, the accompaniment being supplied by the orchestra—generally with the addition of the organ—or by the organ
only. The rise of the oratorio,

about the year 1600, was coincident with that of the Opera ; and while it differs from the latter in being unaccompanied by any scenery or dramatic action, the musical numbers are similar, and consist of recitatives, arias, trios, quartets, etc., with the chorus as one of the most important features.

Orchester (*Ger.*)—Orchestra.

Orchestra.—(1) A body of instrumentalists in a concert-room or theatre. (2) That part of a concert hall in which the instrumentalists and the chorus are seated. (3) That portion of a theatre between the stage and the auditorium where the instrumentalists are placed.

Orchestration.—The art of writing for the orchestra.

Orchestrion.—A mechanical instrument, which aims at producing the effect of an orchestra.

Order.—The expressions *open* and *close order* are sometimes used in the same sense as *open* and *close harmony*.

Ordinario (*It.*)—Ordinary. *Tempo ordinario*, in the usual time, or at an ordinary speed.

Organ.—A keyboard instrument of ancient origin. It consists of a larger or smaller number of pipes, which are constructed of wood or metal, and divided into two classes, flue and reed. The pipes stand on the soundboard which forms the upper part of the wind-chest, into which latter the air is driven by means of the bellows. The sound is produced by the air in the wind-chest being admitted to the pipes by the depression of the keys. These keys are arranged in rows which are called manuals, of which there may be one, two, three, or more, according to the size of the instrument. In an organ of ordinary dimensions there are usually three manuals, called Great, Swell, and Choir ; on larger instruments there is a fourth manual, the Solo organ, and occasionally a fifth, the Echo organ. In addition to the manuals which are acted upon by the fingers, there is a keyboard for the feet, called the Pedals.

Organo (*It.*)—Organ. *Organo pleno* full organ.

Organ-point.—(Pedal-point.)

Organum (*Lat.*)—(1) An organ. (2) The name for the earliest attempts at harmonic progression, which consisted of a succession of perfect fourths and fifths.

Orgel (*Ger.*)—An organ.

Orgelpunkt (*Ger.*)—An " organ-point," a pedal-point, a pedal-note (*q.v.*).

Orgelregister (*Ger.*)—An organ-stop.

Orgue (*Fr.*)—An organ.

Orgue expressif (*Fr.*)—An harmonium.

Ornament.—A grace, an embellishment.

Ornamenti (*It.*) — Ornaments, grace notes.

Ornato (*It.*)—Ornamented, adorned.

Ornements (*Fr.*)—Ornaments, grace notes.

Ossia (*It.*)—Or ; or else. A term which indicates that an alternative reading of a passage may be chosen.

Ostinato (*It.*)—Obstinate. Used in the sense of " frequently repeated," *basso ostinato* means a ground bass.

Ottava (*It.*)—Octave. *All' ottava* (abbreviated 8va) "at the octave," an octave higher. *Coll' ottava*, (*lit.*, "with the octave"), in octaves. *Ottava alta*, an octave higher. *Ottava bassa* (8va bassa), an octave lower.

Ottavino (*It.*)—The piccolo flute.

Ottetto (*It.*)—A composition in eight parts.

Ou (*Fr.*)—Or ; or else.

Ouvert (*Fr.*)—Open. *A livre ouvert*, at sight.

Ouverture (*Fr.*) ⎱ Overture.
Ouvertüre (*Ger.*) ⎰

Overblow.—To force the wind into a pipe so that, instead of the prime or fundamental tone, an upper partial or harmonic is made to sound.

Overstrung.—When the strings of a pianoforte are arranged in two sets, one over the other, in order to obtain a greater length and—as a result—a more sonorous tone.

Overtone. — Another name for a harmonic.

Overtura (*It.*)—An overture.

Overture.—An orchestral introduction to an opera, cantata, oratorio, or other vocal work. A "concert overture" is an independent movement, usually written in sonata-form.

P.

P.—The single letter "p" is used as an abbreviation for Pedal; also for *piano* (soft). The double letter, "pp," indicates *pianissimo* (very soft); "fp," *forte-piano*, (loud, then soft); "mp," *mezzo-piano*, (half-soft).

Padiglione (*It.*)—The bell of a wind instrument.

Padovana (*It.*)—An old Italian dance in triple time. (Other forms of the word are *Padovane, Paduana, Paduane*).

Pæan (*Gk.*)—(1) A hymn in honour of some god, originally addressed to Apollo. (2) A song of triumph.

Pæon.—A metrical foot consisting of one long, and three short syllables. It can be of four varieties, each depending upon the position of the long syllable, as follows :—
(1) — ◡ ◡ ◡, (2) ◡ — ◡ ◡,
(3) ◡ ◡ — ◡, (4) ◡ ◡ ◡ —.

Palco (*It.*)—A stage.

Pandean-pipes.—A primitive wind-instrument, consisting of a series of short hollow reeds closed at one end and graduated in length. They were fastened together so as to form a scale, the open ends being on a level to enable the lips of the player to pass easily from one to the other. The origin, probably, of the organ.

Pandora ⎫ (*It.*) Stringed instru-
Pandura ⎬ ments of the cither
Pandurina ⎭ type played with a quill.

Pantalon (*Fr.*)—One of the movements of the quadrille.

Pantomime.—Originally, a kind of theatrical entertainment in which the performers expressed themselves by gestures to an accompaniment of music; being supplemented at a later period by singing and dancing. The modern pantomime is based upon the same idea, but at the present day may be best described as a musical extravaganza founded on some well-known fairy-tale.

Parallelbewegung (*Ger.*) — Parallel motion.

Parallelen (*Ger.*) — Consecutives. *Parallel Quinten*, consecutive fifths ; *Parallel Oktaven*, consecutive octaves.

Parallel key.—A term sometimes used to indicate the tonic, or relative, major or minor key, as the case may be.

Parallel motion.—The movement of two or more parts at the same intervals, as in thirds, sixths, etc.

Parallel Tonart (*Ger.*)—A relative key.

Paraphrase. — An instrumental arrangement or transcription of a vocal composition, or the transcription of an instrumental composition for some instrument or instruments other than the original.

Parfait (*Fr.*)—Perfect.

Parlando ⎱ (*It.*)—(*lit.*, speaking). The
Parlante ⎰ term indicates—(*a*) in singing, that the words are to be delivered with clear enunciation, as in a declamatory style ; (*b*) in playing, that a given passage is to be played with a clear, crisp touch.

Paroles (*Fr.*) — Words ; as *sans paroles*, without words.

Part.—(1) The notes executed by one single voice or instrument. (2) A division of a work. (3) In musical structure, the simple forms which contain two or three divisions, are spoken of as being in "two part," and "three part," form respectively. In "three part" form, the third part is a reproduction—more or less exact—of the first part.

Parte (*It.*)—A part ; as *Parte corale*, chorus part.

Partie (*Fr.*) — A part ; as *Partie supérieure*, the highest part.

Partial tones.—(Harmonics.)

Partita (*It.*)—(1) A variation. (2) A set of pieces, a kind of suite. There is, however, a difference between the partita and the suite, as the latter consists—with the exception of the first movement — almost entirely of dances, while the former is not so restricted, although the foundation dances of the suite usually appear in it.

Partition (*Fr.*) ⎫
Partitur (*Ger.*) ⎬ A full score.
Partitura (*It.*) ⎭

Part-music.—Music in two or more parts.

Part-singing.—The singing of part-music.

Part-song.—A vocal composition in three or more parts, in which the chief melodic interest is usually sustained by the highest part.

Pas (*Fr.*)—A step, a dance. *Pas redoublé*, a quick step. *Pas seul*, a dance executed by one performer ; *pas de deux*, one executed by two performers.

Passacaglia ⎫ (*It.*) — An old dance
Passacaglio ⎭ in triple time, constructed upon a ground bass.

Passage.—(1) A short portion of a composition. (2) A series of rapid notes, usually formed by the repetition of some musical figure.

Passecaille (*Fr.*)—A Passacaglia.

Passepied (*Fr.*)—An animated dance in triple time. It was a precursor of the minuet.

Passing notes.—Notes foreign to the prevailing harmony, and passing by step from one note of a chord to another. They usually occur upon an unaccented beat, or portion of a beat ; but there are others, called accented passing notes, which occur upon the accented beat, or portion of a beat.

Passionato, -a ⎫ (*It.*) — Passionately,
Passione, con ⎭ with deep intensity of feeling. (Appassionato.)

Passion-music.—The musical setting of that portion of Scripture which records Christ's sufferings and death.

Pas tant (*Fr.*)—Not so much.

Pastorale (*It.* and *Fr.*) ⎫ (1) An in-
Pastoral ⎭ strumental composition in a style suggestive of rural and idyllic scenes. (2) A cantata, or opera, founded on such incidents.

Pastorelle (*Fr.*)—A little pastoral.

Pastourelle (*Fr.*)—One of the figures and movements of the quadrille.

Patetico, -a (*It.*) ⎫
Pathétique (*Fr.*) ⎬ Pathetic.
Pathetisch (*Ger.*) ⎭

Pauke (*Ger.*)—Kettle-drum. *Pauken*, kettle-drums.

Pausa (*It.*)—A rest ; a pause.

Pausa della croma ⎫ (*It.*)—A
Pausa della mezzo-quarto ⎭ quaver rest.

Pause.—A prolongation (indefinite as to length) of (1) a note, or a chord. (2) a rest, or silence.

Pause (*Fr.* and *Ger.*)—A pause or rest.

Pavan ⎫ A stately dance in
Pavana (*It.*) ⎬ duple time, said to
Pavane (*Fr.*) ⎭ have had its origin in Padua.

Paventato ⎫ (*It.*)—With an expression
Paventoso ⎭ of fear.

Pavillon (*Fr.*)—The bell of wind instruments.

Ped.—The abbreviation of the word "pedal"; used in pianoforte music to indicate that the right, or damper, pedal is to be depressed.

Pedal.—(1) On the pianoforte, a lever which is acted upon by the feet. On some instruments there are three pedals, but the usual number is two ; the one to the right being the *damper* pedal (so often incorrectly termed the "*loud*" pedal), which acts upon the dampers, removing them from the strings. The one on the left is the *soft* pedal, which, on a horizontal pianoforte, shifts the action sideways. By this means, wherever a particular sound is produced by three strings tuned in unison (trichord), the hammer strikes only two, thus reducing the volume of tone and modifying its quality. In the case of the lower sounds, which are produced by two strings thus tuned in unison (bi-chord), the hammer strikes only one. (2) On the organ there are three kinds of pedals : (*a*) one of a series in the *pedal keyboard*, which is a set of wooden keys played upon by the feet, having a compass of about two octaves and a - half ; (*b*) the *composition pedal*, one of the metal levers placed above the pedal keyboard, by means of which certain groups of stops are thrown out and drawn in ; (*c*) the *swell pedal*, which opens and closes the shutters of the swell- box, producing a gradual increase and decrease of tone. (3) The pedals of the harp raise the pitch of the strings, and thus change the scale. (4) The word " pedal " is frequently used as an abbreviation of *pedal-point* (*q.v.*).

Pedal-coupler.—A draw-stop which connects the pedals with a particular manual.

Pédale (*Fr.*) } A pedal.
Pedale (*It.*) }

Pédale douce (*Fr.*)—The soft pedal.

Pedale ogni battuta (*It.*)—An indication that the pedal is to be used with each bar.

P e d a l f l ü g e l (*Ger.*)—A horizontal pianoforte with a pedal keyboard attached to it.

Pedalier (*Fr.*)—A set of pedals, either (*a*) connected with the keys of the lower octaves of the pianoforte, or (*b*) provided with a separate set of strings and action.

Pedalklaviatur (*Ger.*)—The pedal keyboard.

Pedal-note.—(Pedal-point.)

Pedal-organ.—The group of stops belonging to, and controlled by, the pedal keyboard.

Pedal-piano.—A pianoforte provided with a set of pedals.

Pedal-point.—A sustained or repeated bass note above which the other parts move with varying harmonies. The dominant and tonic are the notes most frequently used as pedal-points. If the sustained note appear in any part other than the bass, the pedal-point is " inverted.'' In a fugue a pedal-point is a prominent —though not essential—feature in the final section.

Penillion singing.—A system of improvised singing peculiar to the Welsh people.

Pensieroso } (*It.*)—Pensive, thought-
Pensoso } ful.

Pentachord.—A series of five diatonic degrees.

Pentatone.—An interval formed of five whole tones.

Pentatonic scale.—An ancient form of scale, consisting of only five notes, and containing no semitone. The black keys of the pianoforte taken alone would form such a scale.

Per (*Lat.*)—By, through. *Per augmentationem*, by augmentation.

Per (*It.*)—For, by, from, in, through ; *e.g.*, *Per l'organo*, for the organ.

Percussion.—(1) The striking of a discord. (2) The striking of one body against another. *Instruments of percussion* are the pianoforte, drums, bells, triangle, etc.

Perdendo } (*It.*) — Dying away.
Perdendosi } Strictly speaking, the word implies a decrease in tone only, but it is frequently allied with a gradual decrease of speed also.

Perfect.—Complete. (1) *Perfect cadence*, the tonic chord preceded by that of the dominant at the end o- a rhythmical period. (2) *Perfec-concord*, the unison, fifth, octave, and sometimes the fourth. (3) *Perfect interval*, a term applied to the unison, fourth, fifth, and octave.

Perfetto, -a (*It.*)—Perfect.

Period.—A complete musical sentence containing two, three, or four phrases, and ending with a definite cadence, usually the perfect cadence.

Perlé (*Fr.*) } Pearled, brilliant.
Perlend (*Ger.*) }

Perpetual canon.—A canon so constructed as to permit of its being repeated indefinitely without any break.

Perpetuo (*It.*)—Perpetual.

Per recte et retro (*Lat.*)—Imitation by retrogression ; a term used in canonic writing, where the antecedent is found to be repeated by reading the notes backwards.

Pesante(*It.*)—Heavy,firm,ponderous.

Petto (*It.*)—The chest. *Voce di petto*, the chest voice.

Peu à peu (*Fr.*)—Little by little ; by degrees.

Pezzo (*It.*)—A piece. *Pezzi concertanti*, concerted pieces.

Pfeife (*Ger.*)—A pipe ; a small flute. *Orgelpfeifen*, organ pipes.

Phantasie (*Ger.*)—(1) Fancy, imagination. (2) A fantasia.

Phantasiestücke (*Ger.*) — Compositions of a fanciful, romantic nature.

Phantasy (*Old Eng.*)—A fancy.

Phonometer⎫ (*Fr.*)—An instrument
Phonomètre⎭ for determining the number of vibrations of a given sound.

Phrase.—The principal sub-division of a musical sentence. The length of the normal phrase is four bars ; there are, however, numerous exceptions to this, many of which are produced by the extension, or—more rarely—by the contraction of the normal phrase-length.

Phrase-mark.—A term occasionally applied to a slur.

Phrasing. — Musical diction. Included in this are such matters as the intelligent observance of the various rhythmic divisions in the course of the music, attention to the relative strength of the sounds, and the contrasts and differences in their tone-quality.

Phrygian.—(1) In the ancient Greek system, the name of the mode commencing on D. (2) In the Ecclesiastical system, the name of the mode commencing on E.

Piacere, a (*It.*)—At pleasure. A term signifying that the rendering of the passage is left to the individual fancy of the performer.

Piacevole (*It.*)—Pleasant, agreeable ; suggesting a smooth, unobtrusive rendering of a composition.

Pianette (*Fr.*)—A small upright pianoforte.

Piangendo⎫
Piangente ⎬(*It.*) — In a plaintive,
Piangevole⎭ mournful style.

Pianino (*It.*)—(Pianette.)

Pianissimo (*It.*)—Very soft ; indicated by the abbreviation "*pp.*"

Piano. — Abbreviation of *Pianoforte.*

Piano (*It.*)—Soft ; indicated by the abbreviation "*p.*"

Piano (*Fr.*)—A pianoforte. *Piano à queue*, a grand, or horizontal, pianoforte. *Piano carré*, a square pianoforte. *Piano droit*, an upright pianoforte.

Pianoforte. — A keyboard stringed instrument of percussion, distinguished from its predecessors—the harpsichord, spinet, and clavichord—by its hammer mechanism. Its invention is attributed to an Italian named Cristofori, and dates from the year 1711. Each key acts as a lever, and when depressed sets the action in motion, thus throwing the hammer against the strings, the damper being removed at the same moment. The principal parts of a pianoforte are the *Frame, Soundboard, Strings, Action,* and *Pedals.*

Pianoforte score.—A pianoforte arrangement upon two staves of a vocal or instrumental composition, in a more or less condensed form.

Piatti (*It.*)—Cymbals.

Pibroch.—A wild, martial kind of music, which the Scottish Highlanders play upon the bagpipe.

Picchettato ⎫(*It.*) — Detached, stac-
Picchiettato⎭ cato.

Piccolo (*It.*)—Small. (1) A small flute, sounding an octave higher than the orchestral flute. (2) An organ-stop, of 2 ft. pitch.

Piece.—A familiar description of an instrumental composition.

Pièce (*Fr.*)—A piece. *Suite de pièces,* a set of pieces.

Pieds (*Fr.*)—The feet. *Avec les pieds,* with the feet.

Pieno, -a (*It.*)—Full. *Coro pieno,* full chorus ; *a piena orchestra,* for the full band.

Piffero (*It.*)—(1) A fife. (2) A primitive kind of oboe.

Pincé (*Fr.*)—(*lit.,* "pinched.") (1) An indication in French music equivalent to *pizzicato.* (2) The musical ornament indicated by the sign ∿ and usually described in English as the lower mordent. *Pincé bemolisé,* a *pincé* with the auxiliary note flattened ; *Pincé dièsé,* a *pincé* with the auxiliary note sharpened ; *Pincé étouffé,* an acciaccatura ; *Pincé renversé,* the upper mordent.

P i q u é (*Fr.*)—The mezzo-staccato effect produced on stringed instruments by the notes being played with the same stroke of the bow, the movement being slightly broken after each note.

Piston (*Eng.* and *Fr.*)—The valve used in brass instruments, such as the *cornet à pistons, horn, trumpet,* etc., by means of which the pitch of the natural or harmonic notes can be altered.

Pitch.—The position of a sound in the musical scale, or, in other words, its gravity or acuteness. Pitch can be either "*relative*" or "*absolute.*" *Relative* pitch is the position a sound holds with reference to another sound (*i.e.,* either higher or lower). *Absolute* pitch is the fixed position of a sound, as determined by the number of vibrations which produce it. The standard of pitch now most usually adopted is that of the French Diapason

Normal, in which

represents a sound of 522 vibrations per second.

Pitch-pipe. — A small wooden or metal pipe which, when blown, gives one or more notes of fixed pitch. Metal pitch-pipes supplied with a reed are capable of being tuned to the several notes contained in an octave.

Più (*It.*)—More ; as *più allegro,* faster ; *più lento,* slower ; *più vivo,* with more life, *i.e.,* with greater animation.

Pizzicato (*It.*)—(*lit.,* "pinched.") A direction to the performer on any stringed instrument played with a bow, that the tone is to be produced by plucking the string with the finger. It is generally indicated by the abbreviation "pizz."

Placidezza, con ⎱ (*It.*) — Placidly,
Placido ⎰ smoothly ; in a tranquil manner.

Plagal cadence.—The cadence produced by an ending upon the tonic chord, preceded by that of the subdominant. This cadence is sometimes spoken of as the "Church," or "Amen," cadence.

Plagal mode.—The term applied in the Ecclesiastical system to a mode commencing a fourth below an Authentic mode, but having the same "Final" as the latter. A Plagal mode was described by the term "Hypo" prefixed to the name of the corresponding Authentic mode ; *e.g.,* "*Dorian*" (Authentic), *Hypo-Dorian* (Plagal).

Plain chant or Plain song.—The most ancient style of Christian Church music, in which the time is free, the duration and accent of the notes being almost entirely regulated by the metrical accent of the words. The melody is written upon a staff consisting of four lines, the characters used being, the Long ◼, the Breve ◼ and the Semibreve ♦. The clef used, which may be either the C clef ⋿ or the F clef, ⋿, is placed upon that one of the four lines which will bring the compass of the melody within the limits of the staff.

Plainte (*Fr.*)—An elegy or lament.

Plaintif ⎱ (*Fr.*)—Wailing.
Plaintive ⎰

Plaintivement (*Fr.*)—In a complaining manner ; plaintively.

Plectrum (*Lat.*)—A small piece of ivory, horn, quill, or metal, used for setting the strings of certain instruments in vibration.

Plein jeu (*Fr.*)—With the full power.

Pleurant (*Fr.*)—Weeping.

Plötzlich (*Ger.*)—Suddenly.

Pluperfect.—Another term for augmented (applied to intervals).

Plus (*Fr.*)—More. *Plus doux*, softer; *plus fort*, louder; *plus lent*, slower; *plus vite*, faster.

Pneumatic action.—The system of compressed air which is used in modern organs for the action of the keys, couplers, etc., in place of the older system of trackers, etc.

Pochetta (*It.*) ⎱ A small violin.
Pochette (*Fr.*) ⎰

Pochettino ⎱ (*It.*)—The diminutive of
Pochetto ⎰ *poco.*

Pochissimo (*It.*)—A very little.

Poco (*It.*)—A little. *Poco a poco*, little by little; *poco allegro*, rather quickly; *poco forte*, rather loud. If the words *poco meno* stand alone, *mosso* is implied, e.g., *poco meno mosso*, a little less quickly; also, *poco più* would in like manner imply *poco più mosso*, a little faster.

Poggiato (*It.*)—Dwelt upon.

Poi (*It.*)—Then. *A poi la coda*, and then the coda.

Point (*Fr.*)—A dot.

Point d'orgue (*Fr.*)—A pedal-point.

Point de repos (*Fr.*)—A pause.

Pointe (*Fr.*)—(1) A dot. (2) The head or point of a bow.

Pointé (*Fr.*)—Dotted.

Poitrine (*Fr.*)—Chest. *Voix de poitrine*, chest voice.

Polacca (*It.*)—A Polish dance, a polonaise. *Alla polacca*, in the style of a polonaise.

Polka—A dance of Bohemian origin, in 2-4 time, having an accent upon the third quaver of the bar.

Polonaise (*Fr.*)—A Polish dance in 3-4 time, of dignified but animated movement, its characteristic feature being the fall of the cadence-chord upon the weak (third) beat of the bar.

Polymorphous—Having many shapes or forms. A term applied to canons, etc.

Polyphonic ⎱ (1) Music made in many
Polyphony ⎰ parts. (2) The contrapuntal style, in which each part has its own individuality and independent movement, as contrasted with the *Homophonic* style, in which the interest is centred in one part.

Pompa, con ⎱ (*It.*)—Loftily ; in a
Pomposo ⎰ majestic, dignified style.

Ponderoso (*It.*)—With weight ; in a vigorous, impressive style.

Ponticello (*It.*)—The bridge of stringed instruments of the violin family. *Sul ponticello* is an indication that the string must be bowed near the bridge.

Portamento (*It.*)—An effect produced on bowed instruments, or with the human voice, by gliding from one note to another lightly and rapidly through the intervening sounds. The term is sometimes applied to the *mezzo-staccato* touch employed in pianoforte playing.

Portando (*It.*)—(*lit.*, " carrying.") The *portamento* effect. *Portando la voce* = *lit.*, " carrying the voice.' (Portamento.)

Portare la voce (*It.*)—(Portando la voce.)

Portata (*It.*)—The staff.

Portatif (*Fr.*) ⎱ (Portative organ.)
Portativ (*Ger.*) ⎰

Portative organ.—A small organ that can be carried about.

Portato (*It.*)—Lengthened, sustained.

Porte de voix (*Fr.*)—(1) Vocal *portamento*. (2) A term frequently applied to the appoggiatura.

Portée (*Fr.*)—The staff.

Porter la voix (*Fr.*)—(Portando la voce.)

Posato (*It.*)—Sedate, dignified.

Posaune (*Ger.*)—(1) A trombone. (2) A reed-stop on the organ, usually of 8 ft., but sometimes of 16 ft. and 32 ft. tone; these latter belonging, as a general rule, to the pedal-organ.

Posément (*Fr.*)—Sedately.

Positif (*Fr.*)—(1) A " positive " (*i.e.*, stationary) organ, as distinguished from a portative one. (2) A small organ, a chamber organ. (3) The choir manual on an organ having three or more rows of keys.

Position.—The place of the left hand on the fingerboard of the violin, etc., as, *1st position*, *2nd position*, etc. (2) The arrangement of the notes of a chord, with reference to the lowest note, *e.g.*, *1st* or *fundamental position*, when the root is in the bass ; *2nd position*, when the third of the chord is in the bass, etc. ; also, with reference to the distribution of the upper parts, *close position*, being the same as *close harmony* ; *open position*, the same as *open harmony*.

Positiv (*Ger.*)—(Positif.)

Possibile (*It.*)—Possible ; as *il più forte possibile*, as loud as possible.

Post-horn.—(1) A horn without keys or valves, used on coaches. (2) A piece of music in imitation of the notes played on a post-horn.

Posthumous.—A composition published after the author's death.

Postlude } An "after piece,"
Postludium (*Lat.*) } a concluding voluntary.

Pot-pourri (*Fr.*)—A medley ; a collection of tunes strung loosely together.

Poule, la (*Fr.*)—The third figure of a quadrille.

Poussé (*Fr.*)—(*lit.*, "pushed.") The up-stroke of a bow.

Prächtig (*Ger.*)—In a pompous, majestic manner.

Prachtvoll (*Ger.*). — Pompously, grandly.

Præcentor (*Lat.*)—A precentor.

Præludium (*Lat.*)—A prelude.

Pralltriller (*Ger.*)—A transient shake, indicated by the sign w', and consisting of the rapid execution of a principal note, its upper auxiliary and the principal note again. Identical with the upper mordent (*q.v.*).

Präludiren (*Ger.*)—To prelude, to improvise.

Précédent (*Fr.*) } Preceding ;　pre-
Precedente (*It.*) } vious ; as *moto precedente*, in the preceding tempo.

Precentor } The leader and
Préchantre (*Fr.*) } director of a choir.

Precipitando }
Precipitato } (*It.*)—With impetuosity, hurriedly.
Precipitoso }

Précis (*Fr.*)—Precise.

Precisione, con } (*It.*) — With precision ; in an exact
Preciso } manner.

Preghiera (*It.*)—A prayer.

Prelude.—(*lit.*, " something played before.") (1) An instrumental movement designed to precede another, as in the Preludes and Fugues of Bach. (2) The instrumental introduction to an opera, or to an act of the same. The term " Prelude " is also applied to some compositions complete in themselves ; to the introductory bars of a song ; and to the extemporization of a player before commencing the performance of a writtten composition.

Preludio (*It.*) }
Præludium (*Lat.*) } A prelude.

Premi-er, -ère (*Fr.*)—First. *Premier dessus*, first treble ; *première fois*, first time ; *première partie*, first part.

Preparation } When　a　note
Préparation (*Fr.*) } which　is　to appear　as　a
Preparazione (*It.*) } discord in any harmony is sounded in the same part or voice in the preceding chord.

Pressando } (*It.*) Pressing on the
Pressante } speed ; accelerating.

Pressez (*Fr.*) — Hasten the speed. *En pressant*, hastening the speed.

Pressiren (*Ger.*)—To accelerate the speed.

Prestant (*Fr.*)—On French organs a stop of 4 ft. pitch. The name is also synonymous with the English diapason and the German principal, both 8 ft. stops.

Prestissimamente (*It.*)—As fast as possible.

Prestissimo (*It.*)—Extremely fast.

Presto (*It.*)—Fast ; rapid. A degree of speed faster than *allegro*. *Presto assai*, very fast.

Prière (*Fr.*)—A prayer.

Prima (*It.*)—First. *Prima donna*, the principal female singer in the opera. *Prima vista*, at first sight. *Prima volta*, the first time.

Primary accent. — The strongest accent in a bar, the first beat.

Primary triad.—One of the principal triads of a key, viz., those upon the tonic, sub-dominant, and dominant.

Prime.—(1) The first note of a scale. (2) The root of a chord. (3) The generator of a series of harmonics.

Primo (*It.*) — First ; also, the first part, as in a duet. *Tempo primo*, at the original speed. *Violino primo*, the first violin.

Principal.—An organ-stop of open metal flue-pipes ; on the manuals of 4 ft., on the pedal of 8 ft., pitch.

Principal (*Ger.*) ⎱ (1) The principal
Principale (*It.*) ⎰ part.   (2) The foundation-stops of an organ, known as diapasons in this country.

Principal subject.—The chief theme in a movement, as distinguished from a subordinate theme, or episode.

Principio (*It.*) Beginning, first time. *In principio*, at the beginning.

Probe (*Ger.*) A rehearsal.

Processional. — A hymn sung in church during the procession of the choir and clergy.

Programm (*Ger.*) ⎱ A list of the
Programma (*It.*) ⎰ various musical
Programme (*Fr.*) ⎰ items to be per-
formed at a concert.

Programme-music.—Music suggested by, or describing, some incident, or scene in nature ; also that founded upon some subject contained in a poem, or prose composition.

Progression.—The movement of a single part from one note to another (called *melodic* progression) ; or of two or more parts moving together (called *harmonic* progression).

Promptement (*Fr.*) — Promptly, quickly.

Pronunziato (*It.*)—Pronounced. *Bene pronunziato*, clearly articulated.

Proposta (*It.*)—The subject of a fugue.

Proscenium.—The front of a stage ; that portion between the footlights and the curtain.

Prova (*It.*)—A rehearsal.

Psalmody.—The practice of singing psalms or hymns.

Psalter.—A book of psalms.

Psaume (*Fr.*)—A psalm.

Pulse.—A beat. The periodic throb in all music.

Punctum ⎱ (*Lat.*)—A point or dot.
Punctus ⎰

Punkt (*Ger.*)—A dot.

Punktirt (*Ger.*)—Dotted.

Punta (*It.*) — Point. *Colla punta dell' arco*, with the point of the bow.

Puntato (*It.*)—Dotted.

Punto (*It.*)—A dot.

Pyramidon.—An organ-stop of 16 ft. or 32 ft. tone, the pipes of which are more than four times as wide at the top as at the mouth.

Pyrrhic.—A metrical foot, consisting of two short syllables, ⌣ ⌣

Q.

Quadrat (*Ger.*) ⎱ The sign of a
Quadrate (*Lat.*) ⎰ natural, ♮.

Quadriglia (*It.*)—A quadrille.

Quadrille.—A square dance, consisting of five or six figures, named *La Pantalon, L'Eté, La Poule, La Trénise* (and sometimes *La Pastourelle*), *La Finale*.

Quadruple counterpoint. — Counterpoint in four parts, so constructed that all the parts are invertible.

Quadruple croche (*Fr.*) — A semidemisemiquaver.

Quadruple time.—That time in which the bar contains four divisions or beats.

Quadruplet.—A group of four equal notes which do not form a normal division of a bar, indicated by the figure 4 placed over the group. They are played in the time of 6 (or sometimes 3) notes of the same value.

Quarta (*It.* and *Lat.*)—The interval of a fourth. *Quarta toni*, the fourth degree of the scale, the subdominant.

Quart de mesure (*Fr.*)—A crotchet rest.

Quart de soupir (*Fr.*)—A semiquaver rest.

Quarte (*Fr.* and *Ger.*)—The interval of a fourth. *Quarte du ton* (*Fr.*), the fourth degree of the scale, the subdominant.

Quarter-note.—A crotchet.

Quarter-rest.—A rest equal to a quarter-note.

Quarter-tone.—An interval less than a semitone.

Quartet
Quartett (*Ger.*)
Quartetto (*It.*)
} A composition for four solo voices or instruments.

Quartflöte (*Ger.*)—A small flute, a fourth higher in pitch than the one commonly in use.

Quarto d'aspetto (*It.*)—A semiquaver rest.

Quartole (*Ger.*)—A quadruplet.

Quasi (*It.*)—As if ; almost ; as it were ; in the style of. *Andante quasi allegretto*, an andante almost as quick as an allegretto. *Quasi recitative*, in the style of a recitative.

Quatre (*Fr.*)—Four. *À quatre mains*, for four hands.

Quattricroma (*It.*)—A semidemisemiquaver.

Quattro (*It.*)—Four. *A quattro mani*, for four hands.

Quatuor (*Fr.*)—A quartet.

Quaver.—A note equal to one-half of a crotchet and one-eighth of a semibreve.

Quaver rest.—A rest equal in value to the note of the same name.

Quelque (*Fr.*)—Certain, some.

Querflöte (*Ger.*)—The cross-flute, *flûte traversière.*

Querstand (*Ger.*)—False relation.

Queue (*Fr.*)—(1) The tail piece of a violin, violoncello, etc. (2) The stem of a note.

Quieto (*It.*)—Quiet, calm, peaceful.

Quindecima (*It.*)—(1) The interval of a fifteenth. (2) An organ-stop of 2 ft. pitch.

Quint.—(1) The interval of a fifth. (2) An organ-stop 5⅓ ft. length on the manuals, and 10⅔ ft. on the pedals.

Quint (*Ger.*)—(Quinte.)

Quinta (*Lat.* and *It.*)—The interval of a fifth. *Quinta modi*, or *quinta toni*, the fifth degree of the scale, the dominant.

Quintadena
Quintatön (*Ger.*)
} An organ-stop of small, stopped metal pipes, the tone of which is characterised by the prominence of the 2nd harmonic.

Quinte (*Fr.*)—(1) The interval of a fifth. (2) A viola. (3) An organ-stop sounding a fifth higher than the foundation-stops.

Quinte (*Ger.*)—(1) The interval of a fifth. (2) An organ-stop sounding a fifth higher than the foundation-stops. (3) The E string of the violin.

Quintes cachées (*Fr.*) — Hidden fifths.

Quintet
Quintett (*Ger.*)
Quintetto (*It.*)
} A composition in five parts for solo voices or instruments.

Quintole (*Ger.*)—(Quintuplet.)

Quintuor (*Fr.*)—A quintet.

Quintuplet.—A group of five equal notes played in the time of four of the same value.

Quintviole (*Ger.*)—An organ-stop the pitch of which is a twelfth above that of the foundation-stops.

Quinzième (*Fr.*)—The interval of a fifth.

Quire (*Old Eng.*)—A choir.

Quitter (*Fr.*)—To quit, to leave. *Sans quitter la corde*, without quitting the string.

Quodlibet.—A musical medley ; a potpourri.

R.

R.—The abbreviation for right. *R.H.* = right hand.

Raddolcendo ⎫ (*It.*)—Growing calmer
Raddolcente ⎭ and more gentle.

Raddolciato (*It.*)—Calmer.

Raddoppiamento ⎫ (*It.*)—The doubl-
Raddoppiato ⎭ ing of an interval or part.

Radiating pedals.—The pedal keyboard of an organ, in which the pedals are arranged somewhat after the shape of a fan.

Radical bass. — The fundamental bass ; the root of a chord.

Rallentamento (*It.*) — At a slower degree of speed.

Rallentando (*It.*)—Gradually slackening the speed.

Rallentato (*It.*)—At a slower speed.

Rank of pipes.—The term used to indicate the number of pipes belonging to each note on the mixture stop on an organ — as two-rank mixture, three-rank mixture, etc.

Ranz des vaches (*Fr.*)—The tune sung, or played on the alpine horn, by the Swiss herdsmen.

Rapidamente (*It.*) ⎫
Rapide (*Fr.*) ⎪
Rapidità, con (*It.*) ⎬ With rapidity.
Rapido (*It.*) ⎭

Rapsodia (*It.*) ⎫ (Rhapsody.)
Rapsodie (*Fr.*) ⎭

Rasch (*Ger.*)—Quick, rapid. *So rasch wie möglich*, as quick as possible.

Rascher (*Ger.*) — Quicker. *Noch rascher*, still more quickly.

Ratio (*Lat.*)—Relation or proportion, as between the two notes forming an interval.

Rattenendo ⎫ (*It.*) — Holding back,
Rattenuto ⎭ slackening the speed. (Ritenuto.)

R a u s c h e r (*Ger.*)—A passage of repeated notes.

Rauschflöte ⎫ (*Ger.*) — A mixture
Rauschpfeife ⎪ stop on the organ,
Rauschquint ⎬ having two ranks
Rauschwerk ⎭ of pipes sounding the twelfth and fifteenth.

Ravvivando ⎫ (*It.*) — Re-animating.
Ravvivare ⎬ *Ravvivando il tempo*,
Ravvivato ⎭ quickening the speed.

Ray.—The Tonic Sol-fa syllable for the second degree of the scale.

Re (*It.*) ⎫ The second of the Are-
Re (*Fr.*) ⎭ tinian syllables, and the name of the note D in France, Italy, etc.

Real answer.—A fugal answer which is the exact transposition at the fifth above or the fourth below of the theme announced by the first voice. A fugue having such an answer is sometimes spoken of as a " real fugue."

Ré bemol (*Fr.*) ⎫ The note D flat
Re bemolle (*It.*) ⎭

Recessional.—A hymn sung at the close of a service during the departure of the choir and clergy.

Recht (*Ger.*)—Right. *Rechte Hand*, right hand.

Récit (*Fr.*)—(1) A vocal or instrumental solo. (2) The principal part in a concerted piece. (3) The swell manual on an organ.

Recital.—A term frequently used to imply a concert at which all the pieces are executed by one performer.

Recitando (*It.*)—In the style of a recitative.

Récitatif (*Fr.*) ⎫ Recitative.
Recitativ (*Ger.*) ⎭

Recitative.—Musical declamation. A form of vocal writing which does little more than emphasise the rhetorical accent of the words to which it is set, and which thus holds a position midway between speech and rhythmical song.

Recitativo (*It.*)—Recitative. *Recitativo parlando* is that which most nearly resembles speech. *Recitativo secco*, that which is accompanied by a few chords only, usually occurring between the vocal phrases. *Recitativo accompagnato*, or *stromentato*, that supported by a more elaborate accompaniment.

Réciter (*Fr.*)—To perform a vocal or instrumental solo part.

Reciting note.—The first note of a chant, and also the first note after each double bar in the same. In Gregorian Chant this note is the dominant.

Recte et retro.—(Per recte et retro.)

Ré dièse (*Fr.*) ⎱
Re diesis (*It.*) ⎰ The note D sharp.

Redita, or **Reddita** (*It.*)— A return, a repeat.

Redouazka ⎫ A Bohemian dance in 3-4
Redowa   ⎬ time, resembling the
Redowak ⎭ mazurka.

Redundant.—A term applied to an extra entry of the first voice in a fugue, at the close of the normal exposition.

Reed.—A thin strip of metal or cane set in vibration by a current of air. The reeds of the clarinet, oboe, and bassoon, are of cane, the first named having a single reed, and the last two a double reed.

The harmonium and the reed-pipes of the organ have metal reeds. A *free reed* vibrates within the aperture to which it is affixed, as in the harmonium ; a *striking*, or *beating*, *reed* vibrates against the edges, as in the reed-pipes of an organ.

Reed-instrument.—An instrument, the tone of which is produced by the vibration of a reed.

Reel.—A spirited dance, in favour with the Scotch and Irish. It is of Scandinavian origin, and is usually in 4-4 or 6-4 time.

Refrain.—A burden ; the words repeated at the end of each stanza of a song.

Register.—(1) An organ-stop, and the set of pipes controlled by such stop. (2) A certain portion of the compass of the voice, indicated by such terms as *head*, *medium*, or *chest* register. (3) Sóme part of the compass of certain instruments, differing in quality from the other parts, as the *chalumeau* register of the clarinet.

Register (*Ger.*)—(Register (1) and (3).)

Registerzug (*Ger.*)—The draw-stop mechanism on an organ.

Registration.—(1) The art of using and combining the stops of an organ. (2) The combination of stops used for a certain composition.

Registre (*Fr.*)—A stop on an organ. (Register (3).)

Registriren (*Ger.*)—To register (on an organ).

Registro (*It.*)—An organ-stop.

Règle de l'octave (*Fr.*)—(Rule of the octave.)

Regular fugue.—One in which the laws of fugal writing are strictly obeyed, as opposed to a free fugue.

Related, or **Relative, keys.**—Those keys having the most notes in common. The so-called Relative minor key is one which has as its tonic the note a minor third below the tonic of a major key ; the Relative major has as its tonic the note a minor third above the tonic of a minor key.

The relative, or related, keys of any major key are the major keys of the dominant and subdominant, together with the Relative minors of all three; for example, the related keys to C major are G major, F major, A minor, E minor, and D minor. The related keys of a minor key are the minor keys of the dominant and sub-dominant, with their Relative majors ; thus the related keys of A minor are E minor, D minor, C major, G major, and F major.

Religieusement (*Fr.*) ⎫ In a religious
Religiös (*Ger.*)   ⎬ or devout
Religioso (*It.*)   ⎭ style.

Remote key.—An unrelated key.

Rentrée (*Fr.*)—The re-entry of a part after a rest.

Renversé (*Fr.*)—Reversed, inverted.

Renversement (*Fr.*)—Inversion.

Renvoi (*Fr.*)—A repeat.

Repeat. — The sign ┇┇ which indicates that the music between the dots is to be repeated.

Repercussion.—(1) The repetition of a note or chord. (2) The reappearance of the subject of a fugue after the exposition.

Répétition (*Fr.*)—(1) Repetition. (2) Rehearsal.

Repetizione (*It.*)—(Ripetizione.)

Replica (*It.*)–A repeat. *Senza replica*, without repeat.

Replicato (*It.*) — (1) Repeated. (2) Doubled.

Réplique (*Fr.*)—(1) Octave. (2) Answer. (3) The interval produced by the inversion of any given interval.

Reply.—The answer in a fugue.

Réponse (*Fr.*)—(1) Reply. (2) The answer in a fugue.

Repos (*Fr.*)—Repose, rest ; a pause.

Reprende le mouvement (*Fr.*)—To resume the speed.

Reprise (*Fr.*)—(1) Burden of a song. (2) A revival. (3) A repeat. (4) The recapitulation of a theme in a movement.

Requiem (*Lat.*)—A Mass for the dead. It is composed of the following divisions :—(1) Requiem æternam ; (2) Kyrie ; (3) Absolve ; (4) Dies iræ ; (5) Domine Jesu Christe ; (6) Sanctus ; (7) Benedictus ; (8) Agnus Dei ; (9) Lux æterna.

Reservoir.—Part of the wind apparatus of the organ and harmonium.

Résolu (*Fr.*)
Resolut (*Ger.*) } Resolute.

Resolution.—The progression of a discord. *Direct resolution* is its immediate progression to resolution. *Ornamental* or *deferred resolution* takes place when one or more notes intervene between the discord and its resolution.

Resoluzione (*It.*)—The resolution of a dissonance.

Resonance.—Co-vibration or sympathetic vibration. The phenomenon produced by a sounding body causing another body to sound, or to reinforce a sound. If, for example, the notes of a chord (say) 𝄢 be silently pressed down on a pianoforte with the left hand, and so held, while the corresponding notes an octave above 𝄞 are sharply struck with the right hand and immediately released, these latter sounds will be distinctly heard ; *i.e.*, the sympathetic vibration of the strings of the lower chord produces the notes of the higher as harmonics.

Resonanzboden (*Ger.*)
Resonator } Any body, such as the soundboard of a pianoforte, or the body of a violin, which reinforces the tone produced by the vibration of the strings.

Response.—(1) The answer to a fugue subject. (2) The answer to a versicle in the Church service.

Rests.—The signs in musical notation which indicate silence.

Resultant tones.—Tones produced by the vibration of two notes sounded together. Resultant tones are of two kinds, *differential* tones, and *summational* tones. As an example of the former, these notes 𝄢 sounded together would produce 𝄢, the number of the vibrations of this last note being the difference between the vibration numbers of the first two. *Summational* tones are those whose vibration numbers are the sum of the vibration numbers of the two notes ; *e.g.* 𝄢 sounded together would produce

Retardation.—(1) A gradual decrease in speed. (2) A term sometimes applied to a suspension (*q.v.*) resolving upwards.

Retenu (*Fr.*)—Held back.

Retro (*Lat.*)—Backwards.

Retrogrado (*It.*) } Retrograde,
Retrogradus (*Lat.*) } backwards. *Imitatio retrograda*, imitation *per recte et retro.*

Retto (*It.*) — Direct. *Moto retto,* direct, or similar, motion.

Réveil (*Fr.*) } A military morning
Reveille } signal, indicating that the troops are to rise.

Réveillé (*Fr.*)—Awakened.

Reverse motion or movement.—(1) Contrary motion of two parts. (2) A theme presented by inverse movement.

Rhapsodie (*Fr.* and *Ger.*) } An in-
Rhapsody } strumental composition in the style of a fantasia, frequently founded upon national or popular airs, or upon themes taken from an opera or other work.

Rhythm.—The element of *movement* in music towards points of culmination or repose, by means of which sounds are logically grouped into figures, phrases and sentences. Involved in this idea of movement is that of cadence, *i.e.*, the corresponding *arrest* of movement, implied by the points of culmination or repose referred to above.

The term rhythm is also (somewhat loosely) applied to the pattern of the sounds within any metrical bar or measure (*q.v.*) ; for example, the two following passages would often be described as being different in rhythm :—

$$\frac{3}{4} \; \music \quad \text{and} \quad \frac{3}{4} \; \music$$

Ribattuta (*It.*)—An old device for beginning a trill. The principal note was at first dwelt upon and the auxiliary note made short, the two notes gradually approximating in value until a full trill was reached,

Allegro.

Ricercata, Ricercare (*It.*)—(1) The term applied to a fugue in which are employed all the various devices of subject treatment. (2) A species of fantasia or toccata.

Ridotto (*It.*) — Reduced ; arranged from a full score.

Riduzione (*It.*)—Arrangement.

Rigaudon.—A lively dance of French origin, in 2-4 or 4-4 time.

Rigo (*It.*)—A staff.

Rigodino } (*It.*) A rigaudon (*q.v.*).
Rigodone }

Rigore (*It.*) — Strictness, exactness. *Con rigore*, with strictness. *Al rigore di tempo*, in strict time.

Rigoroso (*It.*)—Strictly, exact.

Rimettendo } (*It.*)—Resuming the
Rimettendosi } original speed.

Rinforzando } (*It.*)—Reinforced ; in-
Rinforzare } dicating an increased loudness for a note
Rinforzato } or chord, or for the whole of a phrase.

Ripercussione (*It.*)—(Repercussion.)

Ripetere (*It.*)—To repeat.

Ripetizione (*It.*)—Repetition.

Ripieno (*It.*) — " Filling up." A *ripieno* part is one that is used for the purpose of a *tutti*, and is executed by several performers, as distinguished from a *solo* or *obbligato* part. *Ripienists* are the performers of such parts. In a score, *ripieno* is synonymous with *tutti.*

Riposato } (*It.*)—In a calm, tran-
Riposo, con } quil manner.

Riprendendo (*It.*) — Resuming. *Riprendendo poco a poco il tempo*, gradually resuming the preceding tempo.

Ripresa (*It.*)—A repetition, a repeat.

Risoluto ⎱ (*It.*)—In a reso-
Risoluzione, con ⎰ lute, decided style.

Risonanza (*It.*)—Resonance.

Ristretto (*It.*) — The stretto in a fugue.

Risuonanza (*It.*)—Resonance.

Risvegliato (*It.*) — With increased animation.

Ritardando ⎱ (*It.*)—Gradually getting
Ritardare ⎰ slower.

Ritardato (*It.*)—At a slower speed.

Ritenendo ⎱
Ritenente ⎰ (*It.*)—(Ritardando.)

Ritenuto (*It.*)—Held back, *i.e.*, at a slower rate of speed. The more usual (but less accurate) application of the term is gradually to slacken the speed.

Ritmico (*It.*)—Rhythmical.

Ritmo (*It.*)—Rhythm. *Ritmo di tre battute*, in a rhythm of three bars.

Ritornello (*It.*) ⎱ (1) The burden of
Ritournelle (*Fr.*) ⎰ a song. (2) A repeat. (3) An instrumental prelude, interlude, or postlude, in accompanied vocal music.

Riverso (*It.*)—Reversed. It may imply : (*a*) the contrary motion of two parts ; (*b*) the retrograde movement of a single part.

Rivolto (*It.*)—Inversion.

Robusto (*It.*)—Strong, powerful. *Tenore robusto*, a tenor voice of powerful tone.

Rohr (*Ger.*)—A reed.

Rohrflöte (*Ger.*)—Reed-flute ; an organ-stop.

Rohrwerk (*Ger.*)—The reed-stops on an organ.

Roll ⎱ The rapid beating of a
Rollo (*It.*) ⎰ drum, producing an almost continuous sound.

Romance.—(1) An instrumental piece of a lyrical character. (2) The name often given in France to any short simple song.

Romanesca (*It.*) ⎱ An Italian dance,
Romanesque (*Fr.*) ⎰ a galliard.

Romantic.—Music which appeals to the imaginative and emotional senses to a larger degree than does that of the more severe Classical school. Though romanticism is by no means absent from many of the works of the classic writers, it is generally agreed that the Romantic school, as such, began to flourish in the early part of the nineteenth century.

Romanza (*It.*)—A romance.

Ronda (*It.*)—A round.

Ronde (*Fr.*)—A semibreve.

Rondeau (*Fr.*)—(1) A rondo. (2) An old term used to describe the principal theme in a rondo.

Rondinetto ⎱
Rondino ⎰ (*It.*)—A short rondo.

Rondo (*It.*)—A form of composition in which the principal theme recurs after each digression. The germ of the form may be expressed by the formula, a, b, a, in which " a " represents the principal theme, and " b " a contrasted portion. By adding another contrasted portion, the form a, b, a, c, a, is obtained, and by adding yet another—a, b, a, c, a, d, a. Either of these constitutes what is known as " Old Rondo " form. If, instead of the contrasted theme " d " the first new theme " b " reappears, transposed into the key of the tonic, the form becomes the " Modern " (or " Sonata ") Rondo.

Rondoletto (*It.*)—A short rondo.

Root.—The lowest note of a chord in its fundamental position. Another definition is : " the lowest note of a series of thirds " in chord formation.

Rosalia (*It.*)—A melodic or harmonic progression several times repeated, each repetition being a degree higher or lower in pitch than the previous one. (See Sequence.)

Rosin.—A prepared substance applied to the hairs of a bow in order to obtain a sufficient grip of the strings.

Rotondo (*It.*)—Round, full.

Roulade (*Fr.*) —An embellishment consisting of a rapid series of notes sung to one syllable.

Roulement (*Fr.*)—The roll of a drum.

Round.—An infinite canon at the unison for three or more voices.

Roundel.—A rustic song; a circular dance.

Roundelay. —(1) A poem in which certain lines are repeated at intervals. (2) The musical setting of such a poem.

Rovesciamento } (*It.*)—(1) Contrary
Rovescio } motion between two parts. (2) Inversion of intervals and of chords.

Rubato (*It.*)—(*lit.*, " robbed.") This term indicates that the music is not to be performed in strict metronomic time; certain notes being given more, others less, than their absolute value. (Tempo rubato.)

Rückgang (*Ger.*)—A transition leading to the repetition of a preceding theme.

Rückung (*Ger.*)—Syncopation.

Ruhelos.—Restless.

Ruhepunkt } (*Ger.*)—A pause.
Ruhezeichen }

Ruhig (*Ger.*)—Quiet, calm, tranquil.

Ruhig gehend(*Ger.*)—Gently moving; synonymous with *andante moderato.*

Ruhig verhalten (*Ger.*)—To keep silent.

Rührung (*Ger.*)—Emotion.

Rule of the octave. — An old formula for harmonizing the ascending and descending scale.

Run.—A rapid scale passage; in vocal music usually sung to one syllable.

Running.—A defect in an organ produced by a leakage of the wind in the wind-chest; the pipes sounding when a key is pressed down, although no stop be drawn.

Rustico (*It.*)—Rustic, rural, pastoral.

Rythmé (*Fr.*)—Measured. *Bien rythmé,* the rhythm to be clearly defined.

S.

S.—The abbreviation for *Segno* in the terms *al Segno, dal Segno;* for *Sinistra, Solo, Soprano;* also for *Subito* in the term *Volti subito* (*V.S.*).

Sackbut.—(1) An obsolete name for the trombone or bass trumpet. (2) The Biblical translation of *Sabeca* or *Sabbek,* a stringed instrument supposed to have been akin to the harp.

Sackpfeife (*Ger.*)—A bagpipe.

Saite (*Ger.*)—A string.

Saitenhalter (*Ger.*)—The tail-piece of the violin, violoncello, etc.

Saiten Instrumente (*Ger.*)—Stringed instruments.

Salcional } An organ stop of soft tone,
Salicional } rather reedy in quality. It is frequently met
Salicet } with in place of the dulciana.

Salmo (*It.*)—A psalm.

Saltando (*It.*)—In violin music this indicates the " springing bow."

Saltarella } (*It.*)—(1) An Italian dance,
Saltarello } usually in 6–8 or 12–8 time, characterised by a movement in triplets. (2) A harpsichord " jack."

Saltato (*It.*) —(Saltando.)

Salto (*It.*)—A leap, a skip. *Di salto,* proceeding by skip.

Sampogna (*It.*)—A bagpipe.

Sanctus (*Lat.*)—One of the divisions of the Mass.

Sanft (*Ger.*)—Soft, gentle.

Sanftgedackt (*Ger.*)—An organ-stop of soft tone.

Sänger (*Ger.*)—A male singer. *Sängerin,* a female singer.

Sans (*Fr.*)—Without. *Sans pédale,* without the pedal. *Sans traîner,* without dragging.

Saraband } A stately dance, of
Sarabanda (*It.*) } Spanish
Sarabande(*Fr.*and *Ger.*) } or Oriental origin, in triple time, with an accent upon the second beat of the bar.

Sarrusophone.—A brass wind-instrument played with a double reed.

Sattel (*Ger.*)—The nut of a violin, etc.

Satz (*Ger.*)—(1) A theme, or subject. (2) A phrase. (3) A movement. (4) A composition.

Saut (*Fr.*)—A skip.

Sautillé (*Fr.*)—Springing bow.

Saxhorns.—A family of brass wind-instruments fitted with valves, each horn being capable of producing the complete chromatic scale. The tenor saxhorn in E flat or F is the one most commonly used.

Saxophones.—A family of brass wind-instruments. They have a clarinet mouth-piece with a single reed, the key mechanism also being similar to that of the clarinet.

Saxotrombas. — Brass wind-instruments invented by Sax to supersede the horn in the military band. Their use, however, is not at all general.

Saxtuba.—A deep-toned brass instrument similar to the saxotromba.

Sbalzato (*It.*) — Impetuously, with dash.

Sbalzo (*It.*)—A leap, a skip.

Sbarra (*It.*) — A bar-line. *Sbarra doppio,* a double bar.

Scagnello (*It.*)—The bridge of a stringed instrument.

Scala (*It.*)—A scale.

Scale.—(1) A series of sounds in alphabetical order. The most frequently used are : (*a*) the diatonic scale, which consists of tones and semitones ; (*b*) the chromatic scale, which contains semitones only. (2) The compass of a voice or instrument. (3) The dimension of an organ pipe with regard to the relationship between the width of the bore and the length.

Scena (*It.*)—(1) A scene. (2) A composition for a solo voice, consisting of recitative and arioso passages usually ending with an aria.

Scène (*Fr.*)—A scene.

Schäferlied } (*Ger.*)—A pastoral.
Schäferspiel

Schalkhaft (*Ger.*)—Roguishly, playfully.

Schall (*Ger.*)—Sound, tone.

Schallbecken (*Ger.*)—Cymbals.

Schallkasten (*Ger.*)—The body of an instrument.

Schalmei } (*Ger.*) (1) A reed pipe.
Schalmey } (2) A shawm. (3) A reed-stop on an organ, of 16, 8, or 4-ft. pitch.

Scharf (*Ger.*) — (1) Sharp. (2) A mixture-stop on an organ, containing the acute harmonics.

Scharf betont (*Ger.*) — With emphasis.

Scherz (*Ger.*)—Drollery, fun.

Scherzando }
Scherzante } (*It.*) In a playful manner ; lightly, jestingly.
Scherzevole }

Scherzhaft (*Ger.*)—Playful, jesting.

Scherzo (*It.*)—(*lit.,* a joke, a jest.) An instrumental piece of a playful, humorous character. *Scherzi* occur as single pieces, or as movements of larger compositions.

Schisma (*Gk.*)—The small interval which forms the difference between a true fifth and the fifth of equal temperament.

Schlag (*Ger.*)—A stroke, beat, pulsation.

Schlaginstrumente (*Ger.*) — Instruments of percussion.

Schlechter Taktt(h)eil (*Ger.*) — The unaccented part of a bar.

Schleifer (*Ger.*)—(Slide (2).)

Schleppen (*Ger.*)—To drag, to retard the time. *Nicht schleppen,* do not drag. *Schleppend,* dragging, retarding the time.

Schlummerlied (*Ger.*) — A slumber song.

Schluss (*Ger.*)—(1) The conclusion, finale. (2) A cadence.

Schlüssel (*Ger.*)—A clef.

Schlussfall (*Ger.*)—A cadence.

Schluss-Satz } (*Ger.*)—(1) The con-
Schlusstück } clusion, finale. (2) The final section in the exposition of a movement in sonata-form.

Schlusszeichen (*Ger.*)—(1) A double bar. (2) A pause.

Schmachtend (*Ger.*)—Languishing.

Schmeichelnd (*Ger.*) — Flattering, coaxing, caressing.

Schmelzend (*Ger.*) — Dying away ; diminishing.

Schmerz (*Ger.*)—Sorrow, grief.

Schmerzhaft ⎱ (*Ger.*)—Sorrowful,
Schmerzlich ⎰   plaintive.

Schmerzvoll (*Ger.*) — In a doleful manner.

Schnabel (*Ger.*)—The mouthpiece of a clarinet, or of other instruments blown in a similar manner.

Schnabelflöte (*Ger.*)—A flute played with a mouthpiece like that of a flageolet ; a *flûte à bec.*

Schnarrpfeifen ⎱ (*Ger.*) — The reed-
Schnarrwerk ⎰   stops of an organ.

Schnell (*Ger.*)—Quick. *Sehr schnell,* very quick. *Mässig schnell,* moderately quick.

Schneller (*Ger.*)—(1) Quicker. *Nach und nach schneller,* gradually faster and faster. (2) A transient shake, or Pralltriller (*i.e.,* an upper mordent).

Schnelleres tempo (*Ger.*) — Quicker speed.

Schnell wenden (*Ger.*)—Turn over quickly.

School.—(1) A method of teaching (*e.g.,*Spohr's *Violin School*). (2)Style of composition (as the *Madrigal School, Operatic School,* etc.) (3) A group of composers whose works founded some particular style in the evolution of musical composition.

Schottische.—A round dance, in 2–4 time.

Schreibart (*Ger.*)—Style.

Schrittmässig (*Ger.*)—Slowly, *andante.*

Schrittweise (*Ger.*)—Stepwise (*i.e.,* by conjunct movement).

Schwach (*Ger.*)—Soft, faint, low, weak. *Schwacher Taktteil,* a weak beat.

Schwächer (*Ger.*)—Softer, fainter.

Schwebend (*Ger.*)—Undulating.

Schweizerflöte (*Ger.*)—An 8 ft. metal flue-stop on the organ, of penetrating tone.

Schwellen (*Ger.*)—To increase in loudness.

Schweller (*Ger.*)—The swell organ.

Schwer (*Ger.*)—(1) Heavy, ponderous. (2) Difficult.

Schwermüt(h)ig (*Ger.*)—Sad, melancholy.

Schwindend (*Ger.*)—Dying away.

Schwung, mit ⎱ (*Ger.*) — Swingingly,
Schwungvoll ⎰   buoyantly.

Scialumo (*It.*)—(Chalumeau.)

Scintillante (*It.*)--Sparkling, brilliant.

Sciolezza, con (*It.*)—With freedom, agility, ease.

Sciolto (*It.*)—Free, nimble, easy, fluent. *Fuga sciolta,* a free fugue.

Scivolando (*It.*)—Same as *Glissando* in pianoforte playing.

Scoop.—To slide on to a note, instead of obtaining it by direct attack.

Scordato (*It.*)—Out of tune.

Score.—An arrangement of all the vocal and instrumental parts of a composition one above the other on the same page. Scores are of different kinds :—(1) *Close* or *compressed score, i.e., Short score (q.v.)* (2) *Full score,* one in which all the parts, for orchestra, chorus, etc., are written on separate staves. (3) *Pianoforte,* or *organ, score,* one in which the vocal parts are written on separate staves, the orchestral accompaniment being condensed. (4) *Open score, i.e., Full score (q.v.).* (5) *Short score,* an arrangement of a composition upon two staves, as for the organ or pianoforte ; also, four parts written upon two staves. (6) *Vocal score, (a)* one in which each voice part is written upon a separate stave, (*b*) another name for a pianoforte or organ score.

Scoring. — Instrumentation, orchestration.

Scorrendo ⎱ (*It.*) — Gliding from
Scorrevole ⎰   one note to another. Fluent, flowing.

Scotch snap.—The time-figure ♪♫.
which is characteristic of many
Scotch airs.

Scriva (*It.*)—Written. *Si scriva*, as
written.

Se (*It.*)—If. *Se bisogna*, if necessary.

Sec (*Fr.*) ⎱ Dry, unadorned, plain.
Secco (*It.*) ⎰ *Recitativo secco*, recitative with plain accompaniment.

Sécheresse, avec(*Fr.*)—(*lit.*,"dryly.")
Without embellishment.

Sechsachteltakt (*Ger.*) — Six - eight
time.

Scchssaitig (*Ger.*)—Six-stringed.

Sechst(h)eilig (*Ger.*)—In six parts.

Sechsvierteltakt (*Ger.*) — Six - four
time.

Sech(s)zehntel(note) (*Ger.*)—A semiquaver.

Sech(s)zehntelpause (*Ger.*)—A semiquaver rest.

Second.—(1) The interval from any
note to the one alphabetically next
to it above or below. (2) The alto
part or voice. (3) A part lower in
pitch than the first (*e.g.*, *second
violin*). (4) The highest string but
one on any instrument of the violin
family.

Second, -e (*Fr.*)—Second.

Seconda (*It.*)—The interval of a
second.

Secondary chords.—Subordinate
chords.

Secondo, -a (*It.*)—Second. *Seconda
volta*, second time.

Section.—A subdivision of a phrase,
frequently of two bars in length.

Secunde (*Ger.*)—(Sekunde.)

Seele, mit (*Ger.*)—With soul, with
feeling.

Segno (*It.*)—A sign. *Al segno*, to
the sign. *Dal segno*, from the sign.

Segue (*It.*)—Follows, comes after.
È poi segue la coda, and then
follows the coda.

Seguendo ⎱ (*It.*)—Following. *Attacca
Seguente ⎰ subito il seguente*, begin
the following at once.

Seguenza (*It.*)—A sequence.

Seguidilla (*Sp.*)—A lively Spanish
dance, in triple time.

Sehnlich ⎫
Sehnsucht, mit ⎪ (*Ger.*). — In a style
Sehnsüchtig ⎬ expressive of yearn-
Sehnsuchtsvoll ⎭ ing ; ardently.

Sehr (*Ger.*) — Very. *Sehr langsam*,
very slow. *Sehr bewegt*, very lively.
Sehr markirt, very marked. *Sehr
schnell*, very fast. *Sehr stark*, very
loud.

Sei (*It.*)—Six.

Seitenbewegung (*Ger.*) — Oblique
motion.

Seitensatz (*Ger.*)—A second subject.

Sekunde (*Ger.*)—The interval of a
second.

Semblable (*Fr.*)—Similar.

Semibiscroma (*It.*)—A semi-demisemiquaver.

Semibreve.—Half a breve ; a "whole-
note," equal to two minims.

Semi-chorus.—A small choir used as
a contrast to a full chorus, or large
choir,in choral works of importance.

Semicroma (*It.*)—A semiquaver.

Semi-demisemiquaver.—Half a demisemiquaver, the sixty-fourth part
of a semibreve.

Semiquaver.—Half a quaver ; the
sixteenth part of a semibreve.

Semitone.—Half a tone ; the smallest
interval on the pianoforte or organ
keyboard.

Semitonium (*Lat.*)—Half a tone, a
semitone.

Semitonium fictum (*Lat.*)—A chromatic semitone.

Semituono (*It.*)—A semitone.

Semplice ⎱ (*It.*)—In a simple,
Semplicità, con ⎰ unaffected style.

Sempre (*It.*)—Always, continually.
Sempre forte, always loud.

Sensibile (*It.*)—Sensitive. *Nota
sensibile*, the leading note.

Sensibilità, con (*It.*)—With feeling.

Sensible (*Fr.*) — (*lit.*, "sensitive."*
Note sensible, the leading note.

Sentence.—A musical idea containing two or more phrases.

Sentimentale
Sentimento, con } (*It.*)—With feeling.

Senza (*It.*)—Without ; as *Senza pedale*, without the pedal ; *senza rallentare*, without slackening the speed.

Septet
Septett (*Ger.*)
Septetto (*It.*) } A composition in seven parts, whether for voices or instruments.

Septième (*Fr.*)
Septime (*Ger.*) } The interval of a seventh.

Septimenakkord (*Ger.*)—A chord of the seventh.

Septuor (*Fr.*)—(Septett.)

Septuplet.—A group of seven equal notes to be played in the time of four or six of the same value.

Sequence.—(1) The repetition of a melodic or harmonic progression at a pitch different from that of the original. Sequences are of three kinds : (*a*) *Tonal*, in which the number of the intervals, but not their quality, is preserved in the repetitions, and in which the key does not change ; (*b*) *Real*, in which both number and quality are preserved, and the key changes ; (*c*) *Modulating*, in which the number of the intervals but not their quality, is preserved, and in which the key changes. (2) A kind of hymn used in the Roman Catholic Church.

Sequentia (*Lat.*)
Sequenz (*Ger.*)
Sequenza (*It.*) } A sequence.

Serenade
Sérénade (*Fr.*)
Serenata (*It.*) } (1) An " Evening song " ; music sung or played at night, and usually associated with the idea of a lover singing to his lady from beneath her window. (2) A composition imitative of such idea. (3) Formerly, the title of instrumental compositions containing several movements of varying character.

Serenità, con
Sereno } (*It.*) — In a calm, tranquil style.

Sérieu-x, -se (*Fr.*)—Serious.

Serio, -a (*It.*)—Serious. *Opera seria*, grand or tragic opera.

Serioso (*It.*)—Grave, serious.

Serpent
Serpente (*Fr.*)
Serpentone (*It.*) } (1) A bass wind instrument constructed of wood and covered with leather, with a cup-shaped mouth-piece. It is now practically obsolete. (2) A reed-stop on an organ.

Service. — The musical setting of certain portions of the Church service, such as the canticles, etc.

Sesquialtera (*Lat.*)—(1) The relation of two numbers in the proportion 3 : 2. (2) An organ-stop containing two, or more, ranks of pipes.

Sestet
Sestetto (*It.*) } A sextet (*q.v.*).

Sestina (*It.*)—A sextuplet.

Sesto, -a (*It.*)—Sixth. *Sesta*, the interval of a sixth; the sixth degree of the scale.

Settima (*It.*) — The interval of a seventh.

Seufzend (*Ger.*)—Sighing.

Seventeenth.—(1) The interval of two octaves and a third. (2) Another name for *Tierce*, an organ-stop.

Seventh.—(1) An interval containing seven degrees. (2) The name given to chords formed by adding to a triad the interval of a seventh from its root.

Severamente
Severità, con } (*It.*)–Severely, strictly.

Sext.—(1) A sixth. (2) An organ-stop of two ranks—a twelfth and a seventeenth—having the interval of a sixth between them. (3) One of the canonical hours.

Sexte (*Ger.*)—The interval of a sixth.

Sextet
Sextett (*Ger.*) } A composition for six voices or instruments.

Sextole
Sextolet } A sextuplet (*q.v.*).

Sextuor (*Fr.*)—A sextet.

Sextuplet.—A group of six equal notes played in the time of four of the same value. A true sextuplet is the sub-division into two parts of the units of a triplet, thus—

Sfogarto (*It.*)—(*lit.*, "exhaled.") A term used in vocal music to indicate a light, airy style of performance.

Sforzando } (*It.*)—Abbreviated *sfz.*,
Sforzato } *sf.* These terms indicate that a note or chord so marked is to be emphasised.

Sforzato piano (*It.*)–Abbreviated *sfp.*, indicates an emphasis, followed by an immediate *piano*.

Sfuggita (*It.*) — (*lit.*, "avoided, shunned.") *Cadenza sfuggita*, an interrupted cadence.

Shake.—An ornament produced by the rapid and continued alternation of any note with the note a semitone or tone above.

Sharp.—The sign ♯, which raises the note before which it is placed a semitone.

Sharp (*adjective*).—(1) Applied to notes, voices, or instruments, the term indicates "too high in pitch." (2) An augmented interval is sometimes said to be *sharp*. (3) It also implies shrill or acute, as *sharp mixture*, an organ-stop.

Shawm.—An ancient type of instrument played with a reed. It is said to have been a primitive kind of clarinet.

Shift.—A change of the position of the left hand in playing on stringed instruments, such as the violin, violoncello, etc. The term "position" is now used, and the 2nd position is synonymous with the half shift, the 3rd position with the whole shift, and the 4th position with the double shift.

Short score.—(See Score.)

Si.—(1) The name of the seventh degree of the scale in solmisation. (2) The name of the note B in Italy, France, and some other countries.

Si bémol (*Fr.*)—The note B flat. *Si bémol majeur*, B flat major. *Si bémol mineur*, B flat minor.

Si bemolle (*It.*)—The note B flat. *Si bemolle maggiore*, B flat major. *Si bemolle minore*, B flat minor.

Siciliana }
Siciliano } (*It.*)
Sicilienne (*Fr.*) } A graceful dance in 6–8 or 12–8 time, moderately slow, and pastoral in character.

Side-drum.—A small military drum suspended at the side of the player, and beaten with two sticks.

Si dièse (*Fr.*)—The note B sharp.

Signalhorn (*Ger.*)—A bugle.

Signatur (*Ger.*) } The signs placed at
Signature } the commencement of a piece of music, or of part of a piece. Signatures are of two kinds, *key-signature* and *time-signature*.

Signaturen (*Ger.*)—The figures placed above or below a bass part to indicate the accompanying chords.

Signe (*Fr.*)—A sign.

Silence (*Fr.*) } A rest.
Silenzio (*It.*) }

Si maggiore (*It.*) } The key of B major.
Si majeur (*Fr.*) }

Similar motion.—The progression of two or more parts in the same direction.

Simile (*It.*)—Like; in the same manner.

Si mineur (*Fr.*) } The key of B minor.
Si minore (*It.*) }

Simple.—This word is used in many ways, of which the following are the most important: (1) Not florid; *e.g.*, *simple* counterpoint. (2) Not developed; as *simple* imitation. (3) Not exceeding an octave; as *simple* interval. (4) *Simple* time; when each pulse is divisible into two equal parts, *e.g.*,

(5) *Simple* tone; a sound devoid of harmonics.

Simplement (*Fr.*)—Simply. (Semplice.)

Sin'.—Abbreviation of *Sino*.

Sin' al fine (*It.*)—To the end.

Sin' al segno (*It.*)—To the sign.

Si naturel (*Fr.*)—The note B natural.

Sincope (*It.*)—Syncopation.

Sinfonia (*It.*)—(1) A symphony. (2) In early Italian instrumental writing a term signifying an overture.

Sinfonie (*Ger.*)—A symphony.

Singbar ⎱ (*Ger.*)—Singing. (Canta-
Singend ⎰ bile.)

Single chant.—(Chant.)

Single fugue.—A fugue on one subject ; as distinguished from a *double fugue*, a fugue on two subjects.

Singstimme (*Ger.*) — (1) A voice. (2) A vocal part.

Singübung (*Ger.*)—A singing exercise.

Sinistra (*It.*)—Left. *Mano sinistra*, the left hand.

Sino (*It.*)—To, as far as, until.

Si piace(*It.*)—At pleasure. (A piacere.)

Si replica (*It.*)—Repeat.

Si segue (*It.*)—Go on, proceed.

Sistema (*It.*)—A stave.

Si tace (*It.*)—Keep silent.

Si volta (*It.*)—Turn over.

Six pour quatre (*Fr.*)—A sextuplet.

Sixième ⎱ (*Fr.*)—The interval of a
Sixte ⎰ sixth.

Sixteenth note.—A note the sixteenth part of a semibreve ; a *semiquaver*.

Sixth.—The interval of a sixth. *Chord of the sixth*, the first inversion of a triad. *Chord of the added sixth*, the subdominant triad with the sixth from the lowest note added to it—for example, f a c d in the key of C major. *Chord of the Neapolitan sixth*, the first inversion of the major chord on the minor second of a scale.

Sixty-fourth note.—A note the sixty-fourth part of a semibreve ; a *semidemisemiquaver*.

Skip.—The progression of a part by an interval larger than a second.

Slancio, con (*It.*)—With dash ; impetuously.

Slargando ⎫
Slargandosi ⎬ (*It.*)—Getting slower.
Slentando ⎭

Slide.—(1) The movable part of the trombone and slide trumpet, by means of which the length of the tube can be increased. (2) An old ornament consisting of two or more rapid notes proceeding by degrees to the principal note, thus :—

Slide-trombone ⎱ A trombone or a
Slide-trumpet ⎰ trumpet in which the pitch of the natural (harmonic) notes is altered by means of a slide instead of by valves.

Slur.—A curved line placed above or below a series of notes to indicate that they are to be played *legato*. In *vocal* music a slur indicates that two or more notes are to be sung to one word, or to one syllable of a word. In music for *bowed instruments*, the slur indicates the number of notes to be played with one stroke of the bow. In *pianoforte* playing, when two successive notes are connected by a slur, the first of these is usually played with some additional stress, and the second made slighter and shorter than would otherwise be the case.

Small octave.—The notes beginning with C (the second space on the bass staff), and extending to, but not including, the C next above it. Small letters without an accent mark are used to indicate it, thus : c, d, etc.

Smorzando (*It.*)—Dying away.

Snare-drum.—A side-drum, having gut strings stretched across the lower head. These strings—the "snares"—jar against the head, thus reinforcing the tone.

Soave ⎱ (*It.*) — Gently, softly,
Soavità, con ⎰ sweetly.

Sofort angreifen (*Ger.*)—To attack instantly.

Soggetto (*It.*) — Subject, theme, motive.

Soh.—The Tonic Sol-fa syllable for the fifth degree of a scale.

Sol (*It.*)—(1) The fifth of the Aretinian syllables. (2) The name of the note G in Italy, France, and some other countries.

Sol bémol (*Fr.*) ⎫
Sol bemolle (*It.*) ⎬ The note G flat.

Sol bémol majeur (*Fr.*) ⎫ The key
Sol bemolle maggiore (*It.*) ⎭ of G flat major.

Sol dièse (*Fr.*) ⎫
Sol diesis (*It.*) ⎬ The note G sharp.

Sol dièse mineur (*Fr.*) ⎫ The key of G
Sol diesis minore (*It.*) ⎭ sharp minor.

Solemnis ⎫
Solennis ⎪
Sollemnis ⎬ (*Lat.*)—Solemn.
Sollennis ⎭

Solenne (*It.*)—Solemn, lofty.

Solenne-l, -lle (*Fr.*)—Solemn.

Sol-fa ⎱ Singing, in which use is
Sol-faing ⎰ made of the syllables *do* (or *ut*), *re*, *mi*, *fa*, *sol*, *la*, *si*, to indicate respectively : *C*, *D*, *E*, *F*, *G*, *A*, *B;* or the Tonic Sol-fa syllables *doh*, *ray*, *me*, etc., to indicate the 1st, 2nd, 3rd, etc. degrees of any scale.

Solfège (*Fr.*)—A singing exercise, with the use of the syllables as in Sol-fa.

Solfeggi (*It.*)–The plural of *Solfeggio*.

Solfeggiare (*It.*)—To Sol-fa.

Solfeggio (*It.*)—A singing exercise, either to one vowel, or to syllables as in Sol-fa.

Solfier (*Fr.*)—To Sol-fa.

Solista (*It.*)—A solo player.

Solito (*It.*)—Usual, accustomed. *Al solito,* as usual.

Solmisation.—(1) Sol-faing. (2) An old system of teaching scales and intervals by means of the syllables *ut*, *re*, *mi*, *fa*, *sol*, *la*, devised by Guido d'Arezzo, who lived during the early part of the eleventh century. It was based upon the hexachord, or six-tone scale, the complete compass being obtained by a series of seven hexachords. The syllable *si*, for the seventh degree of the scale, was added during the seventeenth century.

Solo (*It.*)—(*lit.*, "alone.") A piece or passage for one voice or instrument, or in which one part predominates. In orchestral scores the word " Solo " (often abbreviated I) indicates that one instrument (the first of its class) is to take some leading part. *Violino solo* means either "violin alone," or that the principal violin is to perform such part. *Solo quartet,* a composition for four solo parts, vocal or instrumental.

Soloist.—One who sings or performs alone.

Soloiste (*Fr.*)—A solo player.

Solo organ.—The name of the fourth manual on an organ, containing only solo-stops.

Solosänger (*Ger.*)—A solo singer.

Solospieler (*Ger.*)—A solo player.

Solostimme (*Ger.*)—A solo voice or part.

Sombre (*Fr.*)—Dark, veiled.

Sommo, -a (*It.*)—Utmost, highest, greatest. *Con somma espressione,* with the utmost expression.

Son (*Fr.*)—Sound, tone.

Sonabile ⎱ (*It.*)—Sounding, sonorous,
Sonante ⎰ resonant.

Sonare (*It.*)—To sound ; to play.

Sonare alla mente (*It.*)—To play extemporaneously.

Sonata (*It.*)—An instrumental composition for a solo instrument—or for a solo instrument accompanied by some other instrument—consisting of two, three, or four contrasted movements. The four movements would generally be :

(1) An allegro (occasionally with an introduction). (2) A slow movement. (3) A scherzo, or minuet and trio. (4) An allegro.

Sonata da camera (*It.*)—A chamber sonata.

Sonata da chiesa (*It.*)—A church sonata.

Sonata-form.—The form generally used for the structure of the first movement of a sonata, also spoken of as "First Movement form." It is founded upon two themes (or groups of themes), and its broad outline is as follows :—
Part 1.—Principal subject, second subject in new key.
Part 2.—Development of themes, or episodical matter, or both combined.
Part 3.—Principal subject, second subject, usually transposed into the tonic key.

Sonate (*Fr.* and *Ger.*)—A sonata.

Sonatina (*It.*)
Sonatine (*Fr.* and *Ger.*) } A small sonata ; one in which the parts are of smaller dimensions.

Song.—A musical setting of a poem or portion of prose.

Song - form. — A term sometimes applied to a vocal or instrumental composition which contains three sections—A, B, A².

Soni alterati (*It.*) — Chromatically altered notes.

Sono (*It.*)—Sound.

Sonore (*It.*)
Sonore (*Fr.*) } Sonorous, resonant.
Sonoro, -a (*It.*)

Sons étouffés (*Fr.*) — Veiled, or muffled, tones ; sounds produced by muted instruments.

Sons harmoniques (*Fr.*)—Harmonics.

Sopra (*It.*)—Above, on, upon, over. In pianoforte music, the term *sopra* indicates that the hand playing such part is to be held *over* the other hand. *Come sopra*, as above. *Sopra una corda*, on one string.

Sopran (*Ger.*)—Soprano.

Soprano (*Fr.* and *It.*)—The highest voice of women or boys.

Soprano clef.—The name given to the C clef when placed upon the first line of the staff.

Sorda (*It.*)—(Sordo.)

Sordino (*It.*)—(Plur. : *Sordini*.) A mute. *Con sordino*, with the mute. *Con sordini*, with mutes. In pianoforte music the term *senza sordini* ("without mutes") indicates that the damper pedal is to be depressed. Although the above forms of the word are those usually met with, the correct forms are respectively *sordina* (sing.) *sordine* (plur.).

Sordo (*It.*)—Muffled, veiled, damped.

Sortita (*It.*)—(1) The first entrance of any character in an opera ; the first number sung by such person. (2) A concluding voluntary.

Sospirando
Sospirante } (*It.*)—Sighing, sobbing.

Sospirevole (*It.*)—(*lit.*, "sighing deeply.") Plaintive, mournful.

Sospiro (*It.*) — (1) A sigh. (2) A crotchet rest. In old music, a minim rest.

Sospiroso (*It.*)—(Sospirevole.)

Sostenendo
Sostenente } (*It.*)—Sustaining.

Sostenuto (*It.*) — Sustained, prolonged. As an indication of speed, it implies a rate of movement approximately the same as *Andante cantabile* ; it may also imply movement at a speed rather slower than that existing at the moment. *Più sostenuto* is very much the same as *Meno mosso*.

Sotto (*It.*)—Below, under. *Sotto voce*, in an undertone. In pianoforte music, the term *sotto* indicates that the hand playing such part is to be held *under* the other hand.

Soubasse (*Fr.*)—A sub-bass. An organ-stop of 32 ft. pitch.

Sound.—The vibration of air or any other elastic body, acting through the medium of the ear, produces in the brain the sensation of sound. A musical sound is the result of periodic vibration ; irregular vibration produces noise.

Sound-board.—(1) The broad piece of wood placed underneath or behind the strings of an instrument to reinforce the sound. (2) The cover of the wind-chest in an organ.

Sound-body ⎫ The hollow body of
Sound-box ⎬ instruments such as the violin, harp, etc.

Sound-holes.—The holes in the bellies of stringed instruments.

Sound-post. — The small round wooden prop which, in instruments of the violin family, is placed underneath the bridge, connecting the belly with the back of the instrument.

Soupir (*Fr.*)—A crotchet rest. *Demi-soupir*, a quaver rest. *Quart de soupir*, a semiquaver rest. *Demi-quart de soupir*, a demisemiquaver rest.

Soupirant (*Fr.*)—Sighing.

Soupir de croche (*Fr.*)—A quaver rest.

Soupir de double croche (*Fr.*)—A semiquaver rest.

Soupir de triple croche (*Fr.*)—A demisemiquaver rest.

Sourdine (*Fr.*)—(1) A mute. (2) A stop on the harmonium which reduces the supply of wind.

Sous (*Fr.*)—Under ; as *sous-domi-nante*, the sub-dominant.

Soutenu (*Fr.*)—Sustained.

Space.—The distance or interval between two lines on the staff, or between two leger lines. A note written immediately above or below the staff is also said to be in a " space."

Spagnoletta (*It.*)—A Spanish dance.

Spasshaft (*Ger.*)—(Scherzando.)

Spazio (*It.*)—A space (*q.v.*).

Spianato,-a (*It.*)—Smooth, level, even.

Spiccato (*It.*)—(1) Distinct, detached, pointed. (2) A form of detached bowing in violin-playing.

Spielart (*Ger.*)—Manner, style, of playing.

Spielen (*Ger.*)—To play.

Spieler (*Ger.*)—A player.

Spielmanieren (*Ger.*) — Ornaments, graces.

Spindelflöte (*Ger.*)—An organ-stop of 8 ft. or 4 ft. pitch, the tone being thin and reedy.

Spinet ⎫ An ancient keyboard
Spinett (*Ger.*) ⎬ instrument similar in construction to,
Spinetta (*It.*) ⎭ but smaller than, the harpsichord.

Spirante (*It.*)—Expiring ; dying away.

Spirito, con ⎫ (*It.*) — In a spirited
Spiritoso ⎭ manner.

Spitz (*Ger.*)—(1) Point (of the bow). (2) Toe (in organ playing).

Spitzflöte (*Ger.*)—(Spindelflöte.)

Spitzquint (*Ger.*)—A quint-stop on the organ, sounding a twelfth above the fundamental. The pipes are conical in shape.

Spondee (*Lat.*)—A metrical foot, consisting of two long syllables, — —

Springing bow.—A style of bowing in violin playing, in which the bow is made to drop on the string, leaving the string with a rebound after each note. (Sautillé.)

Sprung (*Ger.*)—A skip.

Sta (*It.*)—As it stands ; to be performed as written.

Stabat Mater (*Lat.*)—The name and the first two words of a Roman Catholic hymn, in use since the 13th century, and included in the Roman Missal as a sequence in 1727.

Stabile (*It.*)—Firm, steady.

Staccatissimo (*It.*)—Very detached. The superlative of *staccato*, indicated thus—(♪).

Staccato (*It.*)—Detached, separated ; the notes so marked to be disconnected one from the other.

Staccato-mark.—A dot over or under a note (♪ ♪) indicates *staccato ;* dots with a slur, (♪ ♪ ♪), *mezzo staccato ;* with a dash (♪) *staccatissimo.*

Staff, or Stave.—The horizontal and parallel lines with the intervening spaces, used for musical notation. The staff now in general use has five lines, the "Great staff" has eleven lines, while for plain-song a staff of four lines (or less) is used.

Ständchen (*Ger.*)—A serenade.

Standhaft (*Ger.*)—Firm, steady.

Stanghetta (*It.*)—A bar-line.

Stanza (*It.*)—A verse or sub-division of a poem.

Stark (*Ger.*)—Loud, strong, forcible.

Stärker (*Ger.*)—Louder, stronger; *più forte.*

Steg (*Ger.*)—The bridge of the violin and similar instruments.

Stem.—The perpendicular line drawn from the head of a note.

Stentando (*It.*)—Dragging, delaying, retarding.

Stentato (*It.*)—Forced, emphasized.

Sterbend (*Ger.*)—Dying away. (Morendo.)

Steso (*It.*)—Extended, spread.

Stesso (*It.*)—The same. *Lo stesso* (or *l'istesso*) *tempo,* at the same speed.

Sticker.—A part of the key action of an organ.

Stiel (*Ger.*)—The stem of a note.

Stil (*Ger.*)
Stile (*It.*) ⎱Style.
Stilus (*Lat.*)

Stillgedackt (*Ger.*)—A soft-toned organ-stop.

Stimme (*Ger.*)—(1) A voice. (2) A part. (3) An organ-stop. (4) A sound-post.

Stimmen (*Ger.*)—To tune.

Stimmführer (*Ger.*)—The leader of a choir.

Stimmführung (*Ger.*)—Part-writing.

Stimmgabel (*Ger.*)—A tuning fork.

Stimmhammer (*Ger.*)—A tuning key or hammer.

Stimmholtz (*Ger.*)—A sound-post (of the violin, etc.).

Stimmhorn (*Ger.*)—A tuning cone, used for tuning organ pipes.

Stimmpfeife (*Ger.*)—A pitch-pipe.

Stimmstock (*Ger.*)—A sound-post.

Stimmumfang (*Ger.*)—Compass of a voice.

Stimmung (*Ger.*)—(1) Tuning, or being in tune. *Stimmung halten* to keep in tune. (2) A mood, frame of mind.

Stimmweite (*Ger.*)—Compass.

Stinguendo (*It.*)—Dying away.

Stiracchiato ⎱ (*It.*)—(*lit.,* "strained.")
Stirato ⎰ Holding back, retarding the *tempo.*

Stonante (*It.*)—Discordant.

Stop.—(1) (*a*) Pressure of a finger on a string for the purpose of shortening its vibrating length. (*b*) Covering an aperture in the tube of a wood-wind instrument. (*c*) The placing of the hand in the bell of such an instrument as the horn for the purpose of altering the pitch. (2) A fret upon a guitar or similar instrument. (3) A set of pipes in an organ ; also the handle by the drawing of which a certain set of pipes is brought into play.

Stopped notes.—Notes obtained by "stopping," as distinguished from open notes. (See Stop.)

Stopped pipes.—Organ pipes closed at one end. A closed pipe produces a note an octave lower in pitch than does an open pipe of the same length.

Stracinando (*It.*)—(Strascicando.)

Strain.—Speaking generally, *strain* may mean a tune, an air, a melody, or a portion of such. Technically, the term is sometimes applied to a musical sentence, and also to the various subdivisions of a sentence.

Strascicando (*It.*)—Dragging, drawling.

Strascicato (*It.*)—Dragged.

Strascinando (*It.*)—(Strascicando.)

Strascinando l'arco (*It.*)—Drawing the bow from one string to another so as to bind the notes together.

Strascinare la voce (*It.*) — To sing with an exaggerated *portamento.*

Strathspey.—A spirited Scotch dance in 4–4 time, with a characteristic movement of dotted quavers alternating with semi-quavers.

Stravagante (*It.*)—Extravagant, fantastical, capricious.

Stravaganza (*It.*) — A composition of an extravagant, fantastical character.

Streichinstrument (*Ger.*)—A stringed instrument played with a bow.

Streichquartett (*Ger.*) — A string quartet.

Streichtrio (*Ger.*)—A string trio.

Streng (*Ger.*)—Strict, severe. *Streng im Tempo*, strictly in time.

Strepitoso (*It.*)—In a noisy, boisterous, impetuous manner.

Stretta (*It.*)—A coda ; a concluding passage taken at a quicker *tempo*, and working up to a climax.

Stretto (*It.*)—(*lit.*, "pressed, drawn together.") (1) Applied to the *tempo* of a movement, the term indicates that the speed is to be gradually quickened. (2) A *stretto* in a fugue is that part in which two entries of the theme overlap. This may take place at any interval.

Strich (*Ger.*)—Stroke of the bow.

Strict style.—A style of composition in which all dissonances are prepared and resolved, or appear as passing notes.

String.—Wire or catgut, plain or covered, used for musical instruments. *First string*, the highest of a set. *Open string*, one not stopped.

String band.—(1) The group of stringed instruments played with a bow in an orchestra. (2) A band consisting only of such instruments.

Stringed instruments.—All instruments whose tone is produced by the vibration of strings, whether struck, plucked, or bowed.

Stringendo (*It.*)—Pressing on the time ; getting gradually quicker.

Stringere (*It.*)—To hasten. *Senza stringere*, without hastening.

String-quartet.—(1) A composition in four parts for bowed instruments, usually two violins, viola, and violoncello. (2) An expression, not completely accurate, often applied to the group of bowed instruments in an orchestra.

String-quintet.—(1) A composition in five parts for bowed instruments. (2) The term sometimes applied to the group of bowed instruments in an orchestra.

Strisciando ⎫ (*It.*)—Gliding, smooth,
Strisciato ⎭ slurred ; *legato*.

Strofa (*It.*)—A strophe (*q.v.*).

Stromentato (*It.*) — Instrumented ; scored for an orchestra.

Stromento (*It.*)—An instrument. *Stromenti da corda*, stringed instruments. *Stromenti d' arco*, instruments played with a bow. *Stromenti da percossa*, percussion instruments. *Stromenti di legno*, wood instruments.

Strophe.—A division of a poem. In the Greek drama, a *strophe* is that portion sung by the chorus when dancing from the right to the left ; *antistrophe*, that sung when the movement is reversed.

Stück (*Ger.*)—A piece.

Studie (*Ger.*) ⎫ A study (*q.v.*).
Studio (*It.*) ⎭

Study. — A composition written primarily for the purpose of acquiring technical facility.

Stufe (*Ger.*) — A degree, a step. *Stufen*, degrees. *Stufe der Tonleiter*, a degree of the scale.

Stürmisch (*Ger.*)—Passionate, furious, tempestuous.

Styl (*Ger.*) ⎫ The character of a com-
Style ⎭ position, due to authorship, period, etc.

Styrienne (*Fr.*) — An air in slow *tempo* and in 2–4 time, with a jodler after each verse.

Su (*It.*)—On, upon ; by, near. *Arco in su*, with an up-bow.

Suave ⎫ (*It.*)—In a sweet, plea-
Suavità, con ⎭ sant, gentle style.

Sub (*Lat.*)—Under.

Sub-bass ⎫ A pedal-stop on the
Sub-bourdon ⎭ organ, of 16 or 32 ft.
⠀⠀⠀⠀⠀⠀⠀⠀⠀⠀⠀pitch.

Subdiapente.—The "under fifth."

Subdominant. The "under fifth."
The fourth degree of a scale.

Subitement (*Fr.*)—Suddenly.

Subito (*It.*)—Quick, sudden. *Volti
subito,* turn over quickly.

Subject.—The theme of a fugue or
any other musical composition.

Submediant.—The "under third."
The sixth degree of a scale.

Suboctave. — (1) The octave below
any note. (2) A coupler on the
organ, which connects any sound
played with that an octave lower.
This latter sound may be upon the
same or another manual.

Subordinate chords.—Chords which
are not primary or fundamental :
for example, the triads upon the
second, third, and sixth degrees of
a scale.

Subprincipal. — An organ - stop of
32 ft. pitch on the pedals, and of
16 ft. pitch on the manuals.

Subtonic.—The leading note.

Succentor.—The deputy for the precentor in a choir.

Sugli ⎫ (*It.*)—(Sul.)
Sui ⎭

Suite (*Fr.*)—A set or series of movements in various dance-forms. In
the earlier suites the principal
numbers were the Allemande,
Courante, Sarabande, and Gigue,
frequently preceded by an introductory movement in the shape of
a Prelude. Other dances were
frequently introduced, such as the
Bourrée, Gavotte, Minuet, etc.
Generally speaking, all the dances
of the suite were in the same key.
The modern suite differs from the
older type in that the movements
are not necessarily in dance-forms,
and also that there may be—and
frequently is — contrast of key
between the various numbers.

Suivez (*Fr.*)—(*lit.*,"follow.") An indication that an accompanist is to
follow the soloist, and to render the
accompaniment accordingly.

Sujet (*Fr.*)—A subject ; a phrase.

Sul ⎫ (*It.*)—On, on the, near the.
Sull' ⎪ ⠀*Sul ponticello,* near the
Sulla ⎬ ⠀bridge. *Sulla soprano corda,*
Sulle ⎭ ⠀upon the first string.

Summation, or Summational, tones.
—Resultant tones, the pitch of
which is represented by the sum of
the number of vibrations of the two
tones which give rise to them.

Suo loco (*It.*)— (*lit.*, "in its own place")
i.e., at the pitch as written. A term
sometimes used after an indication
such as *8va.*

Suonare (*It.*)—(Sonare.)

Suoni armonici (*It.*)—Harmonics.

Suono (*It.*)—A sound.

Super (*Lat.*)—Above, over.

Superbo, -a (*It.*)—Proudly, loftily.

Super-dominant.—A term sometimes
used to indicate the sixth degree of
the scale.

Superfluous. — A term sometimes
used to describe an augmented
interval.

Super-octave.—(1) An organ - stop
sounding two octaves above the
diapasons. (2) (Octave-coupler.)

Supertonic ⠀⠀⠀⠀⎫ The note above
Supertonique (*Fr.*) ⎭ the tonic ; the
second degree of the scale.

Supplicando (*It.*)—In a manner expressive of supplication, pleading.

Supplication (*Fr.*)—Prayer.

Sur (*Fr.*)—On, upon, over. *Sur la
quatrième corde,* upon the fourth
string.

Surprise cadence. — An interrupted
cadence.

Sus dominant (*Fr.*) — The sub-
mediant.

Suspension.—A dissonance produced
by holding on a note of a chord
whilst another chord is sounded,
of which it forms no part.
When two or three notes are
thus suspended, a *double* or *triple*
suspension is formed. There are
three stages in the treatment of a
suspension : (*a*) *preparation*—the
appearance or sounding of the note

in the first of the two chords ;
(*b*) *suspension* (or *percussion*)—the
retaining of that note as a dissonance in the second chord ;
(*c*) *resolution* — its progression by
step to the note of the second chord,
whose appearance it has delayed :—

Suspension (*Fr.*)—A suspension.

Süss (*Ger.*)—Sweet(ly).

Sustain.—(1) To hold notes during
their full time-value ; (2) to execute
a passage in a *sostenuto* or *legato*
manner.

Sustaining-pedal. — The right (or
"damper") pedal of the pianoforte.

Susurrando ⎱ (*It.*)-Murmuring, whis-
Susurrante ⎰ pering.

Su-tonique (*Fr.*)—Super tonic.

Svegliato (*It.*) — Awakened, animated, lively.

Svelto (*It.*)—Swift, light, nimble,
easy.

Sviluppo (*It.*) — The development
section of a movement in sonata
form.

Swell.—In an organ, the box containing the pipes which belong to
the stops on the swell manual.
One side of the box consists of a
set of shutters, which can be
opened or closed by means of a
pedal, thereby producing a *crescendo*
or *diminuendo*.

Symphonic.—Resembling, or relating
to, a symphony. *Symphonic ode*, a
symphonic composition for chorus
and orchestra. *Symphonic poem*,
an extended orchestral composition,
founded upon, and descriptive of, a
story or the subject of a poem. It
is not divided into set movements,
nor is it written in any particular
form, the structural outline being
largely dependent upon its poetic
basis.

Symphonie (*Fr.* and *Ger.*) ⎱ (1) A
Symphony   ⎰ composition for the orchestra—usually
in four movements—the structure
of which is similar to that of the
sonata, but, speaking generally,
of vaster proportions, and more
fully elaborated.   (2) Formerly,
overtures were styled symphonies.
(3) The introductory, intermediate,
and final instrumental sections of a
song or any vocal piece are called
symphonies.

Symphonisch (*Ger.*)-(1) Harmonious,
consonant.   (2) Symphonic.

Symphonische Dichtung (*Ger.*)—A
symphonic poem.

Syncopation ⎱ A displacement of the
Syncope (*Fr.*) ⎰ normal accent of
the bar.

Synkope (*Ger.*)—Syncopation.

Syren.—An acoustical instrument
used for the purpose of determining
the number of vibrations corresponding to a note of any particular
pitch.

T.

T.—The abbreviation standing for
Tasto, Tempo, Tenor, Toe (in pedal
playing on the organ), *Tre, Tutti.*

Taa.—A French " time-name " (*see*
page viii).

Taballo (*It.*)—(Timballo.)

Tablature.—(1) The signs and characters used for musical notation
generally.   (2) An early system,
now obsolete, of musical notation
for the lute, viol, and organ.

Table (*Fr.*)—The belly of a violin, etc.

Table d'harmonie (*Fr.*) — A sound-
board.

Tabor
Taboret
Tabouret (*Fr.*) ⎱ (A small drum.)
Tabret

Tabulatur (*Ger.*) ⎱ (Tablature.)
Tabulatura (*It.*) ⎰

Tace (*It.*) ⎱ (*lit.*, "silent.") An in-
Tacet (*Lat.*) ⎰ dication that a part
so marked is not employed during a
movement or piece.

Tail.—(Stem.)

Taille (*Fr.*)—(1) The tenor part or a tenor singer. (2) The viola.

Taille-Trombone (*Fr.*)—Tenor trombone.

Tail-piece.—That part of the violin, etc., to which the strings are fastened, at the end opposite to the head of the instrument.

Takt (*Ger.*)—A beat; a measure (bar); time.

Taktaccent (*Ger.*)—Bar accent.

Taktart (*Ger.*)—The kind of time, whether duple, triple, etc.

Taktmässig (*Ger.*)—In time.

Taktmesser (*Ger.*)—A metronome.

Taktnote (*Ger.*)—A semibreve.

Taktpause (*Ger.*)—A bar rest.

Taktstrich (*Ger.*)—A bar-line.

Taktt(h)eil (*Ger.*)—Part of a bar. *Guter Taktt(h)eil*, the accented part of a bar; *schlechter Taktt(h)eil*, the unaccented part of a bar.

Taktzeichen (*Ger.*)—A time-sign.

Talon (*Fr.*)—The heel of a bow.

Tambour (*Fr.*)—(1) A side drum. (2) A drummer.

Tambourin (*Fr.* and *Ger.*)—(1) A drum longer and narrower than the ordinary side-drum. (2) A lively French dance in 2-4 time, sometimes found in the suite.

Tambourin basque (*Fr.*) — A tambourine (*q.v.*).

Tambourine.—An instrument of the drum class, consisting of a narrow hoop of wood or metal with one head of stretched parchment or skin; the hoop is pierced with holes, in each of which are inserted two loose metal discs called jingles. The jingles are made to sound by the instrument being shaken, and the parchment is struck with the right hand.

Tamburo (*It.*)—A side-drum.

Tamburone (*It.*)—A big, or bass, drum. Also called *cassa grande*.

Tam-tam. — (1) A gong. (2) An Indian drum. Also called *Tom-tom*.

Tändelnd (*Ger.*)—In a playful style.

Tangent.—A metal pin forming that part of the action of the clavichord which strikes against the strings.

Tanto (*It.*)—So much, as much; too (much). *Allegro non tanto*, not too quickly. *A tanto possibile*, as much as possible.

Tanz (*Ger.*)—A dance.

Tarantella (*It.*) ⎫ A lively Neapolitan
Tarantelle (*Ger.*) ⎭ dance in 6-8 time, and rapid *tempo*. Also an instrumental piece in the same time, of a brilliant character.

Tardo (*It.*)—Slow, dragging.

Tarentelle (*Fr.*)—(Tarantella.)

Tastatur (*Ger.*)—A keyboard.

Tastatura (*It.*)—A keyboard; a fingerboard.

Taste (*Ger.*)—A key.

Tastiera (*It.*)—A keyboard; a fingerboard. *Sulla tastiera*, on, or near, the finger-board.

Tasto (*It.*)—Key; fret; touch; fingerboard. *Sul tasto*, on, or near, the finger-board.

Tasto solo (*It.*)—(*lit.*, "one key alone.") A direction in figured-bass playing, that the bass part only is to be played, either in single notes or in octaves, without chords.

Tatto (*It.*)—Touch.

Tattoo.—A military signal executed on the drum, telling soldiers to repair to their quarters for the night.

Tavola armonica (*It.*)—Sound-board.

Te.—The Tonic Sol-fa syllable for the seventh degree of a scale.

Teatro (*It.*)—A theatre.

Technik (*Ger.*) ⎫ All that appertains
Technique (*Fr.*) ⎭ to the mechanical part of instrumental or vocal performance; mechanical training; dexterity. The term also may reasonably be given a wider meaning, and be used to signify all that may be learnt or acquired in connection with an art.

Tedesco, -a (*It.*)—German. *Alla tedesca*, in the German style.

Te Deum (*Lat.*)—A hymn of thanksgiving.

Teil (*Ger.*)—A part. (Theil.)

Teiltöne (*Ger.*)—(Theiltöne.)

Tell-tale.—A movable indicator attached to the bellows of an organ, for the purpose of showing the supply of air.

Tema (*It.*)—A theme, or subject. *Tema principale*, the principal subject.

Temperament.—If, starting from the note C, the G above were tuned as a true perfect 5th and the same tuning continued upwards, the 12th fifth, B♯, would not agree with the note C (the sixth octave above the C started from), but would be rather too sharp. On all keyed instruments, therefore, the fifths are modified—*i.e.*, *tempered*, with the result that the octave is divided into twelve equal parts. This compromise, which dates (approximately) from the Bach period, renders all keys available upon an instrument thus tuned, and is known as *Equal temperament.* Upon the older system of tuning—*Unequal temperament*—the intervals were usually made true for the key of C; the result being that those keys most closely related to C major were fairly accurate, but in the case of keys further removed, discrepancies were apparent which rendered such keys virtually useless for practical purposes.

Tempérament (*Fr.*) ⎫
Temperamento (*It.*) ⎬ Temperament.
Temperatur (*Ger.*) ⎭

Tempestoso (*It.*) — Tempestuous, moved, passionate, impetuous.

Tempo (*It.*)—Rate of speed, movement.

Tempo alla breve (*It.*)—Called also *Alla cappella* time, was chiefly used in the older Church music. Each bar contained four minims, hence its name. Modern *Alla breve* time has two minims in a bar, usually indicated by the time-signature ₵

Tempo beschleunigen (*Ger.*) — Increasing the speed.

Tempo binario (*It.*)—Binary (duple) time.

Tempo commodo (*It.*)—At a commodious, convenient speed.

Tempo composto (*It.*)—Compound time.

Tempo debole (*It.*)—The unaccented part of a bar.

Tempo di ballo (*It.*) — In dance measure.

Tempo di bolero ⎫ (*It.*) — In the
Tempo di gavotta ⎬ time and style
Tempo di marcia ⎪ of a *Bolero*,
⎪ etc., respec-
Tempo di menuetto ⎭ tively.

Tempo di Polacca (*It.*)—In the time of a polonaise, or polacca.

Tempo di prima parte (*It.*)—In the time of the first part.

Tempo forte (*It.*)—The accented part of a bar.

Tempo giusto(*It.*)—Just, appropriate, time; *i.e.*, indicating a moderate rate of speed.

Tempo ordinario (*It.*)—4-4 time, in which the crotchet is the unit of measurement, as distinguished from *alla breve* time, in which the minim is the speed unit.

Tempo primo, or **primiero** (*It.*)—The speed as at first.

Temporeggiato (*It.*)—Accommodating the speed in order to accord with the wish of the solo performer.

Tempo rubato (*It.*)—(*lit.*, "robbed time.") An indication of a relaxation of the mathematical regularity of pulse, for the purpose of heightening the expressive power of the music, and of giving a freer rhythmical rendering of the same. *Tempo rubato* is produced by lengthening, or dwelling upon, some notes of a phrase; and shortening, or hastening, others; the deflection from the strict time being thus counterbalanced.

Tempo semplice in due movement (*It.*)—Duple time.

Tempo ternario (*It.*)—Ternary (triple) time.

Tempo wie vorher (*Ger.*)—The speed as before.

Temps (*Fr.*)—Time; the divisions of a bar.

Temps faible (*Fr.*)—The unaccented part, or beat, of a bar.

Temps fort (*Fr.*)—The accented part, or beat, of a bar.

Temps frappé (*Fr.*)—The down-beat in a bar.

Temps levé (*Fr.*)—The up-beat in a bar.

Tempus (*Lat.*)—Time, measure. In the ancient mensurable music, *tempus* was the time-value of a breve; *tempus imperfectum*, the division of the breve into two semibreves; *tempus perfectum*, the division of the breve into three semibreves.

Tendrement (*Fr.*)—Tenderly, delicately.

Tenendo (*It.*)—Sustaining. *Tenendo il canto*, sustaining the melody.

Tenerezza, con (*It.*)—With tenderness, delicately.

Teneroso (*It.*)—Tenderly, softly, delicately.

Tenete (*It.*)—Sustain, hold.

Tenor.—(1) The highest natural male voice, the normal compass, being

(2) The viola. (3) The largest bell in a peal of bells.

Tenor (*Ger.*)
Ténor (*Fr.*) } Tenor.

Tenor C. — The note indicated by a small c; so called from being the lowest note of the tenor voice, and the pitch of the lowest string of the viola.

Tenor clef. — The name generally applied to the C-clef when it is placed on the fourth line of the staff. Strictly speaking, the term *Tenor* should, under these conditions, be applied to the staff, and not to the clef.

Tenore (*It.*)—(1) A tenor voice. (2) A tenor singer. *Tenore buffo*, a tenor singer rendering a comic part in an opera. *Tenore leggiero*, a tenor singer with a light voice of small quality. *Tenore robusto*, a tenor singer with a powerful, sonorous voice.

Tenore-trombone (*It.*)—Tenor trombone.

Tenori acuti (*It.* and *Lat.*)—" High tenors " (*i.e.*, male altos).

Tenorist (*Ger.*)—A tenor singer.

Tenor-Posaune (*Ger.*)—A tenor trombone.

Tenor Schlüssel (*Ger.*)—(Tenor clef.)

Tenor trombone.—(Trombone.)

Tenor tuba.—(Tuba.)

Tenor violin.—The viola.

Tenth.—A compound interval comprising an octave and a third.

Tenu (*Fr.*)—Held, sustained.

Tenue (*Fr.*)—(1) A holding note. (2) A pedal note.

Tenuto (*It.*)—Held, sustained.

Tepidamente (*It.*)—In a lukewarm, unimpassioned style.

Tercet (*Fr.*)—A triplet.

Ternaire (*Fr.*)
Ternario (*It.*) } Ternary.

Ternary form. — The form of the whole (or a section of) a movement consisting of three parts—A, B, A², the last named being a more or less exact reproduction of the first.

Ternary time, or Ternary measure.— Triple time; each bar containing three pulses or beats.

Terz (*Ger.*)
Terza (*It.*) } The interval of a third.

Terzadecima (*It.*)
Terzdezime (*Ger.*) } The interval of a thirteenth.

Terzett (*Ger.*)
Terzetto (*It.*) } A composition in three parts for either voices or instruments.

Terzflöte (*Ger.*)—A flute sounding a minor third above the written notes.

Terzina (*It.*)—A triplet.

Terzquartsextakkord (*Ger.*) — A $\frac{6}{4}$ chord; the second inversion of a chord of the seventh.

Terzquintsextakkord (*Ger.*) — A $\frac{6}{5}$ chord; the first inversion of a chord of the seventh.

Testa (*It.*)—The head; as *voci di testa*, the head voice.

Tetrachord.— A scale series of four notes, the lowest and highest of which form an interval of a perfect fourth. In its modern sense, the lower or upper half of an octave of a scale.

Tertalogy.—A connected series of four works.

Text.—The words of any vocal musical composition.

T(h)eil (*Ger.*)—(1) A part of a bar. (2) A phrase, or part of a piece.

T(h)eiltöne (*Ger.*)—Partial tones.

Thema (*Ger.*) ⎱ A theme.
Thème (*Fr.*) ⎰

Theme.—(1) A musical idea or subject. (2) The *cantus firmus* against which counterpoint is written. (3) The subject of a fugue. (4) The tune, or subject, upon which variations are written.

Theorbe (*Ger.*) ⎱ A theorbo.
Théorbe (*Fr.*) ⎰

Theorbo.—A species of large, double-necked bass lute.

Thesis (*Gk.*)—The down beat, the strong beat.

Third.—An interval comprising three degrees in alphabetical order.

Thirteenth.—A compound interval comprising an octave and a sixth.

Thirty-second note.—A demisemi-quaver.

Thorough bass.—This—the Italian *basso continuo*—was the system adopted by the composers of the 16th, 17th, and 18th centuries to indicate the harmonies in those cases where (as frequently happened) the accompaniment for the organ or the harpsichord was not written out in full.

Three-lined octave ⎱ The octave
Thrice-accented octave ⎰ extending to the note *b* next above; it is indicated thus:— *c'''*, *d'''*, etc.

Tibia (*Lat.*)—The ancient Roman flute.

Tibia major. — An organ-stop of 16 ft. pitch.

Tibia obliqua (*Lat.*) — The *flauto traverso*.

Tie.—A curved line connecting two or more notes of the same pitch, indicating that they are to be held as one continuous sound. A *tie* is also called a *bind*.

Tief (*Ger.*) — Deep, low. *Tiefer*, lower.

Tiefer Bass (*Ger.*)—A deep bass.

Tierce (*Fr.*)—(1) A third. (2) A mutation-stop on the organ, sounding a seventeenth above the diapason.

Tierce de Picardie (*Fr.*)—The major third in the final chord of a composition in the minor mode.

Timbale (*Fr.*) ⎱ A kettle-drum.
Timballo (*It.*) ⎰

Timbre (*Fr.*) — The quality of a musical sound. *Timbre* depends upon the number, order, and relative intensity of the upper partial-tones which accompany the fundamental note.

Timbrel.—A tambourine or tabor.

Time.—The grouping of sounds by means of periodic accent. The formation of all measures (bars) is based upon two species of such time-groups : (*a*) duple or binary, consisting of two pulses, the first accented, the second unaccented; (*b*) triple or ternary, having three pulses, the first accented, the second and third unaccented. A measure may contain one, or more than one, of such groups. The English system of nomenclature and classification recognises three species of time—*duple*, *triple*, and *quadruple*, each being capable of sub-division into *simple* and *compound*. In *simple* time each pulse is divisible into two parts, in *compound* time into three parts.

Timidezza, con ⎱
Timido
Timoroso ⎰ (*It.*) — In a style expressive of timidity, hesitation, or fear.

Timpani (*It.*)—Kettle-drums. *Timpani coperti*, muffled drums.

Tinto, con (*It.*)—With tone-colour, expressively.

Tirade (*Fr.*) — The filling up of an interval between two notes with a run.

Tirato (*It.*)—A down-bow, in violin playing, etc.

Tiré (*Fr.*)—(Tirato.)

Toccata (*It.*)—A composition for the pianoforte or organ, free in style, with an animated, rapid movement. It is generally constructed out of a figure which runs throughout the whole movement, and serves for the display of technical dexterity.

Toccatina (*It.*)—A short toccata.

Tom-tom.—A gong. (Tam-tam.)

Ton (*Fr.* and *Ger.*)—(1) Tone, sound. (2) The interval of a second.

Tonal.—Pertaining to a tone, key, or mode.

Tonal fugue. — The term used to describe a fugue in which the answer is a modified reproduction of the subject.

Tonalita (*It.*) ⎱
Tonalität (*Ger.*) ⎸
Tonalité (*Fr.*) ⎹
Tonality ⎰ This term has reference to (1) the characteristics of any particular system, mode, or key ; (2) the notes of a scale, their relationship to one another and to one central note—the tonic ; also to chords regarded from the same standpoint ; (3) the preponderance in a composition of one key over the other keys to which modulation is made.

Tonart (*Ger.*)—(1) Key. (2) Mode.

Tonausweichung (*Ger.*)—Modulation.

Ton bas (*Fr.*)—A deep, low tone.

Tone.—(1) A musical sound. (2) A sound of a particular pitch. (3) The quality of a sound. (4) An interval of a second containing two semitones. (5) A Gregorian chant.

Tonfall (*Ger.*)—A cadence.

Tonfarbe (*Ger.*)—Timbre, quality of tone.

Tonfolge (*Ger.*) — A succession of sounds, a melody.

Tonführung (*Ger.*)—(1) A melodic progression. (2) Modulation.

Ton générateur (*Fr.*)—The root of a chord.

Tongeschlecht (*Ger.*)—The mode o. a key or scale (major or minor).

Ton gesteigert (*Ger.*)—Reinforced in tone.

Tongue.—(*Noun*), a reed : (*verb*), to use the tongue in producing the tone on certain wind-instruments.

Ton haut (*Fr.*)—A high sound.

Tonic.—The keynote of a scale. *Tonic pedal.* (Pedal-point.) *Tonic section,* that part of a composition which is in the original key.

Tonica (*It.* and *Ger.*)—The keynote of a scale.

Tonic Sol-fa.—A method for teaching sight-singing on the principle of recognising the several degrees of the scale by the mental impression peculiar to each. Founded on the " Movable-Doh " system, *doh* invariably represents the keynote, which may be at any pitch ; the remaining degrees of the scale in order are *ray, me, fah, soh, lah, te.*

Tonique (*Fr.*)—The keynote of a scale.

Tonleiter (*Ger.*)—A scale.

Ton majeur (*Fr.*) ⎱
Tono maggiore (*It.*) ⎰ A major key.

Ton mineur (*Fr.*) ⎱
Tono minore (*It.*) ⎰ A minor key.

Tono relativo (*It.*)—A relative key.

Tonsatz (*Ger.*) — A musical composition.

Tonschluss (*Ger.*)—A cadence.

Tonschlüssel (*Ger.*)—Key, keynote.

Tons d'église (*Fr.*) — The Church modes.

Tons de la trompette (*Fr.*)—Crooks used for altering the keys of the trumpet.

Tons du cor (*Fr.*)—Crooks used for altering the keys of the horn.

Tons ouverts (*Fr.*) — The natural notes of a horn, etc.

Tonstück (*Ger.*)—A piece of music, a composition.

Tonstufe (*Ger.*)—A degree of a scale.

Tonsystem (*Ger.*)— (1) The arrangement of sounds on a tonal system. (2) A scale.

Tonumfang (*Ger.*) Compass.

Tonus (*Lat.*)—Tone, sound. *Tonus currens*, the reciting note.

Tonverhalt (*Ger.*)—Rhythm.

Tosto (*It.*)—Swift, rapid. *Piùttosto* (usually written *più tosto*), quicker. *Tostissimo*, very rapidly.

Touche (*Fr.*)—(1) A key. (2) A finger-board.

Toucher (*Fr.*) — (*Verb*) To play, (*noun*) touch.

Touches (*Fr.*)—(1) The keys of the pianoforte, or other keyboard instrument. (2) The frets on instruments of the guitar class.

Touches mélodieuses (*Fr.*) — In a singing style (Cantabile).

Toujours (*Fr.*)—Always.

Touquet (*Fr.*)—(Toccata.)

Tournez vivement (*Fr.*)—Turn over quickly.

Trackers.—Strips of wood forming part of the mechanism of an organ connecting the keys with the pallets.

Traîné (*Fr.*)—Slurred, bound, legato.

Trait (*Fr.*)—A run, or division.

Trait de chant (*Fr.*) — A melodic phrase.

Trait d'harmonie (*Fr.*)—A harmonic progression.

Tranquillement (*Fr.*)—Quietly, tranquilly.

Tranquillezza, con ⎫
Tranquillità, con ⎬ (*It.*)—In a quiet, tranquil style.
Tranquillo ⎭

Transcription.—(1) The adaptation of a composition for some voice or instrument other than that for which it was originally written. (2) A composition in the style of a fantasia, on themes from the work of another composer.

Transient modulation. — A temporary modulation, the original key being returned to almost at once.

Transitio (*Lat.*)—Change of key ; modulation.

Transition ⎫ (1) A passage lead-
Transition (*Fr.*) ⎬ ing from one theme to another.
Transizione (*It.*) ⎭ (2) A temporary modulation.

Transitus (*Lat.*)—A transition. *Transitus regularis*, a passing note. *Transitus irregularis*, a changing note.

Transponiren (*Ger.*)—To transpose.

Transponirende Instrumente (*Ger.*)— Transposing instruments.

Transpose ⎫ To perform, or
Transposer (*Fr.*) ⎬ write out, a composition in a different key.

Transposing instruments.—(1) Those instruments which produce notes different in pitch from those written. (2) Instruments having some device by means of which the pitch can be altered.

Transpositeur (*Fr.*)—A transposing keyboard which can be fixed to a pianoforte.

Transposition.—(1) A change of key. (2) The change of the relative position of two or more parts.

Transportare (*It.*)—To transpose.

Transverse flute.—(Flauto traverso.)

Trascinando (*It.*)—Dragging, holding back the speed.

Trauergesang (*Ger.*)—A f u n e r a l hymn.

Trauermarsch (*Ger.*)—A f u n e r a l march.

Trauervoll (*Ger.*)—Mournful, sorrowful.

Traurig (*Ger.*)—Sad, melancholy.

Traversflöte (*Ger.*) — (Flauto traverso.)

Traversière (*Fr.*)—Cross. *Flûte traversière*, the flute held crossways. (Flauto traverso.)

Traverso (*It.*)—Cross. *Flauto traverso*, the flute held crossways.

Tre (*It.*)—Three. *A tre*, for three voices or instruments.

Treble.—(1) The highest part in a composition, vocal or instrumental. (2) Another name for the soprano voice.

Treble clef.—The name given to the G clef on the second line of the staff; also called the *violin* clef.

Tre corde (*It.*)—A term used in pianoforte music to indicate that the soft pedal is to be released.

Treibend (*Ger.*)—Hurrying, pressing on the speed.

Tremblant (*Fr.*)—Tremulous, wavering.

Tremolando (*It.*) ⎫
Tremolato (*It.*) ⎬ Trembling, wavering. (1) An effect produced on
Tremolo ⎭ stringed instruments by a rapid up and down movement of the bow on the strings. (2) The rapid alternation of notes on keyboard instruments such as the pianoforte. (3) Vibration of the voice in singing.

Tremulant.—A mechanical device in an organ, which, acting on the wind supply, produces a trembling effect.

Trénise (*Fr.*)—One of the figures of the quadrille.

Très (*Fr.*)—Very. *Très animé*, very animated. *Très élevé*, very high. *Très peu*, very little. *Très vite*, very fast. *Très pressé*, in haste.

Très égal (*Fr.*)—Smooth.

Triad ⎫
Triade (*It.*) ⎬ A note with a third and fifth added above, or, in other words, a note
Triade (*Fr.*) ⎭ with two superimposed thirds. These added thirds— one of which may be major, the other minor, or both of the same quality—give rise to four kinds of triads, major, minor, diminished, and augmented; the major and minor triads are, however, generally spoken of as common chords, by reason of the fact that the lowest and highest notes form the interval of a perfect fifth.

Triangalo (*It.*) ⎫
Triangel (*Ger.*) ⎬ An instrument of percussion formed of a steel rod bent
Triangle ⎭ into triangular shape, but with one corner left open; it is played by being struck with a metal rod.

Tribrach.—A metrical foot, containing three short syllables, ⌣ ⌣ ⌣

Trichord.—An instrument having three strings. A *trichord pianoforte* is one having three strings (tuned in unison) to each note, throughout the greater part of its compass.

Trill ⎫
Trille (*Fr.*) ⎬ The regular and rapid alternation of a note, and the note next
Triller (*Ger.*) ⎭ above, either a tone or a semitone distant. Also called a "shake."

Trillerkette (*Ger.*)—A chain of trills.

Trillo (*It.*)—A trill, or shake.

Trio (*It.*) ⎫ (1) A composition in three
Trio (*Fr.*) ⎭ parts for voices or instruments. (2) The name applied to the second division of minuets, marches, etc.

Triole (*Ger.*) ⎫
Triolet (*Fr.*) ⎭ A triplet.

Triomphal (*Fr.*)—Triumphal.

Triomphant (*Fr.*)—Triumphant.

Trionfale (*It.*)—Triumphal.

Tripelconcert (*Ger.*)—A triple concerto, *i.e.*, a concerto for three solo instruments with orchestral accompaniment.

Tripelfuge (*Ger.*)—A fugue on three subjects.

Tripeltakt (*Ger.*)—Triple time.

Tripla (*It.*)—A triplet; triple time.

Triple counterpoint.—Counterpoint in three parts, so constructed that each part will serve equally well as the highest, middle, or lowest part.

Triple croche (*Fr.*)—A demisemiquaver.

Triple fugue.—A fugue on three subjects.

Triplet.—A group of three equal notes played in the time of two of the same value, indicated thus— 𝅘𝅥𝅘𝅥𝅘𝅥

Triple time.—The time in which the measure (bar) contains three equal parts, each part being divisible into two notes or their equivalent.

Tripola (*It.*)—(Tripla.)

Trisagion (*Gk.*)—Thrice Holy. The opening words of the Sanctus in the Mass.

Triste (*Fr.*)—Sad. *Tristement*, sadly.

Tristezza, con }
Tristo, -a } (*It.*)—In a style expressive of sadness, melancholy.

Triton (*Fr.*) }
Tritone }
Tritono (*It.*) } An augmented fourth, consisting of three whole tones.
Tritonus (*Ger. and Lat.*) }

Trittharfe (*Ger.*)—A pedal harp.

Trochee.—A metrical foot, containing one long and one short syllable, — ⌣

Trois (*Fr.*)—Three. *Mesure à trois deux*, 3-2 time. *Mesure à trois quatre*, 3-4 time.

Tromba (*It.*)—(1) A trumpet. (2) A reed-stop on the organ, of 8 ft. pitch.

Tromba bassa (*It.*)—A bass trumpet.

Tromba cromatica (*It.*)—A valve or keyed trumpet capable of producing the chromatic scale.

Trombone }
Trombone (*Fr. and It.*) } A brass wind instrument of powerful tone. The natural sounds produced are those of the harmonic series of the key, and by means of a slide the tube can be lengthened, giving seven series of notes including the closed position, thus rendering available the complete chromatic scale. The most important members of the trombone family are the alto in the key of E flat (now rarely used), the compass with the closed slide being from

the tenor in the key of B flat, a perfect fourth below the alto ; and the bass either in the key of G, a minor third below the tenor ; or in F, a tone lower.

Trommel (*Ger.*)—A drum. *Kleine Trommel*, a side-drum. *Grosse Trommel*, a big drum.

Trommelklöppel }
Trommelstöcke } (*Ger.*)—Drumsticks.

Trompe (*Fr.*)—(1) A trumpet. (2) A hunting horn.

Trompete (*Ger.*)—(1) A trumpet. (2) A reed-stop on the organ of 8, sometimes also of 16, and 4 ft. pitch.

Trompette (*Fr.*)—(1) A trumpet. (2) A reed-stop on an organ.

Trompette à clefs (*Fr.*)—A keyed trumpet.

Trompette à pistons (*Fr.*)—A valve trumpet.

Trop (*Fr.*)—Too much.

Troppo (*It.*)—Too much. *Allegro ma non troppo*, quickly, but not too much so.

Troubadours.—Poet-musicians who flourished in France, Italy, and Spain, from the 11th to the close of the 13th centuries.

Trouvères (*Fr.*) }
Trouveurs (*Fr.*) }
Trovadores (*Sp.*) } (Troubadours.)
Trovatori (*It.*) }

Trugkadenz }
Trugschluss } (*Ger.*)—An interrupted cadence.

Trumpet.—(1) A metal wind-instrument of powerful, penetrating tone. It is a transposing instrument. There are three varieties : (*a*) the natural trumpet (now practically obsolete), giving only the notes of the harmonic series ; (*b*) the valve trumpet, on which the chromatic scale is available ; and (*c*) the slide trumpet, which also can produce the chromatic scale. The pitch of the trumpet is approximately an octave above that of the horn. (2) A powerful reed-stop on the organ, of 8 ft. pitch.

Tuba (*Lat.*)—(1) The war trumpet of the Romans. (2) A brass wind instrument with valves, of very powerful tone. The bass tuba is the one most frequently met with in the orchestra; the usual key is E ♭

and the compass is

(3) A powerful reed-stop on the organ, of 8 ft. pitch.

Tuba mirabilis (*Lat.*)—An extremely powerful reed-stop on the organ, of 8 feet pitch. It is on a high pressure of wind.

Tumultuoso (*It.*) — Vehement, agitated.

Tune.—(1) A melody, an air. (2) The expression "to be in tune'" means that a performer must produce the notes at their absolute pitch, or to accord with an accompanying instrument of fixed pitch.

Tuning-cone. — An instrument shaped like a hollow cone, used for tuning the metal pipes of an organ.

Tuning-fork. — An instrument of steel, with two prongs, which when struck sets up a series of vibrations producing a note of definite pitch. The note sounded is usually either a¹ or c².

Tuning-hammer, or Tuning-key.—An instrument used for tuning the pianoforte.

Tuono (*It.*)—The interval of a tone.

Tuoni ecclesiastici (*It.*)—The Church modes.

Turco, -a (*It.*)—Turkish. *Alla turca,* in the Turkish style.

Turn.—A musical ornament, usually consisting of the principal note, the note next above, the principal note, the note next below, and the principal note, played in rapid succession.

Tutte le corde (*It.*)—A direction to play on all the strings, *i.e.,* to release the soft pedal.

Tutti.—All; the whole. In scores this term indicates that all the performers are to take part. It also indicates a passage thus executed.

In a concerto it signifies those portions in which the whole orchestra is engaged, but not the soloist.

Tutto, -a (*It.*)—All. *Tutta la forza,* all the power.

Tuyau à anche (*Fr.*)—A reed-pipe.

Tuyau à bouche (*Fr.*)—A flue-pipe.

Tuyau d'orgue (*Fr.*)—An organ-pipe.

Twelfth.—(1) A compound interval containing an octave and a fifth. (2) An organ-stop sounding a twelfth above the diapasons.

Twice-accented octave ⎱ The octave
Twice-marked octave ⎰ of notes

between   and the *b*

next above; indicated thus :— *c*¹¹, *d*¹¹, or *c*², *d*², etc.

Tympani.—(Timpani.)

Tympanum (*Lat.*)—A drum, a tambourine.

Tyrolienne (*Fr.*)—A Tyrolese song, the feature of which is the rapid change from the notes of the chest-voice to those of the head-voice, which is known as the jodel.

U.

Übergang ⎱ (*Ger.*)—A passage of
Überleitung ⎰ transition, leading from one subject to another, or from one key to another.

Übermässig (*Ger.*)—Augmented.

Überredend (*Ger.*)—Coaxing.

Überreinstimmung (*Ger.*)—Concord or consonance.

Überschlagen (*Ger.*)—To cross the hands in playing on a keyboard instrument.

Übersetzen (*Ger.*)—To pass a finger over the thumb in playing on a keyboard instrument. In pedal playing on the organ, to pass one foot over the other.

Überton (*Ger.*)—Supertonic.

Übung (*Ger.*)—An exercise; a study.

Uguale (*It.*)—Equal, alike, similar. *Canone a tre voci uguale*, a canon for three equal voices.

Ugualità, con (*It.*)—Equally, similarly ; evenly, smoothly.

U m a n o, -a (*It.*) — Human. *Voce umano*, the human voice ; the name of an organ-stop (*vox humana*), and one of the names of the *cor anglais*.

Umfang (*Ger.*)—Compass, extent. *Umfang der Stimme*, compass of the voice.

U m g e k e h r t (*Ger.*)—Reversed, inverted.

Umkehrung (*Ger.*)—Inversion.

Umore, con (*It.*)—With humour.

Umstimmung (*Ger.*)—A change of tuning or of key, *e.g.*, in the case of the horn or of the kettle-drums.

Un, Une (*Fr.*)—One ; a, an.

Un, Un', Una (*It.*)—One. *Una volta*, once. (Uno.)

Unca (*Lat.*)—A quaver.

Unda maris (*Lat.*)—(*lit.*, " wave of the sea.") An organ-stop the pipes of which are tuned a little sharp, and which, when used with another stop, produces an undulating effect.

Undecima (*Lat.* and *It.*)—The interval of an eleventh.

Undecimole⎫An irregular group of
Undecuplet⎭ eleven notes played in the time of eight (or six) of the same value.

Undulazione (*It.*)—The " vibrato " effect produced on stringed instruments.

U n e n d l i c h (*Ger.*)—Infinite, *e.g.*, *Unendlicher Kanon*, an infinite or circular canon.

Unequal temperament. — (Temperament.)

Unequal voices.—Voices of mixed qualities, and of different compass.

Unessential notes.—Notes which do not form a constituent part of the harmony. Included under this head are suspensions and the various forms of passing notes and auxiliary notes.

Ungarisch (*Ger.*)—Hungarian.

Ungebunden (*Ger.*)—Unrestrained. *Mit ungebundenem Humor*, with unrestrained humor.

Ungerader Takt (*Ger.*)—Triple time.

U n g e s t ü m (*Ger.*)—Impetuous(ly), boisterous(ly).

Ungherese (*It.*)—Hungarian.

Unharmonischer Querstand (*Ger.*)—False relation.

Unison.—When two or more voices, instruments, or strings, produce sounds identical in pitch—*i.e.*, having the same number of vibrations. "*In unison*" is the conventional (but hardly accurate) term applied to a passage sung in octaves by male and female voices.

Unisono (*It.*) ⎫
Unisson (*Fr.*) ⎭ Unison.

U n i t i (*It.*) — An indication, after " divisi," that the voices or instruments are to perform their parts in unison.

Unito, -a (*It.*)—United, joined.

Uno, -a (*It.*)—One. *Una corda*, one string, an indication in pianoforte music that the soft pedal is to be used. *Una volta*, once.

Un peu (*Fr.*)—A little.

Un peu haut (*Fr.*)—Moderately loud.

Un peu lent (*Fr.*)—Somewhat slow.

Un peu plus lent (*Fr.*)—A little slower.

Un pochettino (*It.*)—A very, very little.

Un pochino (*It.*)—A very little.

Un poco (*It.*)—A little. *Un poco più allegro*, a little faster.

Unruhig (*Ger.*) — Restless(ly), agitated.

Unter (*Ger.*)—Under.

Unterbass (*Ger.*)—(1) A double-bass. (2) A sub-bass, an organ-stop of 16 or 32 ft. pitch.

Unterbrochener Schluss (*Ger.*)—An interrupted cadence.

Unterdominant (*Ger.*) — The subdominant.

Unterhalbton (*Ger.*) — The leading note.

Untermediante (*Ger.*) — The sub-mediant.

Untersatz (*Ger.*)—Sub-bass. (Unter-bass.)

Untersetzen (*Ger.*) — To pass the thumb under another finger in playing on a keyboard instrument. In pedal-playing on the organ, to pass one foot behind the other.

Unterstimme (*Ger.*)—An under part. The lowest part in a composition.

Unvocal.—Not suitable for singing.

Unvollkommen (*Ger.*) — Imperfect. *Unvollkommener Schluss*, an imperfect, or half, cadence.

Up-beat. — (1) The raising of the hand in beating time. (2) An unaccented part of a bar.

Up-bow.—In playing on a stringed instrument, the movement of the bow across the strings in the direction from point to nut ; indicated V or ʌ.

Ursprung (*Ger.*)—Root.

Ut.—(1) The first of the Aretinian syllables. (2) The name of the note C in France.

Ut bémol (*Fr.*)—The note C flat. *Ut bémol majeur*, the key of C flat major.

Ut dièse (*Fr.*)—The note C sharp. *Ut dièse mineur*, the key of C sharp minor.

V.

V.—The abbreviation standing for *Violino, Volti, Voce.*

Valeur (*Fr.*)⎱ Value of a note, or of a
Valore (*It.*) ⎰ rest.

Valse (*Fr.*)—Waltz.

Value.—The length or duration of a note with relation to (*a*) other notes in any given passage, (*b*) the standard note (*i.e.*, the semibreve), or any fractional part of the same.

Valve. — A contrivance applied to brass wind instruments, by means of which the current of air can be diverted into an extra length of tubing, and the pitch of the natural series of notes lowered accordingly.

The valves are usually three in number, and, when used singly, the pitch is lowered either a semitone, tone, or minor third. Further, by using together the second and third, the first and third, or all three, the pitch can be lowered a major third, a perfect fourth, and a diminished fifth respectively.

Valzer (*It.*)—Waltz.

Vamp.—To improvise an accompaniment.

Variamente (*It.*)—In a different way.

Variation.—The re-stating of a theme under different conditions, *i.e.*, in an embellished and disguised form, by means of melodic, harmonic, and rhythmic devices.

Variato (*It.*)—Varied, changed.

Variazione (*It.*)—A variation. *Tema con variazioni*, a theme with variations.

Varié (*Fr.*)—Varied. *Thème varié*, a theme with variations.

Varsoviana (*It.*) ⎱ A dance in 3-4
Varsovienne (*Fr.*) ⎰ time and moderate tempo, containing some of the features of both the polka and mazurka, but characterised by a strong accent on the first beat of every second bar.

Vaudeville (*Fr.*)—(1) A gay, popular song. (2) A light comedy, the dialogue being interspersed with verses on " topical " events, generally adapted to well-known tunes. (3) A theatre where such comedies are performed.

Veiled tone.—When the tone of a voice does not ring out clearly, but is somewhat obscured, either intentionally or through faulty production.

Velato, -a (*It.*)—Veiled. *Voce velata*, a veiled tone of voice.

Vellutato, -a (*It.*)—Velvety; soft, delicate.

Veloce (*It.*)—Quick, swift, nimble. A term indicating that any passage so marked is to be played at more than normal speed.

Velocissimo (*It.*)—With extreme rapidity.

Velocità, con (*It.*)—With rapidity.

Velocité (*Fr.*)—Velocity.

Ventil (*Ger.*) ⎫ A valve (*q.v.*).
Ventile (*It.*) ⎭

Veränderungen (*Ger.*)—Variations.

Verbindungszeichen (*Ger.*)—A slur, a bind.

Verdeckt (*Ger.*)—Hidden. *Verdeckte Octaven*, hidden octaves. *Verdeckte Quinten*, hidden fifths.

Verdoppelt (*Ger.*)—Doubled.

Verdoppelung (*Ger.*)—Doubling of notes or parts.

Vergnügt (*Ger.*)—Pleasant(ly), cheerful(ly).

Vergrösserung (*Ger.*)—Augmentation.

Verhallend (*Ger.*)—Dying away; decreasing in tone.

Verkleinerung (*Ger.*)—Diminution.

Verlangend (*Ger.*)—Longingly.

Verliebt (*Ger.*)—Lovingly.

Verlöschend (*Ger.*)—Dying away.

Vermindert (*Ger.*)—Diminished ; as *verminderter Dreiklang*, a diminished triad.

Verschiebung, mit (*Ger.*)—With the soft pedal. *Ohne Verschiebung*, without the soft pedal.

Verschleiert (*Ger.*)—Veiled.

Verschwindend (*Ger.*)—Dying away.

Verse.—(1) In Church music, that portion of an anthem or service in which each part is sung by a single voice. (2) A stanza of a song.

Verse-anthem.—One in which "verse" parts predominate.

Versetzen (*Ger.*)—To transpose.

Versetzungszeichen (*Ger.*)—Accidentals.

Versicle.—In the Church service, a short verse with the response.

Verstärkt (*Ger.*)—(Sforzando.)

Verstimmt (*Ger.*)—Out of tune.

Verwandt (*Ger.*)—Related. *Verwandte Tonarten*, related keys.

Verwechselung (*Ger.*)—Change (*e.g.*, of key, time, etc.)

Verweilend (*Ger.*)—Delaying; holding back the time.

Verzieren (*Ger.*)—To ornament.

Verzierungen (*Ger.*)—Ornaments, embellishments.

Verzögerung (*Ger.*)—Retardation.

Vespers.—Evensong; the sixth of the canonical hours.

Vibrante (*It.*)—Vibrating, tremulous.

Vibrato (*It.*)—A tremulous effect, produced—(*a*) by a slight oscillation of the finger stopping the string on bowed-instruments ; (*b*) by singing in an unsteady, tremulous manner.

Vibrazione (*It.*)—Vibration.

Vicar choral.—A lay vicar in a cathedral choir.

Vide (*Fr.*)—Open. *Corde à vide*, an open string.

Viel (*Ger.*)—Much. *Mit vielem Ausdruck*, with much expression. *Viel bewegter*, much more lively.

Vielstimmig (*Ger.*)—In several parts.

Vier (*Ger.*)—Four.

Vierdoppelter Contrapunkt (*Ger.*)—Quadruple counterpoint.

Vierhändig (*Ger.*)—For four hands ; *i.e.*, for pianoforte duet.

Vierklang (*Ger.*)—A chord of the seventh.

Vierstimmig (*Ger.*)—In four parts.

Vierstück (*Ger.*)—A composition for four players ; a quartet.

Viertelnote (*Ger.*)—A quarter note ; a crotchet.

Viertelpause (*Ger.*)—A crotchet rest.

Vierundsechzigstelnote (*Ger.*)—A semidemisemiquaver.

Vif, vive (*Fr.*)—Lively, brisk quick.

Vigore, con ⎫ (*It.*)—With vigour,
Vigoroso ⎭ energy.

Vigoureusement (*Fr.*)—Vigorously.

Viol.—The generic name given to the family of stringed instruments played with a bow, which were the precursors of the violin, viola, violoncello, and double-bass. The viol was invented in the 15th century, and was in favour until the early part of the 18th. The difference between the two groups of instruments lay in their shape and system of tuning. A viol usually had six strings tuned as follows: The three lower and the three upper were tuned a fourth apart, the two groups of three being separated by the interval of a third.

Viola (*It.*)—(1) A viol. (2) The tenor violin. This instrument has four strings, tuned thus—

(3) An organ-stop of 4 or 8 ft. pitch.

Viola da braccio (*It.*)—(*lit.*, " arm-viol "), *i.e.*, a viol which when being played upon was held in position by the arm. The tenor viol.

Viola da gamba (*It.*)—(*lit.*, " leg-viol "), *i.e.*, a viol which when being played upon was held in position between the knees. The bass viol.

Viola d'amore (*It.*)—An obsolete stringed instrument a little larger than the viola. In addition to the catgut strings, metal strings were stretched below the finger-board, producing sympathetic vibrations which gave to the instrument its characteristic quality.

Viola di bardone (*It.*)—The baryton, an obsolete stringed instrument of the viol class.

Viola pomposa (*It.*)—A species of viola da gamba invented by Bach. It had five strings, tuned thus—

Viole (*Fr.*)—(1) A viol. (2) The viola.

Viole d'amour (*Fr.*)—(Viola d'amore.)

Violento ⎱ (*It.*) — In a violent,
Violenza, con ⎰ impetuous style.

Violin.—The most familiar of the group of stringed instruments played with a bow. Its name is derived from the Italian *violino*, which signifies a "small viol." The violin is tuned thus—

and its usual orchestral compass is from g to a''', but soloists reach some notes higher still.

Violin clef.—The G clef placed upon the first line of the staff; now obsolete. The G clef on the second line of the staff is also called the violin clef.

Violin-diapason.—A diapason-stop on the organ, with a rather stringy quality of tone.

Violine (*Ger.*) ⎱
Violino (*It.*) ⎰ A violin.

Violino piccolo (*It.*)—A small violin, tuned a fourth higher than the ordinary violin.

Violino principale (*It.*)—A solo violinist; the leader of a quartet or of an orchestra.

Violino primo (*It.*)—First violin.

Violino ripieno (*It.*)—A violin part used for the purpose of filling in and strengthening the *tutti* in a concerto, etc. (See Ripieno.)

Violino secondo (*It.*)—Second violin.

Violinschlüssel (*Ger.*) — The violin clef.

Violon (*Fr.*)—(1) The violin. (2) An organ-stop of 8 or 16 ft. tone. (3) In Germany the same word is used for the double-bass.

Violoncell (*Ger.*) ⎫ A bowed instru-
Violoncelle (*Fr.*) ⎬ ment of the violin
Violoncello (*It.*) ⎭ family, the bass of the quartet.
It has four strings tuned thus :—

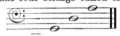

and when played is held between the knees. The word *violoncello* is the diminutive of *violone*.

Violone (*It.*)—(1) The double bass. The violone was the largest of the family of viols, the term itself meaning " big viol." (2) An organ-stop of 16 ft. pitch.

Virginal.—A small keyboard instrument of the same type as the harpsichord and spinet. The tone was produced by the strings being plucked by quills or " jacks," not struck by tangents or hammers.

Virtuos (*Ger.*) ⎱ A highly-skilled
Virtuoso, -a (*It.*) ⎰ performer, either instrumentalist or vocalist.

Vista (*It.*)—Sight. *A prima vista,* at first sight.

Visto, -a (*It.*) — Quick, swift, animated.

Vite (*Fr.*)—Quick, fast. *Plus vite,* faster. *Très vite,* very fast.

Vitement (*Fr.*)—Quickly.

Vivace (*It.*)—Lively, animated, brisk. The term *vivace* is used both in conjunction with some other tempo-mark and also alone ; in the latter case it indicates a speed of movement equal to, or even faster than, *Allegro.*

Vivacezza, con } (*It.*)—Lively, spirit-
Vivacità, con } ed, animated.

Vivacissimo (*It.*)—Extremely lively.

Vive (*Fr.*)—(Fem. of *Vif*)—Brisk, quick, lively.

Vivement (*Fr.*)—Lively, briskly.

Vivente }
Vivido } (*It.*)—Lively, spiritedly, briskly.
Vivo }

Vocal.—(1) Pertaining to the voice. (2) Music suitable to, or effective for, the voice.

Vocal chords.—The two ligaments in the larynx, which, when set in vibration by air expelled from the lungs, produce vocal tone.

Vocale (*It.*)—Belonging to the voice.

Vocalisation.—(1) The practice and art of singing upon the various vowel-sounds. (2) The art and method of singing generally.

Vocalise (*Fr.*)—An exercise for the study of singing to vowels, or to solmisation-syllables.

Vocalizzare (*It.*)—To vocalise.

Vocal score.—The voice parts of a chorus, etc., written one above another on separate staves.

Voce (*It.*)—Voice. *A mezza voce,* with half the power of the voice. *A tre voci,* for three voices, or in three parts.

Voce angelica (*It.*)—(Vox angelica.)

Voce di petto (*It.*)—The chest voice.

Voce di testa (*It.*)—The head voice.

Voce principale (*It.*)—Principal voice.

Voci (*It.*)—Voices. The plural of voce.

Voice.—(1) The sound that issues from the mouth, and which is produced by the vibrations of the vocal chords. The several voices are :— (Female) soprano, mezzo-soprano, contralto ; (Male) alto, tenor, baritone, bass. (2) The word voice is frequently used in the same sense as a "part" in harmony.

Voice-part.—A vocal part.

Voicing.—Regulating the tone of an organ-pipe.

Voilé (*Fr.*)—Veiled. *Voix voilée,* a veiled tone of voice. (Velato.)

Voix (*Fr.*)—Voice.

Voix angélique } (*Fr.*)-(Vox angelica.)
Voix céleste }

Voix de tête (*Fr.*)—Head voice.

Voix humaine (*Fr.*)—(Vox humana.)

Volant (*Fr.*) } Flying ; light, swift.
Volante (*It.*) } A passage so marked is to be played rapidly, and with a delicate touch.

Volata (*It.*) }
Volate (*Ger.*) } A run or division ; a light, rapid series of notes forming an embellishment to a melody.
Volatine (*Fr.*) }

Volkslied (*Ger.*)—A folk-song.

Voll (*Ger.*)—Full. *Volle Kraft,* full power. *Volles Orchester,* full orchestra. *Volles Werk,* full organ. *Mit vollem .Chor,* with full chorus.

Vollkommene Kadenz (*Ger.*)—A perfect cadence.

Vollstimmig (*Ger.*)—Full-voiced ; full-toned.

Volonté (*Fr.*)—Will, pleasure. *À volonté,* at will.

Volta (*It.*)—Turn, time. *Prima volta,* first time. *Secunda volta,* second time. *Una volta,* once. *Due volte,* twice.

Volteggiando (*It.*)—Crossing the hands in pianoforte playing.

Volti subito (*It.*)—Turn over quickly.

Voluntary.—An organ solo played before, during, or at the close of, a service of the Church.

Vom Anfang (*Ger.*)—From the beginning. (Da capo.)

Vom Blatte (*Ger.*)—At first sight.

Von dem Zeichen (*Ger.*)—From the sign.

Vorgeiger (*Ger.*)—Leader; the principal first violin.

Vorgreifung
Vorgriff } (*Ger.*) Anticipation.

Vorhalt (*Ger.*) — (1) Syncopation. (2) Suspension.

Vorher (*Ger.*)—Before, previous. *Vorhergehendes Tempo*, at the previous speed.

Vorig (*Ger.*)—Previous, preceding. *Voriges Zeitmass*, at the preceding speed.

Vorsänger (*Ger.*)—Precentor.

Vorschlag (*Ger.*)—An appoggiatura.

Vorspiel (*Ger.*)—Prelude; introductory movement; overture.

Vortragen (*Ger.*)—To render.

Vorwärts (*Ger.*)—Forwards. *Etwas vorwärts gehend*, somewhat faster.

Vorzeichnung (*Ger.*)—Signature.

Vox (*Lat.*) — (1) A voice; as *vox humana*, the human voice. (2) A part; as *tres voces*, three parts.

Vox angelica (*Lat.*)—An organ-stop containing two ranks of pipes, one of delicate quality of tone, one of which is tuned slightly sharp, producing a wavy, tremulous effect.

Vox humana (*Lat.*)—A delicately toned reed-stop on the organ, intended to imitate the human voice.

Vue (*Fr.*)—Sight. *À première vue*, at first sight. (A prima vista.)

Vuoto, -a (*It.*)—Open; as *corda vuota*, open string (on the violin, etc.)

W.

Wait, or Wayte.—A species of hautboy, now obsolete.

Waits, or Wayghtes.—(1) Players on the above instrument. (2) Street watchmen, who announced their coming by sounding horns. (3) Bodies of performers who sing or play in the streets at night as Christmas time approaches.

Waldflöte
Waldflute } (*Ger.*)—A species of flute-stop on the organ, usually of 4 ft. or 8 ft. pitch.

Waldhorn (*Ger.*)—A hunting horn; the French horn without valves.

Waltz
Walzer (*Ger.*) } A round dance of German origin, in triple time (usually 3-4).

Wärme (*Ger.*) — Warmth. *Mit grosser Wärme*, with great warmth or fervour, very ardently.

Wechselnote (*Ger.*)— A " changing note " (*q.v.*).

Wehmuth
Wehmüthigkeit } (*Ger.*)—Sadness, sorrow.

Wehmüt(h)ig (*Ger.*)—Sadly, sorrowfully.

Weich (*Ger.*) — (1) Soft, tender, mellow. (2) Minor.

Weight of wind.—The wind-pressure used in an organ.

Weinend (*Ger.*)—Weeping, wailing.

Weite Harmonie (*Ger.*)—Dispersed, or extended, harmony.

Well-tempered.—The system of tuning which divides the octave on a keyboard instrument into twelve approximately equal parts.

Wenig (*Ger.*)—Little. *Ein wenig schneller*, a little faster.

Werk (*Ger.*)—Work.

Wert(h) (*Ger.*)—Value.

Wesentlich (*Ger.*)—Essential (in the sense of a component part of a chord).

Whipping bow.—A form of bowing in violin playing, in which the bow is made to fall on the strings with attack, in order to accent sharply certain notes.

Whole note.—A semibreve.

Whole shift. — A term sometimes used to indicate, or describe, the third position on the violin.

Whole tone.—A major second.

Wie (*Ger.*)—As; as if; in the style of.

Wie aus der Ferne (*Ger.*)—As if from the distance.   .

Wieder (*Ger.*)—Again.

Wiederholung (*Ger.*) — Repetition. *Wiederholungszeichen*, sign of repetition.

Wiegend (*Ger.*)—Swaying, rocking.

Wiegenlied (*Ger.*)—A cradle song ; a lullaby.

Wie oben (*Ger.*)—As above.

Wild (*Ger.*)—Fierce, wild.

Wind band.—(1) A body of players on wind instruments. (2) The wind instruments in an orchestra ; also those who play them.

Wind-chest.—The receptacle for the wind in the organ and kindred instruments.

Wind-gauge. — An instrument for testing the wind‑pressure in an organ.

Wind instruments.—Musical instruments whose sounds are produced : (*a*) by the breath of the player (flute, clarinet, horn, etc.) ; (*b*) by means of bellows (organ, harmonium, etc.). The term is generally associated with the first of these groups.

Wind-trunk.—A tube of wood or metal, which serves to convey the wind in an organ from the bellows to the several sound-boards.

Wirbel (*Ger.*) — (1) The peg of a violin, etc. (2) The stopper of a closed organ pipe. (3) The roll of a drum.

Wispernd (*Ger.*)—Whispering.

Wolf. — The term applied to the harsh sound produced in certain chords on keyboard instruments, particularly the organ, when tuned on the unequal temperament system.

Wood-wind ⎱ (1) The flutes,
Wood-wind band ⎰ oboes, clarinets, bassoons, etc., in an orchestra. (2) The players on them.

Working-out.—A term synonymous with "thematic development."

Wrest.—An old name for a tuning hammer.

W u c h t i g (*Ger.*)—Weighty, ponderous, emphasised.

Würde, mit (*Ger.*)—With dignity.

Wurzel (*Ger.*)—Root.

Wüthend ⎱ (*Ger.*)—Furious(ly), fran-
Wüthig ⎰ tic(ally).

X.

Xylophone ⎱ A very ancient instru-
Xylorganum ⎰ ment, found principally in the various parts of Russia. It consisted of a series of flat pieces of wood, tuned to the scale, which were arranged on strips of straw, and struck with two small hammers. The tone produced was sweet, but weak.

Y.

Yodel ⎱ (*See* Jodler.)
Yodler ⎰

Z.

Zampogna (*It.*)—A bagpipe.

Zarabanda (*Sp.*)—(Saraband.)

Zart (*Ger.*) — Soft, delicate, tender. *Mit zarten Stimmen*, with soft-toned stops. *Sehr zart*, very soft.

Zartflöte (*Ger.*)—A delicate toned flute-stop on the organ, of 4 ft. pitch.

Zartheit, mit (*Ger.*)—With tenderness, delicacy.

Zärtlich (*Ger.*)—Tender(ly), soft(ly), delicate(ly).

Zeichen (*Ger.*)—A musical sign.

Zeitmass (*Ger.*)—Speed, time, measure. *Im ersten Zeitmass*, at the original speed.

Zeitmesser (*Ger.*)—A metronome.

Zelo, con ⎱ (*It.*)—In an ardent, ener-
Zeloso ⎰ getic style.

Zerstreut (*Ger.*) — Dispersed, extended. *Zerstreute Harmonie*, extended harmony.

Ziemlich (*Ger.*)—Rather, somewhat. *Ziemlich langsam*, rather slow.

Zierlich (*Ger.*)—Gracefully, elegantly.

Zimbalon.—An improved form of dulcimer, employed in Hungarian music.

Zingara, alla (*It.*)—In the gipsy style.

Zingaresca (*It.*)—A gipsy song or dance.

Zingarese, alla (*It.*)—In the gipsy style.

Zither (*Ger.*)—An instrument constructed of several strings (some 32 or more) stretched over a shallow wooden resonance box. Five of the strings are of metal, and lie over a fretted keyboard ; on these the melody is played. The other strings, of silk covered with silver wire, supply the bass and the accompaniment. The fingers and thumb of the left hand are used to " stop " the melody strings, which are set in vibration by means of a plectrum attached to the thumb of the right hand, the other fingers of this hand plucking the bass and accompaniment strings.

Zitternd (*Ger.*)—Trembling, tremulous, wavering.

Zögernd (*Ger.*)—Retarding the time.

Zoppo, -a (*It.*)—Halting. *Alla zoppa,* syncopated.

Zu (*Ger.*)—To, too. *Zu viel,* too much.

Zufällig (*Ger.*) — Accidental(ly). *Zufällige Versetzungszeichen,* accidentals.

Zug (*Ger.*)—(1) A draw-stop on an organ. (2) A pianoforte pedal. (3) The slide of a trombone.

Zugtrompete (*Ger.*)—Slide trumpet.

Zuklang (*Ger.*)—Unison, consonance.

Zunehmend (*Ger.*)—Working up, increasing the speed and tone.

Zunge (*Ger.*)—The tongue—(*a*) of a reed-pipe ; (*b*) of a reed in the harmonium.

Zurückgehalten (*Ger.*)—Slackening the speed, *ritardando.*

Zurückgehend (*Ger.*) — Returning to the original tempo after an *accelerando.*

Zurückhaltung (*Ger.*)—A retarding of the speed.

Zusammengesetzt (*Ger.*)—Compound. *Zusammengesetzte Taktart,* compound time.

Zusammenschlag (*Ger.*)—A crushed note, or *acciaccatura.*

Zwei (*Ger.*)—Two.

Zweichörig (*Ger.*) — (1) For two choruses (double-choir). (2) Having two strings to each note. *Ein zweichoriges Klavier,* a bichord pianoforte.

Zweifach (*Ger.*)—Twofold ; double. *Zweifacher Kontrapunkt,* double counterpoint. *Zweifache Intervalle,* a compound interval.

Zweifüssig (*Ger.*)—Of two feet—as applied to the pitch of organ pipes.

Zweigesang (*Ger.*)—A duet.

Zweihalbe Takt (*Ger.*)—2-2 time.

Zweihändig (*Ger.*)—For two hands.

Zweistimmig (*Ger.*)—For two voices, or for two parts.

Zweiter (*Ger.*)—A second part.

Zweites Mal (*Ger.*)—Second time.

Zweiunddreissigtel(note) (*Ger.*) — A demisemiquaver.

Zwerchflöte (*Ger.*) — The German flute, or *flauto traverso.*

Zwischenakt (*Ger.*)—An entr'acte.

Zwischenraum (*Ger.*) — (1) An interval. (2) The space between two lines of the staff.

Zwischensatz (*Ger.*)—An episode ; a transition from one subject or theme to another.

Zwischenspiel (*Ger.*)—An interlude.

Zymbel (*Ger.*)—(Cymbal.)

PART II.

A SELECTION OF ENGLISH TERMS AND WORDS

WITH THEIR EQUIVALENTS IN

ITALIAN, GERMAN, AND FRENCH.

NOTE.—*In the following section, whenever a blank space is found in one of the columns, it is to be inferred that the English word has no direct equivalent in the particular language shewn in that column. In such a case, the conclusion is to be drawn that the Italian term would be employed.*

A—Alt

A.

	Italian.	*German.*	*French.*
A (the note)	La	A	La
A flat (A♭)	La bemolle	As	La bémol
A double flat (A♭♭)	La doppio bemolle	A doppel B	La double bémol
A sharp (A♯)	La diesis	Ais	La dièse
A double sharp (Ax)	La doppio diesis	Aisis	La double dièse
Abbreviation	Abbreviatura	Abkurzung	Abréviation
Above	Sopra	Ober	Au-dessus
Abruptly	Brevemente	Abgerissen	Brusquement
Accelerating the speed	{ Accelerando / Stringendo	} Beschleunigend	{ En pressant / Pressez
Accent	Accento	{ Accent / Betonung	} Accent
Accented	Marcato	Markiert	Marqué
Accented part of a bar	} Tempo forte	Guter Taktt(h)eil	{ Bon temps de la / mesure / Temps fort
Accidental	Accidente	{ Versetzungszeichen / Zufällig	} Accident
Accompaniment	Accompagnamento	Begleitung	Accompagnement
Act	Atto	{ Akt / Aufzug	} Acte
Affectionately	Affettuoso	Mit Gefühl	Avec sentiment
Again	Ancora	Wieder	Bis
Agile	Sciolto	Beweglich	Agile
Agility, with	Agilità, con	Leichtigkeit, mit	Agilité, avec
Agitated	Agitato	{ Aufgeregt / Bewegt	} Agité
Air	Aria	Melodie	Mélodie
All (together)	Tutti	Alle zusammen	Tout ensemble
Alone	Solo	Allein	Seul
Also	Anche	Auch	Aussi
Alto clef	Chiave di contralto	Altschlüssel	Clef alto
Alto part	Contralto	Alt	Haute contre

109

	Italian.	*German.*	*French.*
Alto trombone	Alto trombone	Alt Posaune	Haute contre-trombone
Always	Sempre	Immer	Toujours
And	E, Ed	Und	Et
Animated	Animato / Risvegliato	Lebendig / Lebhaft	Animé
An octave higher	All' ottava	Eine Oktave höher	Une octave plus haut
An octave lower	All' ottava bassa	Eine Oktave tiefer	Une octave plus bas
Appropriate (speed)	Giusto	Richtiges Tempo	Juste
Ardently	Ardente / Fervente	Mit Wärme	Avec chaleur
Arrangement	Reduzione	Arrangement	Reduction
As	Come	Wie	Comme
As above	Come sopra	Wie oben	Comme dessus
As before	Come prima	Wie früher	Comme avant
As from a distance	Come da lontano	Wie aus der Ferne	Comme d'une
As if	Quasi	Gleichsam	Comme [distance
As written	Loco	Wie geschrieben	—
At pleasure	A piacere / Senza tempo rigore	Nach Belieben	À plaisir
At sight	A prima vista	Vom Blatte	À livre ouvert / À première vue
Attack instantly	Attacca subito	Sofort angreifen	Attaquez (tout de suite)
At the original speed	Tempo primo	Ursprüngliches Zeitmass	Mouvement original
Augmented	Aumentato	Erweitert / Ubermässig	Augmenté
Augmented(interval)	Eccedente	Vergrösstes Interval	Intervalle augmenté
Awakened	Risvegliato	Erwacht	Réveillé

B.

B (the note)	Si	H	Si
B flat (B♭)	Si bemolle	B	Si bémol
B double flat (B♭♭)	Si doppio bemolle	B doppel B	Si double bémol
B sharp (B♯)	Si diesis	His	Si dièse
Bagpipe	Cornamusa	Dudelsack	Cornemuse
Ballad	Ballata	Ballade	Ballade
Ballet	Balletto	Ballett	Ballet
Band	Banda	Kapelle	Orchestre
Bar	Misura	Takt	Mesure
Barcarolle	Barcarola	Auf dem Wasser / Barcarole	Barcarolle
Baritone	Baritono	Bariton	Bariton
Bar line	Linea	Taktstrich	Barre de mesure
Bass	Basso	Bass	Basse
Bass clef	Chiave di basso	Bass Schlüssel	Clef de basse
Bass, deep	Basso profondo	Tiefer Bass	Basse-contre
Bassoon	Fagotto	Fagott	Basson
Bass trombone	Trombone basso	Bass Posaune	Basse-Trombone
Beat	Battuta	Taktschlag	Battement de mesure
Begin at once	Attacca	Sofort angreifen	Attaquez tout de suite
Beginning, from the	Da capo	Vom Anfang	Du début
Bell	Campana	Glocke	Cloche
Bell, a small	Campanella	Glöckchen	Clochette
Below	Sotto	Unter	Sous

	Italian.	German.	French.
Binary	—	Zweit(h)eilig	Binaire
Bind (a tie)	Fascia	Bindebogen	Liaison
Body (of an instrument)	Corpo	Schallkasten	Coffre
Boisterous	Strepitoso	Geräuschvoll	Impétueu–x, -se
Bold(ly)	Ardito	Mut(h)ig	Hardiment
Boldness	Bravura	Bravour	Bravoure
Bow	Arco	Bogen	Archet
Bound	Legato	Gebunden	Lié
Brass instrument	Instrumento d'ottone	Blechinstrument	Instrument de cuivre
Bridge (of a bowed instrument)	Ponticello	Steg	Chevalet
Brilliant	Brillante	Glänzend	Brillant
Brisk(ly)	{ Vivente { Vivo	} Lebhaft	Vif, vive
Broadening out	Allargando	Breiteres Tempo	En élargissant
Broadly	Largamente	Breit	Largement
Broken chord	Accordo arpeggiato	Gebrochener Akkord	Accord brisé
Brusquely	Bruscamente	{ Barsch { Schroff	} Brusquement
Burlesque	Burlesco	Burlesk	Burlesque
But	Ma	Aber	Mais

C.

C (the note)	Do	C	Ut
C flat (C ♭)	Do bemolle	Ces	Ut bémol
C double flat (C ♭♭)	Do doppio bemolle	Ceses	Ut double bémol
C sharp (C ♯)	Do diesis	Cis	Ut dièse
C double sharp (C x)	Do doppio diesis	Cisis	Ut double dièse
Cadence	Cadenza	{ Kadenz { Schluss	} Cadence
Cadence, Imperfect	Cadenza Imperfetta	Halbschluss	Cadence Imparfaite
Cadence, Interrupted	{ Cadenza Sfuggita { Cadenza d'inganno	} Trugschluss	Cadence Interrompue
Cadence, Perfect	Cadenza Perfetta	Hauptschluss	Cadence Parfaite
Cadence, Plagal	Cadenza Plagale	Plagal Kadenz	Cadence Pleine
Calm	Calmato	Ruhig	Calme
Canon	Canone	Kanon	Canon
Canticle	Cantico	—	Cantique
Caprice	Capriccio	Grille	Caprice
Caressing	Lusingando	Schmeichelnd	Caressant
Certain	Alcuna	Einige	Quelque
Chamber music	Musica da camera	Kammermusik	Musique de chambre
Change	Muta	Wechseln	Mutation
Changing note	Nota cambiata	Wechselnote	Note d'appogiature
Cheerful	Gioviale	Lustig	Gai
Chest	Petto	Brust	Poitrine
Choir	Coro	Chor	Chœur
Chord	Accordo	Akkord	Accord
Chorister	Corista	Chorist	Choriste
Chorus	Coro	Chor	Chœur
Chorus part	Parte corale	Chor Stimme	Partie de chœur
Chromatic	Cromatico	Chromatisch	Chromatique
Church	Chiesa	Kirche	Église
Church style, in the	A cappella	Kirchenstil	—
Clarinet	Clarinetto	Klarinette	Clarinette
Clear(ly)	Distinto	Deutlich	Distinctement

	Italian.	German.	French.
Clef	Chiave	Schlüssel	Clé, Clef
C major	Do maggiore	C dur	Ut majeur
Coaxing (ly)	Accarezzevole	Überredend	Caressant
Comic	Buffo	Komisch	Comique
Comic opera	Opera buffa	Komische Oper	Opéra bouffe
Compass	Compasso	Kompass	Etendue
Complaining	{ Lamentando / Lagrimoso	} Klagend	Plaintivement
Composition	Composizione	Tonsatz	Composition
Compound time	Tempo composto	{ Zusammengesetzte / Taktart }	—
Concert	Concerto	Konzert	Concert
Concerto	Concerto	Concert	Concert
Conductor	Direttore	Kapellmeister	Chef d'orchestre
Conjunct (movement)	Congiunto	Schrittweise	Conjoint
Consecutive fifths	Quinte di moto retto	Parallel Quinten	Quintes consécutives
Consecutive octaves	Ottave di moto retto	Parallel Oktaven	Octaves consécutives
Consonance	Consonanza	Consonanz	Consonance
Continually	Sempre	Andauerend	Toujours
Contrary motion	Rovescio	Gegenbewegung	Mouvement contraire
Convenient speed	Comodo	Gemächlich	—
Cornet	Cornetto	Kornett	Cornet à pistons
Counterpoint	Contrappunto	Kontrapunkt	Contrepoint
Counterpoint, double	Doppio contrappunto	Doppelter Kontrapunkt	Double contrepoint
Counter subject	Contra-soggetto	{ Gegenstimme / Gegensatz }	Contre-sujet
Cradle song	Ninna-nanna	Wiegenlied	Berceuse
Crook	Pezzo di reversa	Krummbogen	Corps de rechange
Crossing hands	Volteggiando	{ Hand übersetzen / Übergreifend }	Croiser les mains
Crotchet	Nota semiminima	Viertelnote	Noire
Crotchet rest	Pausa di semiminima	Virtelpause	Soupir
Crushed note	Acciaccatura	Zusammenschlag	Pincé étouffé
C sharp major	Do diesis maggiore	Cis dur	Ut dièse majeur
C sharp minor	Do diesis minore	Cis moll	Ut dièse mineur
Cymbals	Piatti	Becken	Cymbales

D.

D (the note)	Re	D	Ré
D flat (D♭)	Re bemolle	Des	Ré bémol
D double flat (D♭♭)	Re doppio bemolle	Deses	Ré double bémol
D sharp (D♯)	Re diesis	Dis	Ré dièse
D double sharp (D x)	Re doppio diesis	Disis	Ré double dièse
Damped	Sordo	Gedämpft	Cuivré
Damper	Sordina (commonly, but erroneously, written sordino)	Dämpfer	Étouffoir
Dance	{ Ballo / Danza }	Tanz	Danse
Dash (ing)	Bravura	Mit Bravour	Élan, avec
Decidedly	Deciso	Bestimmt	Décidé
Declamatory	Declamato	Deklamatorisch	Déclamatoire
Decreasing in speed	Ritardando	Abnehmendes Tempo	En retenant
Decreasing in tone	Diminuendo	Abnehmender Ton	{ En diminuant / En s'affaiblissant }

	Italian.	*German.*	*French.*
Deep	Profondo	Tief	Ton bas
Degree	Grado	{ Grad { Stufe	} Degré
Degrees, by (gradually)	} Poco a poco	{ Allmählich { Allmählig	{ Peu à peu { Graduellement
Degrees, by (stepwise)	} Di grado	Schrittweise	Degré conjoint
Deliberately	Deliberato	Entschlossen	Délibérément
Delicate(ly)	{ Delicato { Tenerezza, con	} Zart	Avec délicatesse
Demisemiquaver	Semibiscroma	Zweiunddreis- sigstel(note)	Triple croche
Demisemiquaver rest	Pausa di biscroma	Zweiunddreis- sigstel Pause	Demi-quart de soupir
Design	Forma	Entwurf	{ Dessin { Facture
Detached	Staccato	Abgestossen	Détaché
Development (thematic)	Sviluppo	Durchführung	Développement
Devout(ly)	Religioso	Religiös	Religieusement
D flat major	Re bemolle maggiore	Des dur	Ré bémol majeur
Dignity, with	Pomposo	Mit Würde	Digne
Diminished	Diminuito	Vermindert	Diminué
Discord **Dissonance**	} Dissonanza	Dissonanz	Dissonance
Distinct(ly)	Distinto	{ Deutlich { Klar	} Distinctement
Divided	Divisi	Get(h)eilt	Divisé
Doleful	{ Dolente { Doloroso	} Schmerzvoll	Douloureu-x, -se
Dominant	Quinta	Dominante	Dominante
Dot, a	Punto	Punkt	Point
Dotted	Puntato	Punktirt	Pointé
Double	Doppio	Doppel	Double
Double-bar	Doppia linea	Doppeltaktstrich	Double-barre
Double bass	Contra basso	Kontrabass	Contre-basse
Double flat	Doppio bemolle	Doppel-B	Double bémol
Double sharp	Doppio diesis	Doppel Kreuz	Double dièse
Double the speed, at	Doppio movimento	Doppelte Geschwindigkeit	—
Down beat	Il movimento accentato della battuta	Niederschlag	Temps frappé
Down bow	Arco in giù	{ Herabstrich { Herunterstrich	} Tiré
Dragging, without	Senza rallentare	Nicht schleppend	Sans traîner
Dramatic	Drammatico	Dramatisch	Dramatique
Drawing together (getting faster)	Stringendo	Beschleunigtes Tempo	En pressant
Drum (Bass)	Gran cassa	Grosse Trommel	Grosse caisse
Drum (Kettle)	Timpano	Pauke	Timbale
Drum (Side)	Tamburo	Kleine Trommel	Tambour
Duet	Duetto	Duett	Duo
Duple time	Tempo semplice in 2 movementi	Gerade Takt(art)	À deux temps
Dying away	{ Mancando { Morendo { Perdendosi { Smorzando	} Ersterbend	En se perdant

	Italian.	*German.*	*French.*
	E.		
E (the note)	Mi	E	Mi
E flat (E♭)	Mi bemolle	Es	Mi bémol
E double flat (E♭♭)	Mi doppio bemolle	Eses	Mi double bémol
E sharp (E♯)	Mi diesis	Eis	Mi dièse
E double sharp (Ex)	Mi doppio diesis	Eisis	Mi double dièse
Easily	Con agevolezza / Facilmente	Leicht	Facilement
Easy	Agevole / Facile	Leicht	Facile
Echo	Eco	Echo	Echo
Elegant(ly)	Elegante / Con eleganza	Elegant	Élégant
Elegy	Elegia	Elegie	Élégie
Emotion, with	Affettuoso / Con affetto	Empfindung, mit	Avec émotion
Emphasis	Enfasi	Nachdruck	Emphase
Emphasis, with	Con enfasi	Mit Nachdruck	Avec emphase
End, the	Fine	Ende	Fin
Energy, with	Energia, con / Energico	Energisch	Avec énergie
English horn	Corno Inglese	Englisches Horn	Cor Anglais
Enharmonic	Enarmonico	Enharmonisch	Enharmonique
Enlivening	Animando / Animandosi	Belebend	En animant
Essential note	Nota principale	Hauptnote	Note intégrante / Note réelle
Exact	Preciso	Genau	Juste
Exercise (a study)	Esercizio	Übung	Étude
Expression, with	Affettuoso / Con espressione	Mit Gefühl	Expressi-f, -ve
Extemporise, to	Improvvisare	Extemporieren	Improviser
Extremely	Estremamente	Sehr	Extrêmement

		F.		
F (the note)	Fa	F	Fa
F flat (F♭)	Fa bemolle	Fes	Fa bémol
F double flat (F♭♭)	Fa doppio bemolle	Feses	Fa double bémol
F sharp (F♯)	Fa diesis	Fis	Fa dièse
F double sharp (Fx)	Fa doppio diesis	Fisis	Fa double dièse
False	Falso	Falsch	Faux, fausse
False relation	Falsa relazione	Falsche Verbindung / Querstand	Fausse relation
Fanciful	Capriccioso / Fantastico	Kapriciös / Fantastisch	Capriceu-x, -se / Fantastique
Fantasy	Fantasia	Phantasie	Fantaisie
Fast	Allegro	Rasch / Schnell	Vite
Faster	Più allegro / Più mosso	Schneller	Plus vite
Faster by degrees	Accelerando / Stretto / Stringendo	Allmählich schneller	En animant peu à peu
Fast, extremely	Allegro molto / Presto / Prestissimo	Sehr schnell	Très vite

	Italian.	*German.*	*French.*
Faster, somewhat	Poco più mosso	Etwas schneller	Un peu animé
Feeling, with	Con sentimento	Mit Gefühl	Avec sentiment
Fervent(ly)	{ Ardente { Fervente	} Heftig	Avec ferveur
Fierce	{ Feroce { Fiero	} Wild	Furieu-x, -se
Fiery	Con fuoco	Feurig	Ardent
Fife, a	Piffero	Querpfeife	Fifre
Fifth, a	Quinta	Quinte	Quinte
Figure	Figura	Figur	Figure
Figured	Numerato	Beziffert	Chiffré
Figured bass	Basso numerato	Bezifferter Bass	Basse chiffrée
Finger	Dito	Finger	Doigt
Fingering	Diteggiatura	Fingersatz	Doigter
First	Primo	Erst	Premier, première
First part	Primo	Erster Satz	Première partie
First sight, at	A prima vista	Vom Blatte	A première vue
First time	Prima volta	Erstes Mal	Première fois
Flat	Bemolle	Es	Bémol
Flourish of trumpets	Fanfara	Fanfare Trompeten	Fanfare
Fluent	Sciolto	Geläufig	Fácile
Flute	Flauto	Flöte	Flûte
Flute, cross	Flauto traverso	Traverseflöte	Flûte traversière
Flute, octave	Flauto piccolo	Oktavflöte	Petite flûte
Flying	Volante	Flüchtig	Volant
Following	Seguente	Folgend	Suivant
Force, with	Con forza	Mit Kraft	Avec force
Forcing the tone	{ Sforzando { Forzato	} Verstärkt	—
Four	Quattro	Vier	Quatre
Four hands, for	A quattro mani	Vierhändig	A quatre mains
Fourth (interval)	Quarta	Quarte	Quarte
Four voices, for	A quattro voci	Für vier Stimmen	A quatre voix
Free(ly)	Sciolto	Frei	Librement
Fugue	Fuga	Fuge	Fugue
Full	Pieno	Voll	Plein
Full power	Tutta forza	Volle Kraft	Plein jeu
Full score	Partitura	Partitur	Partition
Fundamental	Fondamentale	Grund	Fondamentale
Fundamental bass	Fondamento	Grundbass	Basse fondamentale
Funeral march	Marcia funebre	Trauermarsch	Marche funèbre

G.

	Italian.	*German.*	*French.*
G (the note)	Sol	G	Sol
G flat (G ♭)	Sol bemolle	Ges	Sol bémol
G double flat (G ♭♭)	Sol doppio bemolle	Geses	Sol double bémol
G sharp (G ♯)	Sol diesis	Gis	Sol dièse
G double sharp (G x)	Sol doppio diesis	Gisis	Sol double dièse
Gaily	Gajamente	Fröhlich	Gaiement
Gavot	Gavotta	Gavotte	Gavotte
Gay	{ Gajo { Giojoso	} Fröhlich	Gai
Generator	Fondamentale	Grundton	Générateur
Gently	Soave	Sanft	{ Doucement { Doux

	Italian.	*German.*	*French.*
Gliding	Glissando	Gleitend	Glissant
Gliding (vocal)	Portamento / Portando / Portare la voce	Gleitend	Port de voix / Porter la voix
Go on at once	Attacca / Attacca subito	Sofort fortsetzen	Attaquez
Gracefully	Grazioso / Con grazia	Anmut(h)svoll / Zierlich	Graceiusement
Grace note	Abbellimento	Verzierung	Ornement / Agrément
Gradually	Poco a poco	Allmälig	Peu à peu
Grandly	Grandioso / Nobilmente	Grossartig	Grandement
Gravely	Grave / Gravemente	Gewichtig	Gravement
Great	Grosso	Gross	Grosse
Great Organ	Principale	Haupt Manual	Grand-orgue
Grief, with	Con dolore / Con duolo	Mit Schmerz	Avec douleur
Grotesque(ly)	Burlesco	Grotesk	Grotesque
Ground bass	Basso ostinato	Grundbass	Basse contrainte
Guitar	Chitarra	Guitarre	Guitare

H.

Half	Mezzo	Halb	Demi
Half cadence	Cadenza imperfetta	Halbschluss	Cadence imparfaite
Half loud	Mezzo forte	Halbstark	—
Hammered	Martellato	Gehämmert	Martelé
Hand	Mano	Hand	Main
Harmonic	Armonica	Harmonisch	Harmonique
Harmonics	Suoni armonici	Übertöne	Sous harmoniques
Harmonious	Armonioso	Harmonisch	Harmonieu-x, -se
Harmony	Armonia	Harmonie	Harmonie
Harp	Arpa	Harfe	Harpe
Harpsichord	Clavicembalo	Kielflügel	Clavecin
Hastening the time	Accelerando / Stringendo / Affrettando / Stretto	Drängend / Treibend	En pressant / Pressez
Heavy, heavily	Pesante	Gewichtig / Schwer	Lourd
Held	Tenuto	Ausgehalten	Tenu
Held back	Ritenuto	Zurückgehalten	Retenu
Heroic	Eroico	Heroisch	Héroïque
High	Alta	Hoch	Haut
High, extremely	Altissimo	Ausserordentlich hoch	Très élevé
Highest part	Parte superiore	Höchste Stimme	Dessus
Holding back the speed	Ritardando / Ritenuto / Slentando	Verweilend	En retenant
Human voice	Voce umana	Menschliche Stimme	Voix humaine
Humour, with	Con umore	Mit Humor	Capricieu-x, -se / Fantastique
Hunting horn	Corno da caccia	Jagdhorn	Cor de chasse
Hurried(ly)	In fretta	Eilig	Pressé

	Italian.	*German.*	*French.*

I.

Idyl	Idillio	Idylle	Idylle
Imitation	Imitazione	Nachahmung	Imitation
Impassioned	{ Appassionato { Con abbandono	Leidenschaftlich	{ Passionné { Avec passion
Imperfect cadence	Cadence Imperfetta	{ Halbschluss { Unvollkommene { Schluss	Cadence Imparfaite
Impetuous(ly)	Impetuoso	Heftig	{ Impétueu-x, -se { Impétueusement
Improvise, to	Improvvisare	Improvisieren	Improviser
Increasing the speed	{ Accelerando { Affrettando { Incalzando { Stringendo	{ Drängend { Tempo beschleunigen	{ En pressant { En serrant
Increasing the tone	Crescendo	Anschwellend	En augmentant
In haste	Con fretta	In Eile	Très pressé
In strict time	In tempo	Abgemessen	En mesure
Instrument, an	Instrumento	Instrument	Instrument
Interlude	Entrata	Zwischenspiel	Intermède
Interrupted cadence	{ Cadenza finta { Cadenza d'inganno	{ Unterbrochener { Schluss	{ Cadence trompeuse { Cadence interrompue
Interval	Intervallo	{ Intervall { Zwischenraum	Intervalle
In the style of	Alla	Im Stil einer	—
In time	A tempo	Im Zeitmass	Au mouvement
Introduction	Introduzione	Einleitung	Entrée
Inversion	Rivolto	Umkehrung	Renversement

J.

Jesting(ly)	{ Burlando { Burlesco { Scherzando	Scherzhaft	En badinant
Jocose(ly)	{ Giocoso { Giochevole	Freudig	En badinant
Joyous(ly)	Giojoso	Fröhlich	{ Joyeu-x, -se { Joyeusement

K.

Kettle drum	Timpano	Pauke	Timbale
Key (Tonality)	Tonalita	Tonart	Tonalité
Key (a finger lever)	Tasto	Taste	Touche
Keyboard	Tastiera	{ Klavier { Klaviatur { Tastatur	Clavier
Keynote	Tonica	Tonica	Tonique

L.

Languid(ly)	Languido	Müde	Langoureusement
Languishing	Languendo	Schmachtend	Languissant
Leader, a	Violino di spalla	Leiter	Chef d'attaque
Leading note	Nota sensibile	Leitton	Note sensible
Left hand	Mano sinistra	Linke Hand	Main gauche
Leger line	Linea aggiunto	Hilfslinie	Ligne ajoutée
Less	Meno	Weniger	Moins
Light(ly)	Leggiero	Leicht	Lég-er, -ère
Like (in the same manner)	Simile	Wie	Même

	Italian.	*German.*	*French.*
Line	Linea	Linie	Ligne
Little, a	Poco	Ein wenig	Un peu
Little, a very	Pochettino	Ein klein wenig	Très peu
Little by litttle	Poco a poco	{ Allmählich { Nach und nach	Peu à peu
Lively	{ Vivo { Vivace	} Frisch	Vif, vive
Lively, very	Vivacissimo	Sehr frisch	Très vif
Lofty	{ Elevato { Nobile	} Erhaben	Élevé
Long	Lunga	Lange	Long, longue
Longingly	Con desiderio	Verlangend	Avec ardeur
Loud	Forte	{ Laut { Stark	} Haut
Louder	Più forte	Stärker	Plus haut
Louder by degrees	{ Crescendo { Più forte poco a { poco	} Anschwellend	{ Enfler { Plus haut { Plus fort
Loud, very	Fortissimo	Sehr stark	Très fort
Lovingly	{ Amorevolo { Amoroso	} Liebend	Affectueusement
Low	Basso, -a	Tief	Basse
Lute	Liuto	Laute	Luth
Lullaby	Ninna-nanna	Wiegenlied	Berceuse

M.

Majestically	Maestoso	Majestätisch	Majestueusement
Major	Maggiore	Dur	Majeur
Major key	Tono maggiore	Dur Tonart	Ton majeur
Major scale	Tono maggiore	Dur Tonleiter	Gamme majeur
Manner	Maniera	Manier	Manière
March, a	Marcia	Marsch	Marche
Marked	Marcato	Markiert	Marqué
Martial	Marziale	Kriegerisch	{ Guerrier { Martial
Master, a	Maestro	Meister	Maître
Mazurka	Mazurka	Masurka	Mazourka
Measure	Misura	Takt	Mesure
Mediant	Mediante	Mediante	Médiante
Melody	Melodia	Melodie	{ Chant { Mélodie
Merry	Giocoso	Lustig	Gai
Metronome	Metronomo	Metronom	Métronome
Minim	Minima	Halbe Note	{ Blanche { Minime
Minim rest	Pausa della minima	Halbe Pause	Demi pause
Minor	Minore	Moll	Mineur
Minor key	Tono minore	Moll Tonart	Ton mineur
Minor scale	Scala minore	Moll Tonleiter	Gamme mineur
Minuet	Menuetto	Menuett	Menuet
Mode	Modo	Tonart	Mode
Moderately fast	Moderato	{ Gemässigt { Mässig schnell	} Modéré
Moderately loud	Mezzo forte	Ein wenig stark	{ Mi fort { Un peu haut
Modulate, to	Modulare	Modulieren	Moduler
Mordent (lower) ♦	Mordente	Mordent	Pincé
Mordent (upper) ♦	Mordente	Pralltriller	Pincé renversé

	Italian.	*German.*	*French.*
More	Più	Mehr	Plus
Motet	Mottetto	Motette	Motet
Motion	Moto	Bewegung	Mouvement
Motion, contrary	Moto contrario	Gegenbewegung	Mouvement contraire
Motion, oblique	Moto obblique	Seitenbewegung	Mouvement oblique
Motion, similar	Moto retto	Gleichebewegung	{ Mouvement semblable Mouvement similaire Mouvement pareil
Motive	Motivo	Motiv	Motif
Mournful	Lamentoso	Klagend	Lugubre
Mouth	Bocca	Mund	Bouche
Mouthpiece (Clarinet, etc.)	Imboccatura	Schnabel	Bec
Mouthpiece (Horn, etc.)	Imboccatura	Mundstück	Embouchure
Movement	Movimento	{ Satz Bewegung	} Mouvement
Much	Molto	Viel	Beaucoup
Muffled	Coperto	Gedämpft	Assourdi
Mute	Sordina (commonly but erroneously written *sordino*)	Dämpfer	Sourdine
Mutes, without	Senza sordine (commonly but erroneously written *sordini*)	Ohne Dämpfer	Ôtez les sourdines
Mysterious(ly)	Misterioso	Mysteriös	Mystérieu-x, -se

N.

Natural (♮)	Bequadro	{ Auflösungszeichen Quadrat	{ Bécarre Béquarre
Nearly	Quasi	{ Beinahe Wie	} Presque
Neck (of the violin, etc.)	Manico	Hals	Manche
Night piece, a	Notturno	Nachtstück	Nocturne
Nimble (fluent)	Sciolto	Flüchtig	{ Agile Léger, –ère
Ninth (interval of the)	Nona	None	Neuvième
Noble	Nobile	Vornehm	Noble
Not	Non	Nicht	Non
Note	Nota	Note	Note
Note, accented	Nota accentata	Betonte Note	{ Note frappée Note accentuée
Note, changing	Nota cambiata	Wechselnote	Note changeante
Note, essential	Nota principale	Wesentliche Note	{ Note intégrante Note réele
Note, grace	Abbellimento	Verzierung	Agrément
Note, leading	{ Nota sensibile Nota caratteristica	} Leitton	Note sensible
Note, passing	Nota di passaggio	{ Durchgangston Übergangsnote	} Note de passage
Note, unaccented	Nota inaccentato	Unbetonte Note	Note non accentuée
Nut (of the fingerboard of a stringed instrument)	Capotasto	Sattel	Sillet

	Italian.	*German.*	*French.*

O.

	Italian.	*German.*	*French.*
Obligato	Obbligato	Obligat	Obligé
Oblique motion	Moto obbliquo	Seitenbewegung	Mouvement oblique
Oboe (or Hautboy)	Oboe	Hoboe	Hautbois
Octave	Ottava	Oktave	Octave
Octave higher	Ottava alta	Oktave höher	Octave plus haut
Octave lower	Ottava bassa	Oktave niedriger	Octave plus bas
Octet	Ottetto	Oktett	Octuor
Of	Di	Von	De
On, upon	Sul	Auf	Sur
Once	Una volta	Einmal	Une fois
One	Uno, -a	Ein	Un, une
Open	Aperto, -a	Offen	Vide
Opera	Opera	Oper	Opéra
Ophicleide	Oficleide	Ophicleide	Basse d'harmonie
Or	Ossia	Oder	Ou
Orchestra	Orchestra	Orchester	Orchestre
Organ	Organo	Orgel	Orgue
Organ-stop	Registro	Registerzug	{ Jeu d'orgue { Registre [début
Original speed	Tempo primo	Erster Zeitmass	Mouvement du
Ornament, an	Ornamento	Verzierung	Ornement
Over	Sopra	Ober	Sur
Overture	Sinfonia	Ouvertüre	Ouverture

P.

	Italian.	*German.*	*French.*
Parallel motion (See also Motion, similar)	Moto retto	Parallelbewegung	Mouvement pareil
Part, a	Parte	Stimme	Partie
Passing note	Nota di passaggio	{ Durchgangston { Übergangsnote	} Note de passage
Passionate(ly)	{ Appassionato { Con passione { Passionata	} Leidenschaftlich	Passionné
Pastoral	Pastorale	Hirtenlied	Pastorale
Pathetic	Patetico	Pathetisch	Pathétique
Pause, a	{ Corona { Fermata { Pausa	} Pause	{ Point d'arrêt { Point d'orgue { Point de repos
Pause, a long	{ Lunga pausa { Punto coronato	} Lange Pause	Longue pause
Pedal	Pedale	Pedal	Pédale
Pedal keyboard	Pedaliera	Pedal Klaviatur	Clavier des pédales
Peg (of violin, etc.)	Bischero	Wirbel	Cheville

Percussion,
  instruments of
	Instrumenti di
	  percussione
		Schlaginstrumente	Instruments à
			      percussion

Perfect	Perfetto, -a	Rein	Parfait
Perfect cadence	Cadenza perfetta	Hauptschluss	Cadence parfaite
Perpetual	Perpetuo	Dauernd	{ Perpétuel { Continuel
Phrase	Frase	Phrase	Phrase
Pianoforte	{ Piano { Pianoforte	} Klavier	Piano
Piccolo	{ Flauto piccolo { Ottavino	{ Oktave-Flöte { Piccolo	} Petite-flûte

	Italian.	*German.*	*French.*
Piece, a	Pezzo	Stück	Pièce, morceau
Placidly	Placido	Ruhig	Tranquillement
Plaintively	Piangendo	Schmerzlich	Plaintivement
Play, to	Sonare	Spielen	Jouer
Player, a	Sonatore	Spieler	Exécutant
Playfully	{ Scherzando { Scherzoso	} Spasshaft	En badinant
Pleasantly	Piacevole	Vergnügt	Agréablement
Pleasure, at	A piacere	Nach Wunsch	{ A plaisir { A volonté
Plucked	Pizzicato	Gepflückt	Pincé
Point (of a bow)	Punta d'arco	Spitze	Pointe
Pompous	Pomposo	Prächtig	Pompeu-x, -se
Position	Posizione	Lage	Position
Possible	Possibile	Möglich	Possible
Powerful	Robusto	Mächtig	Fort
Prayer	Preghiera	Gebet	{ Prière { Supplication
Precise	Preciso	Präcis	Précis
Prelude	Preludio	Vorspiel	Entrée
Preparation	Preparazione	Vorbereitung	Préparation
Pressing on the speed	{ Accelerando { Affrettando { Stretto { Stringendo	} Drängend	{ En pressant { Pressez
Previous	Precedente	Vorhergehend	{ Antérieur { Précédent
Principal theme	Tema principale	Hauptsatz	Thème principal
Prominently	Pronunziato	Hervorragend	En dehors
Psalm	Salmo	Psalm	Psaume

Q.

Quadruplet	Quartina	Quartole	Quadruple
Quality	{ Qualita { Timbro	} Tonfarbe	Timbre
Quartet	Quartetto	Quartett	Quatuor
Quaver	Croma	Achtel(note)	Croche
Quaver rest	{ Pausa della croma { Pausa della mezzo- { quarto	} Achtel-Pause	Soupir de croche
Quick(ly)	Allegro	{ Schnell { Hastig	} Vite
Quicker	{ Più allegro { Più mosso	} Schneller	Plus vite
Quietly	Quieto	Ruhig	Tranquillement
Quintet	Quintetto	Quintett	Quintuor

R.

Rapid(ly)	{ Rapido { Voloce	{ Rasch { Schnell	} Rapide
Rapid(ly), very	Velocissimo	Sehr rasch	Très rapide
Rather (a little)	Poco	Etwas	Un peu
Recitative	Recitativo	Recitativ	Récitatif
Reed stop	Cannello	Rohrwerk	Jeu d'anche

	Italian.	German.	French.
Rehearsal	Prova	Probe	Répétition
Reinforcing the tone	{ Rinforzando { Rinforzato	} Ton gesteigert	Plus fort
Relative key	Tono relativo	Parallel Tonart	Mode relatif
Religiously	Religioso	Religiös	Religieusement
Repeat	{ Replica { Ripresa	} Wiederholung	Reprise
Repeat (sign of)	Replica	Wiederholungszeichen	Bâton de reprise
Repetition	Repetizione	Wiederholung	Répétition,reprise
Resolute	Risoluto	Resolut	Résolu
Rest	{ Pausa { Silenzio	} Pause	{ Pause { Silence
Restless	Inquieto	Ruhelos	Agité
Resume the speed	A tempo	Erste Bewegung	Reprendre le mouvement
Retarding the speed	Ritardando	Verweilend	En retenant
Reversed (inverted)	Riverso	Umgekehrt	Renversé
Rhapsody	Rapsodia	Rhapsodie	Rhapsodie
Rhythm	Ritmo	Rhythmus	Rythme
Right hand	Mano destra	Rechte Hand	Main droite
Robbed time	Rubato	—	—
Roll (of a drum)	Rollo	Wirbel	Roulement
Romance	Romanza	Romanze	Romance
Rondo	Rondo	Rondo	Rondeau
Root	Basso fondamentale	{ Ursprung { Wurzel	} Ton générateur
Rustic	Buccolico	Ländlich	Bucolique

S.

Sad(ly)	{ Dolente { Doloroso { Mesto	Schwermüt(h)ig Traurig Wehmüt(h)ig	} Triste
Same, the	L'istesso	Dasselbe	Même
Scale	Scala	Tonleiter	{ Échelle { Gamme
Scene	Scena	Auftritt	Scène
School of Music	Conservatorio	Musikschule	Conservatoire
Score	Partitura	Partitur	Partition
Second, a	Seconda	Sekunde	Seconde
Second time	Seconda volta	Zweites Mal	Deuxième fois
Sedately	Posato	Gemessen	Posément
Semibreve	Semibreve	Taktnote	Ronde
Semi-demisemi-quaver	Semi biscroma	Vierundsechzigstel-note	Quadruple-croche
Semiquaver	Semicroma	Sech(s)zehntelnote	Double-croche
Semitone	Semituono	Halbton	Demi-ton
Septet	Settetto	Septett	Septuor
Sequence	Sequenza	Sequenz	Marche harmonique
Serenade	Serenata	Ständchen	Sérénade
Serious	Serioso	Ernst	Sérieu-x, -se
Set of pieces, a	Partita	Partie	Suite
Seventh(interval of a)	Settima	Septime	Septième
Seventh (chord of the)	Accordo di settina	Septimenakkord	L'accord de septième
Sextet	Sestetto	Sextett	Sextuor
Shake, a	Trillo	Triller	Trille
Shake (transient)	Trillo	Pralltriller	Cadence

	Italian.	German.	French.
Sharp (♯)	Diesis	Kreuz	Dièse
Short	Corta	Kurz	Court / Sec
Short grace note (a)	Acciaccatura	Zusammenschlag	Pincé étouffé
Sighing	Sospirando	Seufzend	Soupirant
Sign	Segno	Zeichen	Signe
Signature	Chiave	Vorzeichnung	Armure de la clef
Sign, from the	Dal segno	Von dem Zeichen	—
Silent, keep	Tace	Ruhig verhalten	Gardez le silence
Similar	Simile	Ähnlich	Semblable / Similaire
Similar motion	Moto retto	Geradebewegung	Mouvement semblable / Mouvement similaire
Simple	Semplice	Einfach	Simple
Sing, to	Cantare	Singen	Chanter
Singer, a female	Cantatrice	Sängerin	Chanteuse
Singer, a male	Cantatore	Sänger	Chanteur
Singing exercise	Solfeggio	Singübung	Solfège
Singing style, in a, or with a singing tone	Cantabile / Cantando	Singend	Touche mélodieuse
Sixth, the interval of a	Sesta	Sexte	Sixte
Skip	Salto	Sprung	Saut
Sliding	Glissando	Gleitend	Glissant
Slow	Adagio / Grave / Largo / Lento	Langsam	Lent
Slower	Meno mosso / Piu lento	Langsamer	Plus lent / Moins vite
Slower by degrees	Rallentando / Ritardando	Zurückhaltend	En retenant
Slow, rather	Andante	Etwas langsam	Un peu lent
Slur	Legatura	Legatobogen	Coulé
Slurred	Legato	Gebunden	Lié
Small	Piccolo	Klein	Petit, -e
Smooth(ly)	Legato	Gebunden	Très égal
Softer	Meno forte / Piu piano	Schwächer	Plus doux
Softer by degrees	Meno forte, poco a poco	Allmählich schwächer	Graduellement plus doux
Softly	Piano	Leise / Zart	Doucement / Doux
Softly, very	Pianissimo	Sehr zart	Très doux
Soft pedal	Una corda	Mit Verschiebung	Céleste / Petite pédale / Pédale douce
Soft pedal, release of	Tre corde / Tutte le corde	Ohne Verschiebung	—
Solemn	Solenne	Feierlich	Solennel, -le
Solo player, a	Solista	Solospieler	Soloiste
Solo singer, a	Cantante solista	Solosänger	Chanteur soloiste
Somewhat	Poco	Ziemlich	Un peu
So much, not	Non tanto	Gemässigt	Pas tant
Sonata	Sonata	Sonate	Sonate
Sonata, Chamber	Sonata da camera	Kammer Sonate	—
Sonata, Church	Sonata da Chiesa	Kirchen Sonate	—

	Italian.	*German.*	*French.*
Song	Canzona	Lied	Chanson / Chant
Sonorous	Sonore	Kligend	Sonore
Soprano	Soprano	Sopran	Dessus / Soprano
Soprano, first	Primo soprano	Erster Sopran	Première Soprano
Soprano, second	Secundo soprano	Zweiter Sopran	Deuxième Soprano
Sorrowfully	Dolente / Doloroso / Mesto	Leidvoll / Schmerzlich	Triste
Soul, with	Con anima	Mit Gefühl	Avec âme
Sound	Suono	Schall	Son
Soundboard	Tavola armonica	Resonanzboden	Table d'harmonie
Sound-post	Anima	Stimmstock	Âme
Space	Spazio	Zwischenraum	Espace
Sparkling	Brillante	Glänzend	Étincelant
Speed	Tempo	Zeitmass	Mouvement
Spinet	Spinetta	Spinett	Épinette
Spirited	Con spirito / Spiritoso	Lebhaft	Animé
Sportive (*see* PLAYFUL).			
Staccato (*see* DETACHED).			
Staff (or Stave)	Rigo / Sistema	Liniensystem	Portée
Still	Ancora	Noch	Encore
Stop (on an organ)	Registro	Registerzug	Registre
Strict time, in	A rigore di tempo / Tempo rigoroso	Streng im Tempo	Exactement
String	Corda	Saite	Corde
Stringed-instruments	Instrumenti da corda / Stromenti da corda	Streich-instrumente	Instruments à cordes
String, open	Corda vuota	Offene Saite	Corde à jour / Corde á vide
Strong	Robusto	Stark	Fort
Study, a	Studio	Studie	Étude
Style	Genere	Stil	Manière
Style of, in the	Alla	Wie	A la
Sub-dominant	La quarta	Unterdominante	Quarte du ton
Subject	Soggetto	Motiv / Satz	Sujet
Sub-mediant	Sesta	Untermediante	Sus-dominant
Suddenly	Subito	Plötzlich	Subitement
Supertonic	La seconda	Überton	Su-tonique
Suspension	Ritardo	Vorhalt	Suspension
Sustained	Sostenuto	Gehalten	Soutenu
Sweet(ly)	Dolce / Soave	Süss	Doux, douce
Swift(ly)	Veloce / Volante	Eilig	Rapidement
Symphony	Sinfonia	Symphonie	Symphonie
Syncopation	Sincope	Synkope	Syncope

T.

	Italian.	*German.*	*French.*
Tambourine	Tamburino	Tambourin	Tambourin basque
Tearful(ly)	Piangendo	Traurig	Triste
Temperament	Temperamento	Temperatur	Tempérament
Tempestuous(ly)	Tempetuoso	Stürmisch	Orageu-x, -se

	Italian.	*German.*	*French.*
Tenderly	{ Amorevole { Con tenerezza	} Zärtlich	Tendrement
Tenor clef	Chiave di tenore	Tenor Schlüssel	Clef de Ténor
Tenor singer	Tenore	Tenor	Ténor
Ternary	Ternario	Dreit(h)eilig	Ternaire
Theme	Tema	Thema	Thème
Third (the interval of a)	Terza	Terz	Tierce
Three	Tre	Drei	Trois
Tie	Legatura	Bindebogen	Liaison
Time	Tempo	Takt	Mesure
Time (speed) as before	Tempo primo	Erste Bewegung	Mouvement précédent
Time, duple	Tempo binario	Gerade Takt(art)	Double temps
Time, first	Prima volta	Erstes Mal	Première fois
Time, in	A tempo	Taktmässig	Au mouvement
Time, second	Secunda volta	Zweites Mal	Deuzième fois
Time, the same	L'istesso tempo	Dasselbe Tempo	Même mouvement
Tonality	Tonalitá	Tonalität	Tonalité
Tone (quality)	Tono	Ton	{ Son { Ton
Tone (an interval)	Tuono	Ton	Ton
Too much	Troppo	Zu viel	Trop
Touch	Tasto	Anschlag	Toucher
Tranquil(ly)	Tranquillo	Ruhig	Tranquil, -le
Transition	Transizione	Übergang	Transition
Transpose, to	Transportare	Transponiren	Transposer
Trembling	Tremolo	Tremolierend	} Tremblant
Tremulous	Vibrato	Zitternd	
Triad	Triade	Dreiklang	Triade
Triangle	Triangolo	Triangel	Triangle
Trill	Trillo	Triller	Trille
Trio	Terzetto	Terzett, Trio	Trio
Triplet	Terzina	Triole	Triolet
Tritone	Tritono	Tritonus	Triton
Trombone	Trombone	Posaune	Trombone
Trombone (Alto)	Contralto-Trombone	Alt-Posaune	Alto-Trombone
Trombone (Tenor)	Tenore-Trombone	Tenor-Posaune	Taille-Trombone
Trombone (Bass)	Basso-Trombone	Bass-Posaune	Basse-Trombone
Trumpet	Tromba	Trompete	Trompette
Tune (*see* Melody)			
Tune, to	Accordare	Stimmen	Accorder
Turn over quickly	Volti subito	Schnell wenden	Tournez vivement
Twice as fast	Doppio movimento	Doppel so schnell	{ Double mouvement { Le double plus rapide
Two	Due	Zwei	Deux

U.

Unaccented beat	Movimento in unaccentato	{ Schwacher Taktt(h)eil { Schlechter Taktt(h)eil	Temps faible
Unaffected	Semplice	Naiv	Naï-f, -ve
Under	Sotto	Unter	Sous
Undulating	Ondeggiante	Schwebend	Ondulé
Unison	Unisono	Einklang	Unisson
Unrestful	Inquieto	Ruhelos	Inqui-et, -ète
Until	Sino	Bis	Jusqu'à
Up-beat	Accento debole	Aufschlag	Levé
Up-bow	Arco in su	Aufstrich	Poussé
Upon	Sopra	Auf	Sur

	Italian.	German.	French.

V.

Value	Valore	{ Geltung { Wert(h)	} Valeur
Variations	Variazioni	Variationen	{ Doubles { Variations
Vehemently	Con violenza	Heftig	Fortement
Veiled	Velato	Verschleiert	Voilé
Velocity	Velocità	Geläufigkeit	Vélocité
Very	{ Assai { Molto	} Sehr	Très
Very fast	{ Molto allegro { Prestissimo	Sehr schnell	Très vite
Very loud	Fortissimo	Sehr stark	Très fort
Very slowly	{ Adagio { Grave { Largo { Lento	} Sehr langsam	Très lentement
Very soft	{ Molto piano { Pianissimo	{ Sehr sanft { Sehr zart	} Très doux
Vigourously	{ Con brio { Vigoroso	Kräftig Mit Kraft	Fortement Vigoureusement
Viola	Viola	Bratsche	Alto
Violin	Violino	{ Geige { Violine	} Violon
Violoncello	Violoncello	Violoncell	Violoncelle
Voice	Voce	Stimme	Voix

W.

Wailing	Piangendo	Klagend	Plainti-f, -ve
Waltz	Valzer	Walzer	Valse
Wavering	Tremolando	Zitternd	Tremblant
Weak	Debole	Schwach	Débile
Weeping	Piangendo	Weinend	Pleurant
Weight, with	{ Pesante { Ponderoso	} Gewichtig	{ Avec poids { Pesant
Well	{ Ben { Bene	} Gut	Bien
Whimsically	{ Bizzarramente { Capriccioso	Bizarr Mit Humor	} Capricieusement
Whispering	Susurrando	Wispernd	Murmurant
Wild(ly)	Feroce	Wild	Féroce
Wind-instrument	Instrumento da fiato	Blasinstrument	Instrument à vent
With	Con	Mit	Avec
Without	Senza	Ohne	Sans
With the left hand	Colla sinistra	Mit der linken Hand	Avec la main gauche
With the right hand	Colla destra	Mit der rechten Hand	Avec la main droite
With the solo part	Colla parte	Mit dem solo Part	—
With the voice	Colla voce	Mit der Singstimme	Avec la voix
Wood-wind Instrument	} Instrumento da fiato	Holzblasinstrument	—
Work	Opus (*Lat.*)	Werk	Œuvre
Worked up	{ Incalzando { Risvegliato	} Zunehmend	En animant

ADDENDA TO PART I.

A.

Accento (*It.*)—Accent.

Accidente (*It.*)—Accidental.

Accordo arpeggiato (*It.*)—Broken chord.

Accordo di settina (*It.*)—A chord of the seventh.

Agevole (*It.*)—Easy. *Con agevolezza*, easily.

Agile (*Fr.*)—Agile, nimble.

Agréablement (*Fr.*)—Pleasantly.

Allein (*Ger.*)—Alone.

Alle zusammen (*Ger.*)—All together.

Allmählich schneller (*Ger.*)—Faster by degrees.

Animé (*Fr.*)—Spirited.

À plaisir (*Fr.*)—At pleasure.

Attaquez tout de suite (*Fr.*)—Begin at once.

Auch (*Ger.*)—Also.

Au-dessus (*Fr.*)—Above.

Auf dem Wasser (*Ger.*)—A barcarolle (*q.v.*).

Aufzug (*Ger.*)—An act.

Ausgehalten (*Ger.*)—Held.

Aussi (*Fr.*)—Also.

Avec chaleur (*Fr.*)—Ardently.

Avec énergie (*Fr.*)—With energy.

Avec ferveur (*Fr.*)—Fervently.

Avec force (*Fr.*)—With force.

Avec passion (*Fr.*)—Impassioned.

Avec poids (*Fr.*)—With weight.

Avec sentiment (*Fr.*)—With sentiment.

B.

Basse d'harmonie (*Fr.*)—An ophicleide.

Beinahe (*Ger.*)—Nearly.

Betonte Note (*Ger.*)—Accented note.

Beweglich (*Ger.*)—Agile.

Binaire (*Fr.*)—Binary.

Bis (*Fr.*)—Again.

Bischero (*It.*)—A peg (of violin, etc.).

Breiteres Tempo (*Ger.*)—Broadening out the time.

Brevemente (*It.*)—Abruptly.

Burlesque (*Fr.*)—Burlesque.

C.

Cadenza plagale (*It.*)—Plagal cadence.

Cadenza sfuggita (*It.*) }
Cadence trompeuse (*Fr.*) } Interrupted cadence.

Canon (*Fr.*)—A canon.

Cantate solista (*It.*) }
Chanteur soloiste (*Fr.*) } A solo singer.

Chiave di basso (*It.*)—Bass clef.

Clavier des pédales (*Fr.*)—Pedal keyboard.

Clé }
Clef } (*Fr.*)—Clef.

Clef alto (*Fr.*)—Alto clef.

Clef de basse (*Fr.*)—Bass clef.

Coffre (*Fr.*)—Body of an instrument.

Comique (*Fr.*)—Comic.

Comme (*Fr.*)—As, as if.

Comme avant (*Fr.*)—As before

Comme dessus (*Fr.*)—As above.

Comme d'une distance (*Fr.*)—As from a distance.

Compasso (*It.*)—Compass.

Composition (*Fr.*)—Composition.

Conjoint (*Fr.*)—Conjunct. *Mouvement conjoint*, conjunct movement.

Consonance (*Fr.*)—Consonance.

Continuel (*Fr.*)—Perpetual.

Corda vuota (*It.*)—An open string.

Cor de chasse (*Fr.*)—A hunting horn.

Corista (*It.*)—A chorister.

Cornamusa (*It.*) }
Cornemuse (*Fr.*) } A bagpipe.

Corps de rechange (*Fr.*)—A crook.

Croiser les mains (*Fr.*)—To cross the hands.

D.

Danse (*Fr.*) }
Danza (*It.*) } A dance.

Dauernd (*Ger.*)—Perpetual.

De (*Fr.*)—Of.

Debole (*It.*)—Weak.

Début (*Fr.*)—The beginning. *Mouvement du début,* at the original speed (Tempo primo).

Deuxième soprano (*Fr.*) — Second soprano.

Développement (*Fr.*)—Development.

Dissonance (*Fr.*) }
Dissonanz (*Ger.*) } Dissonance.

Divisé (*Fr.*)—Divided.

Do bemolle (*It.*)—The note C flat.

Do diesis (*It.*)—The note C sharp.

Do diesis maggiore (*It.*)—C sharp major.

Do diesis minore (*It.*)—C sharp minor.

Do doppio bemolle (*It.*)—The note C double flat.

Do doppio diesis (*It.*)—The note C double sharp.

Do maggiore (*It.*)—C major.

Doppelter Kontrapunkt (*Ger.*)— Double counterpoint.

Doppia linea (*It.*)—A double bar.

Doppio bemolle (*It.*)—A double flat.

Doppio contrappunto (*It.*)—Double counterpoint.

Doppio diesis (*It.*)—A double sharp.

Double contrepoint (*Fr.*) — Double counterpoint.

Doubles (*Fr.*)—Variations.

Dramatique (*Fr.*)—Dramatic.

Dudelsack (*Ger.*)—A bagpipe.

E.

Église (*Fr.*)—A church.

Ein klein wenig (*Ger.*)—A very little.

Elegant (*Ger.*)—Elegantly.

En augmentant (*Fr.*)—Increasing the tone.

En diminuant }
En s'affaiblissant } (*Fr.*)-Decreasing the tone.

Erwacht (*Ger.*)—Awakened.

Et (*Fr.*)—And.

Exécutant (*Fr.*)—A player.

F.

Fa diesis (*It.*)—The note F sharp.

Fa doppio bemolle (*It.*)—The note F double flat.

Fa doppio diesis (*It.*) — The note F double sharp.

Fa double bémol (*Fr.*) — The note F double flat.

Fa double dièse (*Fr.*)—The note F double sharp.

Falsa relazione (*It.*)—False relation.

Fanfara (*It.*)—A flourish of trumpets.

Fausse relation (*Fr.*)—False relation.

Figura (*It.*) }
Figure (*Fr.*) } A figure.

Finger (*Ger.*)—A finger.

Flûte (*Fr.*)—A flute. *Petite flûte,* an octave flute (Piccolo).

Freudig (*Ger.*)—Jocose, merry.

Fugue (*Fr.*)—A fugue.

G.

Gajo (*It.*)—Gay.

Gamme (*Fr.*)—A scale.

Gepflückt (*Ger.*)—Plucked. (Pizzicato.)

Geräuschvoll (*Ger.*)—Boisterous.

Glöckchen (*Ger.*)—A small bell.

Grandement (*Fr.*)—Grandly.

Gravement (*Fr.*)—Gravely, sadly.

Gros, grosse (*Fr.*)—Large, great.

Grotesque (*Fr.*)—Grotesque(ly).

Guerrier (*Fr.*)—In martial style.

H.

Hand (*Ger.*)—The hand.

Harmonie (*Fr.*)—Harmony.

Harmonieu-x, -se   (*Fr.*)—Harmonious.

Hirtenlied (*Ger.*)—Pastoral.

Haut contre trombone (*Fr.*) — An alto-trombone.

I.

Il movimento accentato della battuta (*It.*)—The down beat in a bar.

Imitation (*Fr.*)—Imitation.

Impétueusement (*Fr.*)—Impetuously.

Improvisieren (*Ger.*)—To improvise.

Instrument (*Ger.*)—An instrument.

Instrument de cuivre (*Fr.*)—A brass instrument.

Instrumenti da corda (*It.*)—Stringed instruments.

Instrumenti di percussione (*It.*)— Instruments of percussion.

Instrumento d'ottone (*It.*)—A brass instrument.

J.

Jeu d'anche (*Fr.*)—A reed-stop.

Jouer (*Fr.*)—To play.

K.

Kapriciös (*Ger.*)–Fanciful, capricious.

Kielflügel *Ger.*)—A harpsichord.

Klar (*Ger.*)—Clear, distinct,

Klaviatur (*Ger.*)—A keyboard.

Klingend (*Ger.*)—Sonorous.

Komisch (*Ger.*)—Comic.

Komische Oper(*Ger.*)—A comic opera.

Kompass (*Ger.*)—Compass.

Kontrabass (*Ger.*)—A double-bass.

Kontrapunkt (*Ger.*)—Counterpoint.

Kornett (*Ger.*)—A cornet.

L.

La doppio bemolle (*It.*)—The note A double flat.

La doppio diesis (*It.*)—The note A double sharp.

La double bémol (*Fr.*)—The note A double flat.

La double dièse (*Fr.*)—The note A double sharp.

Lage (*Ger.*)—Position.

La quarta (*It.*)—The subdominant.

Le double plus rapide (*Fr.*) — At double the speed. (Doppio movimento.)

Leichtigkeit, mit (*Ger.*)—With agility.

Longue pause (*Fr.*)—A long pause.

Luth (*Fr.*)—A lute.

M.

Mächtig (*Ger.*)—Powerful.

Marche funèbre (*Fr.*) } A funeral
Marcia funebre (*It.*) } march.

Martial (*Fr.*)—In a martial style.

Mazourka (*Fr.*)—A mazurka.

Menuett (*Ger.*)—A minuet.

Mi doppio bemolle (*It.*)—The note E double flat.

Mi doppio diesis (*It.*) — The note E double sharp.

Mi double bémol (*Fr.*)—The note E double flat.

Mi double dièse (*Fr.*) — The note E double sharp.

Minime (*Fr.*)—A minim.

Mit Wärme (*Ger.*)—Ardently.

Mode (*Fr.*)—Mode, as applying to a scale, or key.

Modulare (*It.*)—To modulate.

Mouvement du début (*Fr.*)—At the original speed.

Musica da camera (*It.*) } Chamber
Musique de chambre (*Fr.*) } music.

N.

Nach Wunsch (*Ger.*)—At pleasure.

Niederschlag (*Ger.*)—The down beat.

Noble (*Fr.*)—Noble.

Non (*Fr.*)—Not.

Nota semiminima (*It.*)—A crotchet.

Note accentuée (*Fr.*)—An accented note.

Note changeante } *(Fr.)*—A chang-
Note d'appogiature } ing note.

Note de passage *(Fr.)*—A passing note.

Note frappée *(Fr.)*—An accented note.

Note non accentuée *(Fr.)*—An unaccented note.

Note réelle *(Fr.)*—An essential note.

Numerato *(It.)*—Figured.

O.

Octave *(Fr.)*—An octave.

Octave plus bas *(Fr.)*—An octave lower.

Octave plus haut *(Fr.)*—An octave higher.

Octaves consécutives *(Fr.)* — Consecutive octaves.

Opera *(It.)*—An opera.

Orchestra *(It.)*—An orchestra.

Orchestre *(Fr.)* — An orchestra ; a band.

Ôtez les sourdines *(Fr.)*—Without mutes.

Ottave di moto retto *(It.)*—Consecutive octaves.

P.

Parte *(Ger.)*—A set of pieces.

Parte corale *(It.)*—A chorus part.

Parte superiore *(It.)*—The highest part.

Partie de chœur *(Fr.)*—A chorus part.

Passionné *(Fr.)*—Impassioned, passionately.

Pausa della minima *(It.)*—A minim rest.

Pausa di biscroma *(It.)*—A demi-semiquaver rest.

Pausa di semiminima *(It.)*—A crotchet rest.

Pedal *(Ger.)*—A pedal.

Pedaliera *(It.)*—A pedal keyboard.

Perpétuel, -le *(Fr.)*—Perpetual.

Pesant *(Fr.)*—With weight, heavily.

Petit, -e *(Fr.)*—Small.

Petite-flûte *(Fr.)*—A piccolo.

Pezzo di reversa *(It)*—A crook.

Phrase *(Fr.* and *Ger.)*—A phrase.

Plagal Kadenz *(Ger.)* — A plagal cadence.

Plein, pleine *(Fr.)*—Full.

Point d'arret *(Fr.)* }
Point d'orgue *(Fr.)* } A pause.

Pompeu-x, -se *(Fr.)*—Pompous.

Position *(Fr.)* }
Posizione *(It.)* } Position.

Possible *(Fr.)*—Possible.

Präcis *(Ger.)*—Precise.

Presque *(Fr.)*—Nearly.

Pressé *(Fr.)*—Hurried(ly).

Primo soprano *(It.)*—First soprano.

Principale *(It.)*—The "great" manual on an organ.

Psalm *(Ger.)*—A psalm.

Punto coronato *(It.)*—A long pause.

Q.

Quadruple *(Fr.)*—A quadruplet.

Qualita *(It.)*—Quality.

Quartina *(It.)*—A quadruplet.

Querpfeife *(Ger.)*—A fife.

Quinte di motto retto *(It.)* } Consecu-
Quintes consécutives *(Fr.)* } tive fifths

R.

Rapsodia *(It.)*—A rhapsody.

Re bemolle *(It.)*—The note D flat.

Re bemolle maggiore *(It.)* } The key
Ré bémol majeur *(Fr.)* } of D flat major.

Re diesis *(It.)*—The note D sharp.

Re doppio bemolle *(It.)*—The note D double flat.

Re doppio diesis *(It.)*—The note D double sharp.

Ré double bémol *(Fr.)*—The note D double flat.

Ré double dièse *(Fr.)*—The note D double sharp.

Reduction *(Fr.)* }
Reduzione *(It.)* } Arrangement.

Rein *(Ger.)*—Perfect.

Rhythmus (*Ger.*)—Rhythm.

Richtiges Tempo (*Ger.*) — Appropriate speed.

Ripresa (*It.*)—A repeat.

Ritardo (*It.*)—A suspension.

Romanze (*Ger.*)—A romance.

Rondo (*Ger.*)—A rondo.

Rythme (*Fr.*)—Rhythm.

S.

Schroff (*Ger.*)—Brusquely.

Secundo soprano (*It.*) — Second soprano.

Senza tempo rigore (*It.*)—Not in strict time ; at pleasure.

Settetto (*It.*)—A septet.

Seul, seule (*Fr.*)—Alone.

Si (*It.*)—The note B.

Si bemolle (*It.*)—The note B flat.

Si dièse (*Fr.*)
Si diesis (*It.*) } The note B sharp.

Si doppio bemolle (*It.*) } The note B
Si double bémol (*Fr.*) } double flat.

Sillet (*Fr.*)—The nut on the fingerboard of a stringed instrument.

Similaire (*Fr.*)—Similar.

Singen (*Ger.*)—To sing.

Sofort fortsetzen (*Ger.*)—Go on at once.

Sol doppio bemolle (*It.*)—The note G double flat.

Sol doppio diesis (*It.*)—The note G double sharp.

Sol double bémol (*Fr.*)—The note G double flat.

Sol double dièse (*Fr.*)—The note G double sharp.

Sonatore (*It.*)—A player.

Sons harmoniques (*Fr.*)–Harmonics.

Stimmstock (*Ger.*)—A sound post.

T.

Taktschlag (*Ger.*)—A beat.

Tamburino (*It.*)—A tambourine.

Ternario (*It.*)—Ternary.

Timbro (*It.*)—Quality.

Tono (*It.*)—Tone.

Tout ensemble (*Fr.*)—All together.

Traurig (*Ger.*)—Sad, mournful.

Traverseflöte (*Ger.*)—A cross-flute.

Tremolierend (*Ger.*)—Trembling.

Très doux (*Fr.*)—Very soft.

Très fort (*Fr.*)—Very loud.

Très lentement (*Fr.*)—Very slow.

Trombone basso (*It.*)—A bass trombone.

U.

Übergangsnote (*Ger.*). — A passing note.

Übergreifend (*Ger.*) — Crossing hands.

Und (*Ger.*)—And.

Une fois (*Fr.*)—Once.

Une octave plus bas (*Fr.*) — An octave lower.

Une octave plus haut (*Fr.*) — An octave higher.

Ursprüngliches Zeitmass (*Ger.*)— At the original speed.

Ut dièse (*Fr.*)—The note C sharp.

Ut dièse majeur (*Fr.*) — C sharp major.

Ut dièse mineur (*Fr.*) — C sharp minor.

Ut double bémol (*Fr.*)—The note C double flat.

Ut double dièse (*Fr.*) — The note C double sharp.

Ut majeur (*Fr.*)—C major.

V.

Variationen (*Ger.*)
Variations (*Fr.*) } Variations.

Vergrösstes Interval (*Ger.*)—An augmented interval.

Voce umana (*It.*) — The human voice.

Von (*Ger.*)—Of.

Vorbereitung (*Ger.*)—Preparation.

Vorhergehend (*Ger.*)—Previous.

Vornehm (*Ger.*)—Noble.

W.

Wechseln (*Ger.*)—To change.

Weniger (*Ger.*)—Less.

Wie geschrieben (*Ger.*)—As written.

Z.

Zweit(h)eilig (*Ger.*)—Binary.

Zweiunddreissigstel Pause (*Ger.*)— A demisemiquaver rest.